D0758131

The Shawnee Prophet

Open Door, Known as the Prophet, Brother of the Great Chief, by George Catlin. Courtesy National Museum of Art, Smithsonian Institution.

The Shawnee Prophet

by R. David Edmunds

University of Nebraska Press

Lincoln and London

EB

Library of Congress Cataloging in Publication Data

Edmunds, R. David (Russell David), 1939–
The Shawnee Prophet.

Bibliography: p.
Includes index.
1. Tenskwatawa, Shawnee Prophet, 1775?–1834
2. Tecumseh, Shawnee, Chief, 1768–1813.
3. Shawnee Indians – Wars – 1750–1815.   4. Indians
of North America – Wars – 1750–1815.   I. Title.
E99.S35T463 1983   970.004'97 [B]   82–23830
ISBN 0-8032-1850-8

*In heartfelt
thanksgiving for
God's infinite mercy
in the miraculous
recovery of my
daughter, Katie*

Contents

Preface

Several years ago, while conducting research on the history of the Potawatomi Indians, I examined a large number of primary sources that discussed the Potawatomis' relationship with Tecumseh and the Shawnee Prophet in the years before the War of 1812. Like most other American historians I had read secondary accounts of Tecumseh's career and I was interested in his contacts with the Potawatomis. Tecumseh fascinated me for other reasons. Of all the Indians in American history, he has always seemed the most admirable. His white contemporaries, both British and American, described him in glowing terms, and since his death historians have echoed their praises. Tecumseh's attempts to unite the western tribes seemed both perceptive and logical. He obviously was a magnetic individual, a leader whose personal qualities attracted large numbers of followers and enabled him to forge them into a multitribal confederacy.

When I began to examine primary materials from the decade preceding the War of 1812, I expected to find ample evidence that Tecumseh both initiated and dominated the Indian movement, but I was surprised. Although the movement obviously began in 1805, documents from this period make almost no mention of Tecumseh. He does not emerge as an important leader until 1810, following the loss of Indian lands at the Treaty of Fort Wayne. In contrast, primary materials from these early years indicate that Tecumseh's brother, Tenskwatawa, the Shawnee Prophet, was the leading figure in the Indians' efforts to resist the Americans. I was vaguely familiar with the Prophet and his teachings, but like most historians I always had considered him to be entirely secondary, a religious fanatic whose efforts detracted from Tecumseh's grand plan to unify the western tribes.

Several questions regarding Tecumseh and the Shawnee Prophet slowly emerged. Was Tenskwatawa really responsible for beginning the movement and did he dominate it during the early years? Did his religious teachings, which seemed so bizarre to white Americans, appeal to the Indians? If so, how did these doctrines specifically meet the Indians' needs? If Tenskwatawa was the dominant leader in the formation of the movement, why have historians minimized his role? And, finally, if the Prophet was responsible for starting the movement, why have historians portrayed Tecumseh as the most important Indian leader in the decade prior to the War of 1812?

Intrigued by these questions, I decided to examine the careers of these two Shawnee brothers at greater length. After extensive readings in Shawnee ethnography, I turned to the primary materials scattered in depositories across the eastern United States and Canada. The research proved fascinating, for it not only provided answers to many of my questions, but also helped me better understand how different peoples interpret the same events within their own particular cultural framework. Like all of us, both Indians and white Americans were the products of their own cultures and had difficulty in comprehending each others' perspective. This problem was not unique to the nineteenth-century American frontier, for it has continued to plague humanity for centuries. It is hoped, however, that this volume will provide some insights into the Shawnees' perspective. I also hope it will enable its readers to gain a better understanding of the development of Indian-white relations during the first quarter of the nineteenth century.

Several institutions and persons were especially helpful in the completion of this project. The Center for the History of the American Indian, at the Newberry Library, awarded me a postdoctoral fellowship that provided both financial and intellectual support as I began the research for the volume. I am also indebted to the Texas Christian University Research Foundation, which provided me with stipends enabling me to visit archives and manuscript collections throughout the Midwest and Canada. Special thanks is extended to Don Worcester, who took time from his own research and writing to read the manuscript, and who offered many valuable suggestions.

In collecting materials for this volume, I received invaluable assistance from many people. Special recognition is extended to James Kellar and Cheryl Munson of the Great Lakes-Ohio Valley Indian Archives; to John Aubrey of the Edward E. Ayer Collection at the Newberry Library; to Helen Tanner, Jackie Peterson Swagerty, and William Swagerty of the "Great Lakes Indian Atlas" project at the Newberry Library; to Robert Kvasnicka of the National Archives, and to Kent Carter, Barbara Rust, Debbie Fowler, Jeanette Ford, and Overnice Wilks of the Federal Records Center, Fort Worth, Texas. I also wish to thank H. J. Bosveld, Eleanor Gignac, and Mary Lou Brown of the Fort Malden National Historic Park; John Dan and Arlene Shy of the William L. Clements Library; Clarke Evans and Jan Fouts of the Tippecanoe Battleground Historical Association; Harriet Castrataro, Wilma Etnier, and Geneva Warner of the Lilly Library; Ted Appel, Ed Rider, and Laura Chace of the Cincinnati Historical Society; David Levine of the Ohio State Archives; Charles Isetts and Conrad Weitzel of the Ohio Historical Society; Joe Oldenburg and Alice Dalligan of the Burton Collection, Detroit Public Library; Leona Alig and Tom Rumer of the Indiana Historical Society Library; Molly McCarty, Edith

Walden, and Jean Singleton of the Indiana State Library; Michelle Corbett of the Public Archives of Canada; Mrs. E. A. Stadler and Beverly Bishop of the Missouri Historical Society; Bob Knecht of the Kansas State Historical Society; and Johnoween Gill, Janna Ferguson, and Ruth Morgan of the Interlibrary Loan Office, Mary Couts Burnett Library, Texas Christian University.

A note of recognition is extended to Terry Wilson and Gerald Vizenor of the Native American Studies Department, the University of California at Berkeley, who have helped me keep my sense of humor, and to my students at both Texas Christian University and Berkeley, who have listened to my ideas and have helped me keep them in perspective.

Finally, special thanks to my wife, Jeri, and my daughter, Katie, who allow me to write and to neglect my household chores, and who also help me remember what is important in life.

Fort Worth, Texas.
March 4, 1982.

The Shawnee Prophet

Chapter One

The Spawn of
the Serpent

The closing decades of the eighteenth century were dark
years for the Indian peoples of the Old Northwest. Anxious
to preserve their hunting lands, red warriors watched in anger as the Long Knives crossed through Cumberland Gap to
build their cabins along the Licking and Kentucky rivers.
During the American Revolution war parties from north of
the Ohio crossed the broad river to strike at white settlements in the Bluegrass Country, and although the Americans retaliated by burning several Indian villages in central
Ohio, British spokesmen at Detroit assured their red allies
that the war would end in victory. But in 1783, at the Treaty
of Paris, British promises were broken. When they acknowledged American claims to territory west of the Appalachians, the British made no effort to protect Indian lands in
Ohio. Although the tribesmen had fought in the war, they
had no part in the treaty making.

Jubilant over the prospect of acquiring new lands, white
frontiersmen poured over into southern Ohio. Meanwhile,
the fledgling government in Philadelphia offered to meet
with the tribesmen, hoping to gain Indian acquiescence in
American claims to the region. But tribal leaders refused to
acknowledge the government's claims and actively opposed
the new settlements north of the river. Between 1784 and
1789 a few chiefs met with government officials and signed

a series of questionable treaties relinquishing Indian control of lands in southern and eastern Ohio, yet most tribesmen denounced the agreements and continued their raids against outlying farms and villages.

Hoping to force a military solution to the land problem, in 1790 and 1791 the government sent armed expeditions against the Indian villages along the Maumee River. The tribesmen turned back both forces, inflicting catastrophic losses on Governor Arthur St. Clair's command in November 1791, but their victory dances were short-lived. In August 1794, Major General "Mad Anthony" Wayne's legions defeated a multitribal force at the Battle of Fallen Timbers, and the resulting Treaty of Greenville forced the Indians to give up their claims to most of Ohio. The loss of lands not only demoralized the tribesmen, it also forced many to relocate along the Wabash-Maumee waterway, crowding newcomers into a region already occupied by other tribes.

The expanded Indian population in northern Indiana and northwestern Ohio made increased demands on the dwindling supply of game in the region. Moreover, red hunters were forced to compete with growing numbers of whites who systematically crossed over onto Indian lands to kill deer and other animals. The declining game population not only denied the tribesmen fresh meat, it also limited their ability to purchase needed commodities. Most Indians relied on the fur trade, but after 1797 the supply of pelts declined and many warriors were hard pressed to provide for their families.[1]

The Indians also suffered under the American system of justice. Although white poachers killed deer on Indian lands with impunity, tribesmen trespassing on white property were deemed fair game for frontier marksmen. Many Indians on peaceful trading ventures within the settlements were robbed and murdered by American citizens, but frontier courts systematically acquitted culprits accused of such crimes. Indian leaders complained about such injustice, but their pleas were generally ignored. Admitting he could do little to stop the carnage, Governor William Henry Harrison of Indiana Territory confessed that "a great many of the Inhabitants of the Fronteers (sic) consider the murdering of the Indians in the highest degree meritorious."[2]

Yet white men's rifles killed far fewer Indians than white men's diseases. Since the colonial period, smallpox, measles, and influenza had ravaged up and down the Ohio Valley, taking a dreadful toll among the native peoples of the region. With no natural immunity to these epidemics, many tribesmen succumbed within a few days after contracting the maladies. Smallpox was probably the greatest killer, but other diseases also claimed many victims. Contemporary accounts describe entire villages stricken with influenza, while consumption was a common ailment among the adult population. In the 1790s missionary John Heckewelder commented that far fewer tribesmen were surviving until "old age," and Indian leaders complained to white officials that their kinsmen were suffering from "many diseases that our forefathers were ignorant of, before they saw you."[3]

Pressures engendered by the loss of lands, food shortages, white injustice, and disease caused serious rifts within the tribal communities. The traditional fabric of interpersonal relationships, formalized roles, and elaborate kinship groups came apart because the tribes were unable to cope with the rapid changes swirling around them. Orderly, cooperative villages degenerated into violence as stress-ridden warriors vented their frustration. Some tribesmen blamed their problems on witchcraft, declaring that the social deterioration was caused by local sorcerers. Others, unable to adjust to the chaos, withdrew from reality and adopted passive behavior patterns that led toward indolence and depression. Even worse, many tribesmen sought solace in alcohol, which only added to the anarchy. Drunken warriors bartered their few pelts for jugs of whiskey, then fought among themselves in top-heavy brawls. Serious injuries or death were not uncommon, and many Indians of both sexes bore terrible scars, mute testimony to their participation in the bloody free-for-alls.[4]

Aware that their traditional way of life no longer provided economic or social stability, some tribesmen sought an accommodation with the Americans. During the latter half of the eighteenth century, Moravian missionaries had labored among the Delawares, converting many members of the tribe to Christianity and teaching them white agricultural techniques. By 1800 many other Indians were willing to try the white man's road. Late in 1801 a delegation of chiefs from the Potawatomis, Miamis, Delawares, Shawnees, Kickapoos, and Kaskaskias visited the East, where Little Turtle, a Miami chief, and Five Medals, a Potawatomi leader, asked government officials for assistance. Since both the government and the Quakers had earlier urged a program of acculturation on the tribesmen, they were delighted with the request. During the next decade the federal government and various religious organizations sent funds, farming implements, and "agricultural experts" to the tribes of Ohio and Indiana.[5]

Yet most of these efforts produced minimal results. Some of the agricultural programs were mismanaged by unscrupulous Indian agents who juggled government accounts and sold the Indians' farm implements to white settlers. Other programs failed because of the well-intentioned but bumbling ignorance of those officials appointed to supervise them. In 1804 Quaker Phillip Dennis established a "model agricultural station" among the Miamis and Potawatomis, but he ordered Indian women away from his fields and became angry when their husbands refused to take the women's places. Other missionaries ignored tribal protocol and alienated Indian leaders, whose support they desperately needed. But the primary cause for the programs' failures rested within the Indian communities. A few chiefs such as Little Turtle or Five Medals may have sincerely wanted their people to adopt white agriculture, but the majority of the tribesmen rejected such acculturation. Regardless of their socioeconomic situation, many clung tenaciously to their traditional lifestyle. Still roaming the forests, hungry warriors continued to search for game and check their empty trap lines. Others remained in their villages, bitterly mourning a romanticized past, dreaming of the golden age of their forefathers.[6]

The Shawnees shared in the problems of their Indian neighbors. The early history of the Shawnees, who were known as "the Southerners" by other Algonquian-speaking peoples, is shrouded in uncertainty. Ethnographers disagree over what areas the tribe occupied before the mid-seventeenth century, but by the 1650s they were living in southern Ohio and northern Kentucky. There they remained for several years, until quarrels with neighboring tribes caused their dispersal, scattering bands of Shawnees from the Gulf Coast to the Delaware Valley in western New Jersey. Some went south, occupying parts of Georgia and South Carolina, where they assisted the English in their wars against the Westos. Others fled first to Illinois, then to eastern Pennsylvania and Maryland, settling near their "grandfathers," the Delawares. By 1725 most of the southern bands had rejoined their kinsmen in Pennsylvania, but pressure from the expanding white frontier and from the Iroquois slowly pushed the Shawnees westward, where they established new villages in the Wyoming and Susquehanna valleys. During the second quarter of the eighteenth century, part of the tribe again moved south, seeking refuge among the Upper Creek towns in Alabama. Although some of these Shawnees settled permanently among the Creeks, kinship ties drew many others back to the north, and by mid century, most of the tribe were living in villages scattered along the Scioto River in central Ohio.[7]

The Shawnee possession of the Scioto Valley during the third quarter of the eighteenth century occupies a bittersweet place in tribal history. For the first time in many years almost all the Shawnees were living in close proximity. But unfortunately, the decades between 1750 and 1780 also mark the last time that such tribal cohesion would occur. By 1750 the Shawnees were divided into five semiautonomous political units or bands, each occupying a special place within the tribal confederacy. Traditionally, the Thawegila and Chalahgawtha bands supplied leaders for the entire tribe, sometimes competing with each other for positions of prominence. These two bands supposedly concerned themselves with "things political, or things affecting the nation as a whole." The Maykujays, at different times, served as priests, doctors ("health and medicine"), and "counselors." The Kispokothas generally controlled matters relating to warfare, a duty they sometimes shared with the Piqua people. The Piquas also had "charge of the maintenance of order or duty, and . . . the celebration of things pertaining to . . . religion." In the rivalry between the Thawegilas and Chalahgawthas for leadership of the tribe, the Shawnees often split into two groups. The Kispokothas and Piquas usually supported the Thawegilas, while the Maykujays joined with the Chalahgawthas.[8]

All of the bands took an active part in the French and Indian War. Although some of the Shawnees had formed tenuous friendships with the British while living in Pennsylvania, most of the tribe supported the French during the conflict. In 1755, at Braddock's Defeat, Shawnee warriors fought beside Captain Daniel de Beaujeu, firing from the underbrush as the ill-fated British column was cut to pieces near Fort Duquense. During the next four years they joined with bands of Delawares to raid the English frontier in Pennsylvania and Virginia. They also attempted, unsuccessfully, to lure the Iroquois Confederacy into the French alliance, serving as emissaries between the French in Montreal and Seneca villages near Niagara. After the fall of Quebec, most Shawnees withdrew from the warfare and accepted

British trade goods in return for neutrality. Although many tribesmen still mistrusted the British, they realized that the French had been beaten.[9]

But in 1763, with the outbreak of Pontiac's Rebellion, the Shawnees again raised their war clubs against the Redcoats. They sent runners as far west as Illinois, urging the tribes of the Wabash Valley to attack British forts and traders. Shawnee war parties led by Cornstalk also ascended the Kanawha River into West Virginia, killing settlers and burning farms near Greenbriar, Big Levels, and Muddy Creek. Many captives were carried back to the Scioto, but most were relinquished in 1764, after Colonel Henry Bouquet's expedition forced the tribe to sue for peace.[10]

During the decade following Pontiac's Rebellion, most of the Shawnees made a sincere effort to remain at peace. Although they bitterly resented the sale of their hunting lands in Kentucky by the Iroquois at the 1768 Treaty of Fort Stanwix, the Shawnees muzzled their anger and did not strike out at the few Virginians brave enough to hunt along the Kentucky and Licking rivers. Yet Cornstalk and other chiefs warned colonial officials that the Shawnees would not tolerate white settlements in Kentucky. Meanwhile, runners from the villages along the Scioto journeyed to the Cherokees, Mingos, and Delawares, inviting them to oppose the Virginians. In early 1774 delegates from these tribes met at the Shawnee towns in Ohio. They hoped that a united front would frighten the Long Knives and keep them east of the mountains.[11]

Their efforts came too late. In January 1774, while the council fires were burning on the Scioto, frontiersmen attacked a party of friendly Shawnees at Fort Pitt. None of the Indians were injured, but the attack caused considerable apprehension among both Indians and whites in the Ohio Valley. In April a group of traders was ambushed by a Cherokee war party, causing Captain John Connolly, a Virginia militia officer, to issue a circular declaring that the Shawnees were on the warpath. Following Connolly's directive, on April 30, 1774, white frontiersmen slaughtered an encampment of Mingos who had been peacefully hunting on the Ohio near modern Wheeling, West Virginia. Among the dead was the Shawnee wife of the famous Mingo chief Logan, an outspoken friend of the British. Several days later other whites lured another group of Indians across the Ohio under the pretext of a friendly conference, then plied the tribesmen with liquor and murdered them. Logan's brother and pregnant sister were among the second group of victims.[12]

His family annihilated, Logan sought revenge and during the early summer of 1774 Shawnee and Mingo war parties killed several settlers on the Muskingum, in eastern Ohio. But the reprisals were only a part of Shawnee justice and did not signal a general Indian war. In July, Logan informed colonial officials that the killing had ended, and Cornstalk asked the British Indian Department to mediate a peace. Yet too much blood already had been spilled. In October, Lord Dunmore, the governor of Virginia, mustered a force of eleven hundred Virginia militiamen at the juncture of the Kanawha and Ohio rivers. Fearing a campaign against their villages, the Shawnees assembled three hundred warriors across the Ohio from the Virginians, and on October 10 Cornstalk attacked, hoping to defeat Dunmore before the latter could receive any reinforcements. The Battle of Point Pleasant was fiercely fought, but the Shawnees finally were forced to withdraw across the Ohio. For all practical purposes, Lord Dunmore's War had ended.[13]

Disheartened by their lack of success, most of the Thawegila Shawnees withdrew from Ohio and fled to the south, seeking refuge among the Creeks in Alabama. Meanwhile, Cornstalk met with colonial officials in October 1774, pledging his friendship and giving up all Shawnee claims to Kentucky. The agreement was mediated through the efforts of Matthew Elliott, a trader living in the Shawnee villages who later served as an Indian agent for the Crown. Elliott's ability to live peacefully within the tribe amid the turmoil of Lord Dunmore's War was significant. Shawnee anger had been directed at the "Virginians," those whites intent on occupying Kentucky. They had no quarrels with traders and remained on good terms with the British Indian Department.[14]

Shawnee hatred of the Virginians virtually assured that those tribesmen remaining in Ohio would oppose the colonists during the Revolutionary War. Although Cornstalk favored neutrality, he was murdered by frontier riffraff in 1777 and his successor, Blackfish, was an outspoken enemy of the Long Knives. In January 1778, a war party from the Chalahgawtha village (Chillicothe) captured Daniel Boone and several companions at the Blue Licks on the Licking River. Although Boone later escaped, throughout the summer of 1778 Shawnee warriors fell upon Kentucky with a vengeance. Settlements were besieged, farms burned, horses captured, and many scalps taken. During the following year smaller war parties again scourged the Bluegrass Country, and in October 1779, a large force of Shawnees attacked Captain David Rodgers's supply flotilla on the Ohio River, killing forty soldiers and capturing six others.[15]

The war also took its toll on the Shawnees. During July 1779, Colonel John Bowman and two hundred mounted volunteers crossed the Ohio and raided the Chalahgawtha village. Although few Indians were killed, the Americans captured many horses and a considerable amount of Indian property. More important, the raid surprised the Shawnees and evidently demoralized many of the tribesmen. Although their villages were not attacked, most members of the Kispokotha and Piqua bands withdrew from the war and left Ohio. Descending the Ohio Valley, they eventually crossed the Mississippi and established new villages in Spanish territory, near Cape Girardeau, Missouri. There they were joined by many Thawegilas from the Creek towns in the south. Those Kispokothas and Piquas who elected to stay and fight the Long Knives now joined with the Chalahgawtha and Maykujay bands.[16]

The remaining Shawnees, although diminished in numbers, represented the most anti-American elements of the tribe. In June 1780, they accompanied Captain Henry Bird in his successful invasion of Kentucky, and in 1782 they joined with the Delawares, Wyandots, and other tribes to defeat Captain William Crawford and the Pennsylvania militia in their ill-fated expedition against the Indian towns near Sandusky, Ohio. Shawnee warriors also fought with Captain William Caldwell in the attack on Bryan's Station (near modern Lexington, Kentucky) and assisted in the subsequent ambush of American forces at the Battle of the Blue Licks, in August 1782. Although the Kentuckians later burned several Shawnee villages, the Indians suffered few casualties.[17]

The Treaty of Paris, which ended the American Revolution, caused considerable confusion among those Shawnees remaining in Ohio. Although the Indians believed they had won the war, U.S. officials informed them that the British had relinquished all lands west of the Appalachians, and Ohio now belonged to the United States. Denouncing the U.S. claims, the Shawnees turned to British Indian agents, who assured them that the Crown had only given up political control of the western regions: the Shawnees still owned their lands. But while their envoys were meeting with British officials at Detroit, word reached Shawnee villages along the Mad and Auglaize rivers that white settlers already were crowding onto Indian lands in southern Ohio.[18]

Hoping to forestall bloodshed, the United States negotiated a series of treaties with the western tribes. After meeting with the Iroquois, Wyandots, and other tribes during 1784 and 1785, American officials assembled a delegation of Shawnees at Fort Finney, at the mouth of the Great Miami, in January 1786. The Shawnees soon learned that the council was not a meeting of equals. American agents informed the Indians that they must give up their claims to lands east of the Miami and acknowledge the sovereignty of the United States over all their villages. Astonished at the terms, Kekewepellethe, a village chief, replied that the Shawnees did not understand the American demands and had no intention of giving up their lands in Ohio. In reply Indian agent Richard Butler threatened the destruction of the Shawnee women and children. Intimidated, on January 31, 1786, Kekewepellethe and other Shawnee leaders signed the document.[19]

The Shawnees returned to their villages amid much confusion and bewilderment. Angered by the treaty, a small war party of young warriors journeyed to the Ohio, where they periodically fired on American shipping and stole a few horses. Meanwhile, Kentucky was overrun by large numbers of Cherokee and Mingo raiders from Tennessee. Not surprisingly, the Kentuckians blamed the Shawnees, and in October 1786, Colonel Benjamin Logan launched a surprise attack against the villages along the Mad River, destroying the Shawnee corn crop and killing several Indians. Among the victims was Melanthy, an old village chief, who was shot down while approaching the Kentuckians to arrange an armistice. When he fell he was carrying an American flag and holding a copy of the Treaty of Fort Finney before him.[20]

The twin tragedies of the Treaty of Fort Finney and Logan's raid convinced the Shawnees that they needed assistance to hold their lands in Ohio. In December 1786, they met with other tribes at Detroit, attempting to forge a new confederacy to safeguard Indian interests in the region. Repudiating the postwar treaties, the tribesmen sent a message to Congress asking the government to withdraw its surveyors from Ohio. They also requested a new council to discuss problems of land tenure. But political unity came slowly to a people traditionally fragmented by tribal interests, and following the conference in Detroit, Indian solidarity disintegrated. Although the Shawnees and Miamis insisted that the Americans withdraw from all lands north of the Ohio, the Wyandots, Delawares, and Senecas were willing to give up the region east of the Muskingum River.[21]

The proposed council was held at Fort Harmar in December 1788. Once again the Indians fell victim to the American policy of "divide and conquer." Learning that the government had no intention of giving up its claims to Ohio, the Shawnees finally refused to attend the proceedings. The Indians who did meet with white officials included a scattering of warriors from the Detroit region and the Wyandots, Delawares, and Senecas—those tribes willing to compromise. On January 9, 1789, they signed the Treaty of Fort Harmar, validating the government's claims to eastern Ohio. In discussing the conference with his superiors, Governor Arthur St. Clair of the Northwest Territory assured them that the Shawnees and Miamis had been isolated. According to St. Clair, the Indian confederacy was "entirely broken."[22]

Embittered by the treaty, the Shawnees lashed out at white settlers in southern Ohio. In response, federal officials launched a major campaign against Shawnee and Miami villages along the Wabash-Maumee waterway. In October 1790, General Josiah Harmar led an expedition of about 1,450 men toward the Miami towns near modern Fort Wayne. Although the expedition burned several villages, it eventually was ambushed by a mixed force of Shawnees, Miamis, and other Indians who killed over 180 Americans. Harmar declared that he was "exceedingly pleased" with the outcome of his venture, but his efforts only encouraged the Shawnees to further resistance. Harmar had destroyed one of their villages, but the Shawnees had evacuated their families and property. Moreover, many Shawnee warriors had taken scalps from the ill-fated Americans.[23]

Aware of Harmar's failure, in 1792 the government sent a second expedition against the Shawnees and their allies. Under the command of Governor St. Clair, almost 2,000 regulars, militia, and volunteers marched north from Fort

Washington in September 1791, again destined for the Indian villages along the Maumee. Although one-third of the militiamen and volunteers deserted en route, by early November the expedition had reached the headwaters of the Wabash in extreme eastern Ohio. They were surprised and routed by an immense intertribal war party composed of Shawnees, Miamis, Potawatomis, Delawares, and other Indians. From the American point of view Harmar's campaign had been a failure, but St. Clair's expedition was disastrous. On November 4, 1791, the Shawnees and their allies killed over 630 Americans.[24]

Shawnee morale soared. They had beaten the best warriors the Long Knives could send against them. Moreover, the Indian victories seemed to vindicate the Shawnees' hardline stance against ceding tribal lands in Ohio. Even the Wyandots, Delawares, and Senecas now supported the Shawnee position on the territory east of the Muskingum. When Shawnee and other tribal delegates again met with American emissaries at Detroit in July 1793, they confidently refused any compromise. Only if all settlers withdrew south and east of the Ohio would the Indians promise peace. Meanwhile, British agents assured the tribesmen that His Majesty's government would support them in their struggle. During the spring of 1794 the British built a new post, Fort Miamis, on the Maumee at modern Toledo. Elated by what they interpreted as a sure indication of British military assistance, the Shawnees dared the Americans to come again. More warfare seemed inevitable.[25]

Unfortunately for the Indians, their new adversary was a leader of considerably different mettle. "Mad Anthony" Wayne spent two years rebuilding the American army, and in 1794, when he led his "Legion" north toward the Maumee, they were well trained and spoiling for a fight. Once again the Shawnees and their allies assembled to meet the Long Knives. They first made a futile attack on Fort Recovery, an American post in eastern Ohio, then took positions at Fallen Timbers, where a tornado had recently felled a grove of trees on the north bank of the Maumee, southwest of Fort Miamis. The fallen trees formed a natural breastwork, but on August 20, 1794, Wayne's army swept through the barricades, and the hopes of the Shawnees were shattered. Retreating down the Maumee, the Indians sought sanctuary in the British fort, but the commander refused to admit them. Bewildered by the refusal, the tribesmen dispersed into the forest. Shawnee morale, which had reached such peaks after St. Clair's defeat, now plummeted. Embittered, the Indians had no choice but to make peace with the Long Knives. On August 3, 1795, the Shawnees signed the Treaty of Greenville. In exchange for most of their former homeland the tribe received a present of trade goods and an annuity of one thousand dollars. Shawnee lands east of the Mississippi were now reduced to the northwest quadrant of Ohio.[26]

The Treaty of Greenville was an important turning point for those Shawnees remaining in the east. Unable to forget the closed doors at Fort Miamis, most of the Maykujays finally abandoned the British and sought an accommodation with the United States. Led by the aging Black Hoof, a war chief prominent since the colonial period, these Shawnees decided that their only salvation lay in adopting white agricultural techniques and settling permanently in western Ohio. Following the treaty they established new villages at the headwaters of the Miami and at Wapakoneta, on the upper reaches of the Auglaize. But other Shawnees, including many Chalahgawthas and dissidents from other bands, clung to the ways of their forefathers. Although they begrudgingly remained at peace with the Long Knives, they continued to visit representatives of their British father at Fort Malden, across the river from Detroit. Here they complained about the new influx of American settlers into Ohio and received trade goods from His Majesty's Indian agents. Unwilling to try the white man's road, these Shawnees persisted in their hunting and planted small patches of corn at villages scattered from the Auglaize Valley into eastern Indiana.[27]

Black Hoof made a concerted effort to lead his people toward a new way of life. During the winter of 1802–3 he visited Washington and asked federal officials to provide the Shawnees at Wapakoneta with farming implements and livestock so that his followers could learn white agricultural methods. He also requested assistance in erecting permanent log houses modeled after the cabins of white settlers in the region. Black Hoof evidently believed that if the Shawnees settled down on farms like their white neighbors, the government would allow them to remain permanently in their homeland. On February 5, 1802, he startled Secretary of War Henry Dearborn by asking for a specific deed to the remaining Shawnee lands in western Ohio. According to the old chief, such a document would give them a good piece of land, "where [they] may raise good Grain and cut Hay for our Cattle," and guarantee "that nobody would take advantage" of them.[28]

Unwilling to provide the Shawnees with any legal document that might strengthen their claim to the Auglaize Valley, Dearborn informed the tribesmen that the government did not have the authority to grant such a request. Yet he assured Black Hoof that the Indians could rely on the protection of the United States, promising him, "Your Father the President will take care to have ploughs and other useful tools provided for such of his red children, as may be disposed to make good use of them, and he will furnish you with some Cattle and other articles equally beneficial." Following the conference, Black Hoof and his companions returned to the Auglaize.[29]

Since the government and various Quaker groups had received similar petitions from other Indians, federal officials took measures to honor the requests. Yet most of the initial agricultural assistance was not distributed to the Shawnees.

Between 1802 and 1807 both the government and the Quakers funneled their efforts through Fort Wayne, providing both farm implements and agricultural advisers to the Potawatomis and Miamis. Although Black Hoof and his followers were able to acquire a few farm implements, their pleas for technical assistance went largely unanswered. Frustrated, in February 1807 Black Hoof returned to Washington, again soliciting agricultural experts for his people. Ironically, by this time it was apparent to the government that its endeavors among the Potawatomis and Miamis had failed. Envisioning the Shawnees as a more fertile field for their labors, federal officials authorized William Kirk, a Quaker missionary previously active at Fort Wayne, to establish a mission at Wapakoneta.[30]

Kirk arrived on the Auglaize River in July 1807, where he was warmly welcomed by Black Hoof and his followers. Unlike the Potawatomis and Miamis, the Shawnees at Wapakoneta eagerly sought Kirk's advice in clearing farmland and in planting crops of corn and vegetables. Under the Quaker's tutelage the five hundred Indians at Black Hoof's village split the timber from their newly cleared farmland into rails, erecting fences to protect their fields from horses and wild animals. In the fall, over thirty acres of corn were harvested, and by conserving their crop, Black Hoof and his people passed the winter with an adequate food supply.[31]

During the next year the Shawnees at Wapakoneta prospered. In the spring of 1808 they cleared an additional four hundred acres, cultivating such new crops as potatoes, cabbage, and turnips. They also started an orchard, planting several rows of apple seedlings outside their village. Following Kirk's advice the Shawnees purchased breeder stock of hogs and cattle, hoping the domestic animals eventually would supply them with the fresh meat they formerly had secured through hunting. Although most of the fields and animals were held in common by all of Black Hoof's people, a few Shawnees laid out small tracts of land and attempted to establish individual farms like their white neighbors.[32]

Many white Ohioans were genuinely impressed at the "industry and rapid progress of civilization" among the Indians at Wapakoneta. During the summer of 1808 Kirk hired a blacksmith who established a permanent shop among the Shawnees, repairing their farm implements and providing them with the many metal utensils necessary for a settled, agricultural way of life. Meanwhile, Black Hoof and his people erected "log houses with chimneys" resembling those built by white frontiersmen. But after his visits to Washington, Black Hoof was dissatisfied with such primitive accommodations and persuaded Kirk to begin the construction of a sawmill so that his tribesmen would have sawed planks to "finish" their dwellings. Plans also were laid for a gristmill, and by October, Kirk had purchased a grinding stone and the machinery necessary for its operation. Many of the Shawnees had exchanged their traditional skin garments for white men's clothing, and their trips to the settlements were marked by "sobriety and good behavior." Kirk was so encouraged with the Shawnees' progress that he planned similar ventures among the Wyandots and Ottawas.[33]

But in December 1808, Kirk's mission among the Shawnees was terminated. Although the Quaker had been successful in bringing white agriculture to the Indians, he was lax in his paperwork. Busy with the everyday problems at Wapakoneta, Kirk had failed to send adequate financial statements to Washington, and federal officials believed he was mismanaging government funds. On December 22, 1808, Secretary of War Henry Dearborn dismissed the missionary, and although the Shawnees and many white Ohioans petitioned the government in Kirk's favor, the Quaker was forced to leave the Auglaize. At first, Black Hoof's people attempted to continue on the white man's road, but they soon became discouraged. With Kirk's departure the Shawnees lost their primary source of technical advice and their experiment in agriculture waned.[34]

Although Black Hoof and his followers were willing to try the white man's road, their more traditional kinsmen scoffed at the prospect of becoming farmers. Distrusting the missionaries as agents of the federal government, these Shawnees rejected the Quakers' invitations to join in the "civilizing" process. In the summer they continued to pitch their wigwams along the river bottoms, fishing and planting small patches of corn. During the cold months they often scattered through the forests, hunting and trapping furs, which were bartered to white traders for various necessities. But the years following the Treaty of Greenville were not happy ones for these people. As the white population of Ohio and Indiana increased, game animals diminished. White hunters from the settlements frequently crossed over into the Auglaize and upper Miami valleys, killing deer and other animals. In 1802, with their food supply dwindling, Shawnee leaders complained bitterly to the government: "Hear the lamentations of our women and children. . . . Stop your people from killing our game. At present they kill more than we do. They would be angry if we were to kill a cow or hog of theirs, the little game that remains is very dear to us."[35]

Yet federal officials were powerless to change the hunting habits of their citizens, and the illegal slaughter continued. Dodging the issue, American agents suggested that if the Indians could not provide for themselves by hunting, perhaps they should try agriculture. They reminded the Shawnees that the government was supplying them with one thousand dollars in annuities each year. If the amount was too small, the Indians could cede additional lands. As an alternative, President Jefferson urged the tribesmen to purchase goods on credit from government factories (trading posts). Privately, he assured Harrison that such transactions would benefit the government. It would lure the Indians into debt: "When these debts get beyond what the individuals can pay, they become willing to lop them off by a cession of lands."[36]

Ironically, few of the Shawnees traded at the government factories. Although small numbers of Black Hoof's people visited the government post at Fort Wayne, most other Shawnees continued to barter their decreasing harvest of fur to British traders from Canada. Some of the Indians regularly journeyed to Malden, where they traded their pelts to Matthew Elliott and other merchants. Others were visited in their villages by Canadian middlemen anxious to undercut their American competition. In most cases, the British traders were successful. The Shawnees found that the British offered higher prices for their fur and supplied more durable trade goods. Even American traders admitted the British wares were "better calculated for the market than [those of the Americans], the patterns, the quality and prices of the articles [had] been so long fixed that the manufacturers in England [knew] the kind of goods that [would] answer as well as if they were on the spot." Using their economic leverage to great advantage, the British traders worked to maintain the Crown's political influence within the tribe. Although the traders did not openly advocate that the Shawnees take up arms against the United States, they willingly agreed with the tribesmen that the Long Knives were the source of most of their problems. There is no doubt that the traders added fuel to the fires of Shawnee resentment.[37]

The Americans did little to snuff out such flames. Embittered by a quarter-century of warfare, and suspicious of the Shawnees' continued association with the British, the frontier citizens of Ohio and Indiana declared an "open season" on Shawnee property. In addition to the slaughter of game animals on Indian lands, white horse thieves preyed on the Shawnee herds, for once a stolen animal reached the settlements the tribesmen were powerless to recover it. Undoubtedly, a few of these animals had previously been stolen by the Indians, but in the decade after Greenville, most of Ohio's traffic in pilfered horses seemed to originate in the Indian camps and end in the settlements.[38]

Horses were not the only object of white opportunists. Any Shawnee camp left unattended while its owners were hunting or fishing was fair game to mounted frontiersmen seeking deer on Indian lands. The settlements provided a ready market for contraband furs, food, or trade goods. Of course the Shawnees sometimes pilfered white property, but claims for such thefts were deducted from the tribes' yearly annuities. In contrast, Shawnee victims had no such recourse against the frontiersmen. Although white officials attempted to intervene in the Indians' behalf, they could not force payment from their frontier citizens. Seeking stronger penalties for such crimes, Governor St. Clair pointed out that the Shawnees and their Indian neighbors daily were subjected to "injustice and wrongs of the most provoking character, for which I have never heard that any person was ever brought to justice and punishment, and all proceeding from the false principle that, because they had not received the light of the gospel, they might be abused, cheated, robbed, plundered, and murdered at pleasure, and the perpetrators, because professed Christians, ought not to suffer from it."[39]

Other crimes were of a more serious nature. In 1802 a delegation of Shawnee chiefs visited Washington, reporting that a hunting party from Kentucky had kidnapped a Shawnee child. Assuring Jefferson that "the child was born and bred in our town," they asked the president to return "the little girl stole from us . . . , we think it very hard that our children should be taken by force." Other Shawnees were seized as hostages for crimes committed by their Indian neighbors. In 1800 an intoxicated Shawnee warrior killed his white drinking partner in a drunken brawl near Cincinnati. Although the warrior fled, whites arrested three Shawnee men and a woman who were trading nearby. The hostages had no knowledge of the killing, but were kept in confinement several weeks before federal officials obtained their release. Yet these tribesmen were fortunate; they escaped with their lives. Angered that the Indians had been given their freedom, settlers from Hamilton, Ohio, sought revenge against other members of the tribe and in August murdered a small party of Shawnees camped along the Miami River. St. Clair attempted to prosecute the murderers, but was unsuccessful.[40]

If the Shawnees paid dearly for spilling American blood, the opposite was rarely the case. In 1802 a drunken Shawnee was lured into a cabin in eastern Indiana, robbed, and then bludgeoned to death with a piece of firewood by the cabin owner. Although eyewitnesses testified against the man, he was acquitted of the crime. One year later the aged Wawilaway, who earlier had guided American surveyors, was shot down while trading near Frankfort, Ohio. Before he died, the old Shawnee managed to kill one of his assailants, but two of the man's accomplices went free. Other Shawnees fell victim to similar ambushes, and American agents continually worried about widespread Shawnee retaliation. In discussing the problem with his associates, St. Clair admitted, "The number of those unhappy people who have been killed since the peace at Greenville . . . is great enough to give a very serious alarm for the consequences."[41]

It is not surprising that much of the Shawnee-white violence was triggered by alcohol, for after 1800 growing numbers of the tribesmen were addicted to the raw frontier whiskey readily available along the Auglaize and Wabash rivers. Indian agents were ordered to suppress the liquor trade, but their efforts were both halfhearted and ineffectual. White travelers visiting the tribe reported that the Shawnees had acquired "a passion for drink which acknowledges no bounds or moderation," an opinion dolefully reiterated by Indian agents and missionaries in the region. Moravian brethren among the Delawares on the White River in Indiana complained that neighboring Shawnees were buying whiskey in fifty-gallon barrels, drinking one keg after another. Often the bacchanalia lasted several days, interspersed with drunken brawls and other sorry occasions. Passing through a Shawnee camp, one missionary commented that the Shawnees had consumed so much whiskey they had painted themselves black and "screamed all night in the woods and acted like madmen."[42]

As in most cases, the excessive drinking took a heavy toll on all parts of Shawnee society. Brawls generated at drinking bouts spilled over onto other tribal members, and even Indians who abstained from whiskey sometimes suffered. Drunken warriors spread havoc amid the villages, injuring their kinsmen and threatening their friends. Some women took part in the carousing, but others hid in their wigwams, shielding their children from the violence. Meanwhile, much of the Shawnees' dwindling economic base was squandered for whiskey, a malevolent luxury they could ill afford.[43]

Aware that stability within their villages was disintegrating, the Shawnees searched for the cause. Although many realized that most of their problems arose from identifiable sources—the loss of land, economic deterioration, injustice, and alcohol—others suspected darker elements and probed inward, examining the fabric of tribal society. Not surprisingly, some concluded that their woes resulted from witchcraft. A fear of witches and their evil power permeated Shawnee culture, and other Algonquian-speaking peoples believed the Shawnees to have a particular attraction to sorcery and the supernatural.[44]

The roots of such apprehensions lay deep in tribal tradition. Some Shawnees believed that in the dim past, when they first crossed the Great Water in search of their homeland, they had been opposed by a huge water serpent who represented the evil powers in the universe. Although the Indians eventually killed the serpent, part of its body had been saved "and the flesh, tho many thousand years old, [was] as fresh as if it had just been killed." Since the Great Serpent had been the servant of evil, the remaining portions of its flesh possessed powerful medicine and had been preserved by those people practicing witchcraft. The witches kept the flesh in bundles wrapped in cloth or skins and used their magic against other tribe members. A bundle enabled witches to become invisible, or to transform themselves into animals. Witches could direct the bundle's power at their enemies, causing illness or death. In return, the bundle required a periodic nourishment, of human flesh and blood, which the witches would supply, usually at a relative's expense. The Shawnees were certain that these bundles had been passed down through the ages and were used by witches to spread disorder throughout the tribe.[45]

The interplay of order and chaos formed a focal point for the Shawnees' conception of their world. Shawnee cosmology asserted that they were a people chosen by the Master of Life or Good Spirit to occupy the center of the earth (the Shawnee homeland) and to bring harmony to the universe. To assist his chosen people, the Good Spirit provided the Shawnees with sacred bundles containing objects possessing a powerful medicine that could be used for good. He also gave them a series of laws instructing the Shawnees how to live. If the tribe used the sacred bundles properly and followed the precepts of Shawnee law, they would prosper and their world would be orderly. But if witches and their evil power gained the upper hand, or if the Shawnees abandoned the laws of their fathers, their lives would be full of turmoil. By 1805 many traditional Shawnees were certain that the witches were in the ascendancy.[46]

In retrospect, it is apparent that the traditional Shawnee culture no longer could cope with the changes swirling around it. Although the tribe's hunting-gathering-horticultural way of life had easily adapted to the fur trade, in the decades following the American Revolution the Shawnees had been inundated by white men and their technology. The Shawnee economic system, which for years had provided the tribesmen with material self-sufficiency, faltered. Moreover, a social organization that venerated hunters and warriors broke down under new conditions that afforded little opportunity for either role. Unable to provide for their families through hunting or the fur trade, once skilled hunters were forced to rely on the demeaning annuity system. To add to their shame, they no longer could strike back in the time-honored manner of warriors. Subjected to white injustice, the Shawnees now were forced to submit their complaints to the very leaders of those who oppressed them.[47]

Frustrated in their culture's inability to provide for their basic needs, Black Hoof and his followers stumbled along the white man's road. But more conservative Shawnees sought other outlets for their anxieties. Mired in alcoholism, they vented their frustrations on each other. Violence flared while Shawnee society came apart. Kinship and family relationships deteriorated. Sexual mores declined. Demoralized by the chaos around them, some tribesmen retreated into indolence or depression. Others lashed out at witches. But deep in their hearts, all knew that something was seriously wrong.[48]

Huddled around their campfires, the Shawnees sought solace in their traditions. Were they not the chosen people of the Master of Life? Hadn't their fathers assured them that when the Master of Life made mankind he had formed the Shawnees from his brain? As a token of his favor, had not the Master of Life given their ancestors part of his heart? To keep them pure had he not provided the Shawnees with sacred bundles and tribal laws? They knew that in the past they had been "masters of the continent . . . strong, swift and valiant in war, keen and patient in the chase." But the Shawnees feared they had become inferior to their forefathers. Now they were lesser men, both in strength and in intellect. Fallen from grace, the Shawnees pondered the cause of their degeneration.[49]

Not surprisingly, many blamed the Americans. The Shawnees believed that the sea was the home of the Great Serpent, the embodiment of evil. Tribal traditions always had warned that pale-skinned invaders might arrive from the water to threaten the harmony of the Shawnee homeland. Since the Long Knives had first appeared on the eastern seashore, many tribesmen now were certain they were the spawn of the Serpent, intent on the Indians' downfall. In 1803 a Shawnee delegation at Fort Wayne informed American officials that their forefathers had stood on the shores of the Atlantic, watching as a strange object appeared on the horizon.

At first they took it for a great bird, but they soon found it to be a monstrous canoe filled with the very people who had got the knowledge which belonged to the Shawnees. After these white people had landed, they were not content with having the knowledge which belonged to the Shawnees, but they usurped their land also. They pretended, indeed, to have purchased these lands but the very goods they gave for them were more the property of the Indians than of the white people, because the knowledge which enabled them to manufacture these goods actually belonged to the Shawnees. But these things will soon end. The Master of Life is about to restore to the Shawnees their knowledge and their rights and he will trample the Long Knives under his feet.

And even Black Hoof, the staunch friend of the Americans, admitted, "The white people has spoiled us. They have been our ruin." [50]

Chapter Two

The Open Door

The winter of 1804–5 seemed endless to the Delawares scattered along the headwaters of the White River in eastern Indiana. In addition to the usual icy nights and dreary, overcast days, another of the white man's nameless diseases had ravaged through their midst in February and March, taking the lives of the old and weak and debilitating even the strongest of warriors. Camped near the Delawares, a small village of Shawnees had shared in their fate, also giving up lives to the coughing sickness. By early April the illness, probably influenza, had run its course and although nights remained cold, the afternoon sunshine hinted that spring was imminent. In the Shawnee village a heavyset man of thirty years sat cross-legged before the hearth in his wigwam, a blanket wrapped around his shoulders against the chill of the approaching evening. During the recent epidemic he had treated his ailing kinsmen, but with little success. Pondering the causes of his failure, he knew that other Shawnees considered him a ne'er-do-well, a man who flagrantly violated sacred tribal laws. Because of his boasting they had nicknamed him Lalawethika, "the Rattle," or "Noisemaker," a name he did not relish. As he reflected on his sins, the Shawnee reached into the fire and withdrew a brand, intending to light the tobacco in the long-stemmed pipe in his lap. But as he raised the pipe to his lips, Lalawethika gasped, dropped the blazing twig, and toppled over on his side. Believing her husband to be seriously ill, his wife fled from the lodge to summon help from their neighbors. Lalawethika lay sprawled by the fire, as still as death.[1]

At first the neighboring Shawnees were skeptical that Lalawethika was seriously ill. Most knew him as a notorious alcoholic and assumed that Lalawethika had fallen into a drunken stupor, a condition not uncommon for the man. Many of the tribesmen had known Lalawethika all their lives. Although they were disgusted by his degeneracy, they knew he came from good stock. He had been born in early 1775, a triplet with two brothers, at Old Piqua, a Shawnee village on the Mad River in western Ohio. His father was Puckeshinwa, a leading war chief of the Kispokotha division of the tribe; his mother, Methoataske ("Turtle Laying Its Eggs"), was a woman of Creek descent. One of the triplets had died within his first year, but there were several older children in the Shawnee family, for Methoataske had given birth to at least three daughters and three other sons in addition to Lalawethika and Kumskaukau, the other surviving triplet.[2]

Lalawethika's childhood had not been easy. In October 1774, several months before Lalawethika was born, his father, Puckeshinwa, had fallen at the Battle of Point Pleasant. Depressed over her husband's death and frightened by the American Revolution, Methoataske abandoned her Shawnee offspring and either returned to the Creeks or accompanied most of the Kispokothas west when they left Ohio in 1779. Regardless of her motivation, Methoataske's desertion of her family must have been traumatic for the two remaining triplets. Also affected was Tecumseh, a brother seven years older than Lalawethika and Kumskaukau.[3]

Other Shawnees attempted to take the vanished parents' place. Black Fish, the leading war chief in the raids against Kentucky, took an interest in the boys, while Tecumpease, Lalawethika's oldest sister, a woman already married, took the young Shawnees into her wigwam. But Tecumpease and her husband, Wasabogoa ("Stand Firm"), favored Tecumseh over either of the younger brothers and although the Shawnee woman spent hours with Tecumseh, she generally ignored the young Lalawethika. Of course Lalawethika and Kumskaukau, who soon fades into obscurity, received adequate food and shelter, but Lalawethika never developed a close relationship with his sister such as existed between Tecumseh and Tecumpease.[4]

Lalawethika also must have been envious of the affection shown to Tecumseh by Chiksika, the boys' eldest brother, who already had achieved some distinction as a warrior. About fifteen years older than Lalawethika, Chiksika had been present at Point Pleasant when his father was killed. Vowing revenge on the Long Knives, the young Shawnee warrior took an active part in Black Fish's raids into Kentucky, and after the revolution he remained one of the most militant anti-American members of the tribe. Like Tecumpease, Chiksika also expressed a particular affinity with Tecumseh and seemingly ignored the younger brothers. He took special pains to see that Tecumseh was properly trained in the skills of hunting and warfare, and often allowed Tecumseh to accompany him on hunting trips or small war parties. But Lalawethika was too young for such excursions and was forced to remain at home, brooding over being left behind. What little training as a warrior he received evidently was acquired from mimicking other small boys in his village. There is no evidence to suggest he ever possessed enough skill as a hunter to provide for either himself or his family.[5]

And so Lalawethika passed his childhood amid much uncertainty. Either abandoned or ignored by parent figures, he overcompensated for his insecurity through boastful harangues on his own importance. To add to his woes, while playing with a bow and iron-tipped arrows, he suffered an accident and lost the sight of his right eye. Moreover, during his adolescence, Lalawethika acquired a taste for the white man's firewater, a habit that both increased his bragging and decreased his popularity among the Shawnees. He remained on good terms with Tecumseh, but Chiksika would not associate with him. In late 1787, when Chiksika organized a war party of younger warriors to strike at white settlements in Tennessee, Lalawethika was not invited to join. Although Tecumseh accompanied his elder brother into the South and was present in 1788 when Chiksika was killed in an assault on a frontier outpost, Lalawethika remained in Ohio. There is no evidence to suggest that he was deeply grieved at Chiksika's passing.[6]

Lalawethika did not participate in either of the Indian victories over General Harmar or Governor St. Clair, but he did make a minor contribution to the tribes' opposition to "Mad Anthony" Wayne. In August 1794, the nineteen-year-old Shawnee formed part of the Indian army opposing Wayne's legions at the Battle of Fallen Timbers. His performance in the encounter remains unknown, but he accompanied two older brothers, Tecumseh and Sauwauseekau, into the engagement, where the Shawnees were in the thick of the fighting. Sauwauseekau was killed and Tecumseh led a small party of warriors that covered the Indian retreat down the Maumee toward Fort Miamis. Although Tecumseh refused to participate in the subsequent Treaty of Greenville, Lalawethika probably was in attendance. The treaty was negotiated amid presents of trade goods and free-flowing whiskey, attractions holding a powerful enticement for the impressionable young Shawnee.[7]

Following the Treaty of Greenville, Lalawethika joined a small band of Shawnees, led by Tecumseh, residing on Deer Creek, a tributary of the Mad River in west-central Ohio. In the spring of 1796 the Shawnees moved to the Great Miami, where they raised and harvested a crop of corn, but in the fall they abandoned their summer camp and established a new village on the headwaters of the Whitewater, in eastern

Indiana. Lalawethika and his kinsmen remained on the Whitewater through 1797, but in the following year they moved westward to the White River, near the site of modern Anderson. The new White River village was located in a fertile region where game was more abundant, and the Shawnees remained in the area for several years.[8]

The decade following the Treaty of Greenville was not a happy time for the maturing Lalawethika. No longer a child, he now was forced to leave his sister's family and make his way in the world. During this period he took a wife and sired several children, but his growing family demanded support, and Lalawethika was ill equipped to provide for them. He made a desultory attempt at hunting, but the deer herds were diminishing and he often returned to his lodge empty-handed. Drowning his sense of failure, Lalawethika turned more and more to the whiskey keg, a response that only angered his wife and did little to resolve his problems. Finally, after settling on the White River, Lalawethika became acquainted with Penagashea ("Changing Feathers"), an old Shawnee highly respected as a prophet and medicine man. At first Penagashea disliked the alcoholic young braggart, but eventually the two men became friends, and although Lalawethika had not experienced a vision, the aging Shawnee evidently shared some of his knowledge of medicine with him. But in 1804 Penagashea died, and when Lalawethika attempted to take his place and cure the Shawnees, the aspiring new medicine man met with little success. In early 1805 the white man's illness again spread through the Shawnee village. Some who received Lalawethika's herbs and incantations recovered, but many did not. Meanwhile, many tribesmen questioned if a man who so often had broken the sacred Shawnee laws could ever wear the mantle of healer or prophet.[9]

When Lalawethika's wife and neighbors rushed back into the lodge they found the Shawnee still prostrate before the fire. Although his wife spoke to him, he did not answer. Other tribesmen rolled the Shawnee over onto his back, but his eyes remained closed and he did not seem to be breathing. Believing the man to be dead, neighbors led his grieving wife from the wigwam and made plans to wash the body in preparation for the two-day period before burial. But before the funeral arrangements were completed, the assembled Indians gasped in amazement as the supposedly dead Lalawethika first stirred, then awakened. Although dazed, he obviously was very much alive.[10]

Slowly regaining his senses, Lalawethika told a strange tale of death, heaven, and resurrection. The Shawnee claimed that the Master of Life had sent two handsome young men to carry his soul into the spirit world, where he had been shown both the past and the future. Although the Master of Life did not allow Lalawethika to enter heaven, he was permitted to gaze on a paradise, which he described as "a rich, fertile country, abounding in game, fish, pleasant hunting grounds and fine corn fields," a realm where the spirits of virtuous Shawnees could flourish, "pursuing the same course of life which characterized them here. They [could] plant, . . . hunt, [or] play at their usual games and in all things [could remain] unchanged." But not all Shawnee spirits proceeded directly to heaven. The souls of sinful tribesmen also followed the road toward paradise, but after glimpsing the promised land they were forced to turn away and enter a large lodge where an enormous fire burned continually. Here the sinners were subjected to fiery torture in accordance with their wickedness. The most evil were reduced to ashes. Unrepentant drunkards were forced to swallow molten lead until flames shot from their mouths and nostrils. Lesser offenders had their limbs burned, but all evildoers were compelled to repeat their suffering until they had atoned fully for their sins. Finally, they would be permitted to enter heaven, but could never share in all the pleasures enjoyed by more virtuous tribesmen.[11]

As he finished his story, Lalawethika began to weep and tremble. Overcome by emotion, he vowed to renounce his evil ways and never again to drink the white man's whiskey. A changed man, he no longer was the drunken braggart known as Lalawethika. Henceforward he would be called Tenskwatawa, "the Open Door," a name symbolizing his new role as a holy man destined to lead his people down the narrow road toward paradise. Some of his audience remained skeptical, but many others were convinced of his sincerity and readily subscribed to the new prophet's doctrines.[12]

In the following months Tenskwatawa experienced additional visions and enlarged on his doctrine of Indian deliverance. Other Shawnees, demoralized by the changes swirling around them, flocked to the new messiah, seeking stability in a world full of chaos. Since Shawnee social and political systems could not cope with the onrushing frontier, they grasped at the hope that the Master of Life had provided Tenskwatawa with a new faith to revitalize his chosen people. During the summer of 1805 Moravian missionaries in eastern Indiana reported that their congregations were shrinking in the face of a renewed "heathenism" spreading through the nearby Indians. Meanwhile, the Prophet and his followers left the White River to establish a new village near Greenville, in western Ohio.[13]

In late November 1805, the new Shawnee holy man met with delegations of Shawnees, Ottawas, Wyandots, and Senecas at Wapakoneta, on the Auglaize River, where he expounded on his religion at some length. Since his initial vision in April, several similar experiences had provided Tenskwatawa with additional insights, which he incorporated into a well-defined pattern of religious and social doctrines. Much of the Prophet's dogma attacked the decline of traditional moral values among the Shawnees and neighboring tribes. Declaring he "was particularly appointed to that office by the Great Spirit," Tenskwatawa asserted that his "sole object was to reclaim the Indians from bad habits and to cause them to live in peace with all mankind." First and foremost, he denounced the consumption of alcohol. Admitting that he once had been a drunkard, Tenskwatawa asserted that he now was cured and would never again partake of the white man's firewater. He warned the tribesmen that frontier whiskey "was poison and accursed," and described in vivid detail the special tortures awaiting the souls of unrepentant alcoholics. Moved by the Shawnee's exhortations, many of the audience were greatly alarmed and vowed to follow the Prophet's example.[14]

Tenskwatawa also condemned the violence that recently had so permeated tribal society. He instructed his listeners to always treat tribal elders with respect and to provide for kinsmen who were injured, diseased, or incapable of caring for themselves. He admonished his followers to refrain from intertribal violence, urging warriors to treat each other as brothers, stop their quarreling, and never pilfer the belongings of fellow tribesmen. They must remain truthful and not strike their wives or children. Only if a married woman behaved so badly that she brought disrespect to her husband could the man "punish her with a rod," but afterward "both husband and wife was to look each other in the face and laugh and to bear no ill will to each other for what had passed." Concerned about sexual promiscuity, the Prophet warned Shawnee women to remain faithful to their husbands and decreed that warriors were not "to be running after women; if a man was single let him take a wife." He also advised against polygamous marriages, stating that in the future warriors were only to have one wife. Those Shawnees currently married to more than one woman "might keep them," but they should realize that such a union displeased the Master of Life.[15]

In contrast, Tenskwatawa assured his followers that the Master of Life favored the performance of certain rituals and ceremonies. He informed them that they should extinguish the fires in their lodges and light new ones, the new flames to be kindled in the traditional manner, without using the white man's flint and steel: "The fire must never go out. . . . Summer and winter, day and night, in the storm or when it is calm, you must remember that the life in your body, and the fire in your lodge are the same and of the same date. If you suffer your fire to be extinguished, at that moment your life will be at its end." The Prophet also denounced many of the traditional tribal dances as corrupt, but suggested new ones that would both please the Master of Life and bring joy to the dancers. Moreover, Tenskwatawa instructed his listeners that they should pray to the Master of Life both morning and evening, asking that the earth be fruitful, the streams abound in fish, and the forests be full of game. To assist his followers with their prayers, he provided them with prayer sticks inscribed with certain symbols that epitomized the new faith. If the Indians were faithful, then the Master of Life would smile upon them and they would prosper.[16]

Especially suspect were traditional shamans and their "juggleries." Those medicine men who might oppose Tenskwatawa's new doctrines were described as misguided fools or false prophets, men who would never know happiness. To destroy any vestige of the corrupt old ways, the Prophet ordered his followers to throw away their medicine bundles. Although these parcels contained items traditionally sacred to individual Shawnees, Tenskwatawa declared that this medicine "which had been good in its time, had lost its efficacy; that it had become vitiated through age." Those who abandoned their bundles would eventually "find [their] children or . . . friends that have long been dead restored to life."[17]

Although the Prophet's new creed attacked some facets of traditional Shawnee culture, it attempted to revitalize others. Indeed, much of Tenskwatawa's preaching was nativistic in both tone and content. If shamans and medicine bundles were forbidden, the Shawnees were encouraged to return to many other practices followed by their fathers. Tenskwatawa urged them to renounce their desire to accumulate property and to return to the communal life of the past. Those who accumulated "wealth and ornaments" would "crumble into dust," but tribesmen who shared with their brothers, "when they die[d] [were] happy; and, when they arrive[d] in the land of the dead, [would] find their wigwam furnished with everything they had on earth."[18]

The Shawnees and other Indians also were admonished to return to the food, implements, and dress of their ancestors. Although white men kept such domestic animals as cattle, sheep, or hogs, such meat was unclean and not to be consumed by Indians. Even dogs were suspect, for he advised his followers that they were evil creatures and should be destroyed. In contrast, the Master of Life had given the tribesmen "the Deer, the Bear, and all wild animals, and the Fish that swim in the river." These species would provide meat for Shawnee cooking pots. Neither were the Indians "on any account, to eat Bread. It is the food of the Whites." Instead, the tribesmen were to cultivate corn, beans, and other crops raised by their fathers, and to gather maple sugar, which was a special food, favored by both the Master of Life and Tenskwatawa.[19]

In a similar manner, the Prophet instructed his followers to relinquish the white man's technology. Although guns might be used for self-defense, warriors were to hunt with bows and arrows. Stone or wood implements should replace metal ones and the tribesmen were to discard all items of European or American clothing. "You must not dress like the White Man or wear hats like them. . . . And when the weather is not severe, you must go naked Excepting the Breach cloth, and when you are clothed, it must be in skins or leather of your own Dressing." Moreover, the warriors were ordered to shave their heads, leaving only the scalp lock worn in the past.[20]

While praising the culture of his forefathers, Tenskwatawa warned against any close association with the Americans. He informed the assembled Indians that although the
British, French, and Spanish had been made by the Master
of Life and should be considered friends, the Americans had
been created by "another spirit who made and governed the
whites and over whom or whose subjects he [the Master of
Life] had no control." Indeed, the Master of Life assured Tenskwatawa, "The Americans I did not make. They are not
my children, but the children of the Evil Spirit."[21]

The Prophet assured his followers that the Master of Life
had revealed the true character of the Americans to him in
a vision. According to Tenskwatawa, in the vision the Long
Knives had taken the form of a great ugly crab that had
crawled from the sea, its claws full of mud and seaweed.
Meanwhile, the Master of Life had spoken, saying, "Behold
this crab. It comes from Boston and brings with it part of
the land in that vicinity. If you Indians will do everything
which I have told you, I will overturn the land, so that all the
white people will be covered and you alone shall inhabit the
land." Continuing the association of the Americans with
the sea, the home of the Great Serpent, Tenskwatawa claimed
that the Master of Life also had informed him: "They [the
Americans] grew from the scum of the great Water when it
was troubled by the Evil Spirit. And the froth was driven
into the Woods by a strong east wind. They are numerous,
but I hate them. They are unjust. They have taken away
your lands, which were not made for them." Only if the
Indians rejected the influence of the Americans would order
ever be returned to the Shawnee world.[22]

The Indians were instructed to have as little contact with
the Long Knives as possible. When meeting an American in
the forest, a Shawnee might greet him from a distance, but
on no occasion was he to touch him or shake hands. Neither
were the tribesmen to sell any of their provisions to the
settlers, for such foods as corn and maple sugar were the

special gifts of the Master of Life and not to be wasted upon the Americans. Only if the Long Knives were starving could small portions of such foodstuffs be supplied to them, and then the rations must be given, never sold. Tenskwatawa also admonished his disciples to cut their ties with white traders. Although the tribesmen were heavily indebted to frontier merchants, the Prophet ordered them to pay "no more than half their Credits, because [the Americans] have cheated you. You must pay them in Skins, Gums, Canoes, etc., but not in meat, corn, or sugar." Moreover, the Shawnee expressly forbid Indian women to have any sexual contacts with American men, stating: "All Indian women who were living with White Men was to be brought home to their friends and relatives, and their children to be left with their Fathers, so that the Nations might become genuine Indian."[23]

If the Americans were "the children of the Evil Spirit," Indian witches still remained the most active agents of that spirit on earth, and Tenskwatawa, like other Shawnees, was concerned about their role in tribal society. For the Prophet, politics and religion were merged. The sacred Shawnee laws, the formula for order within the tribe, were the gift of the Master of Life. Therefore, order in tribal society reflected the will of the Master of Life, and the Prophet felt obligated to restore and protect such stability. In contrast, Tenskwatawa believed that the Evil Spirit sought to spread disorder among the Indians, using witches as the primary instigators of such chaos. Since he believed that the Master of Life had chosen him to lead his kinsmen back to righteousness, the Prophet warned that those who opposed him also opposed the Master of Life and would be suspected of witchcraft. Unless they repented, they should be destroyed.[24]

Anxious to spread his doctrines beyond his immediate audience, Tenskwatawa made provisions to carry the new faith to distant tribes. No longer should warriors raid enemy villages, but all Indians should live in peace. Messengers

would then be sent to the different nations, enlisting converts and sending them to Ohio. Those unable to journey to
the Prophet's village would be taught the new religion in
their homeland and, after performing certain sacred rituals,
would be allowed to join in the Prophet's cause.

The rituals probably reflect the Shawnee's contact with
Roman Catholicism. The new converts were asked to first
confess all their sins and then to solemnize their regenera-
tion by "shaking hands with the Prophet," a ceremony out-
wardly similar to saying the rosary. After the confession the
neophytes were brought into a lodge where the Prophet's
messengers had assembled certain holy items, including an
effigy of the Prophet under a blanket. Extending from the
blanket were several strings of beans. An eyewitness to the
ceremony among the Chippewas described it:

After a long harangue, in which the prominent features of the new
revelation were stated and urged upon the attention of all, the four
strings of beans, which we were told were made of the flesh itself
of the prophet, were carried, with much solemnity, to each man in
the lodge, and he was expected to take hold of each string at the
top, and draw them gently through his hand. This was called shaking hands with the prophet, and was considered as solemnly engag-
ing to obey his injunctions, and accept his mission as from the
Supreme.

The new disciples were then sworn to secrecy, forbidden
ever to discuss the sacred rituals with whites. Moreover,
they were admonished to send one or two men from each
village to be personally trained by Tenskwatawa as his min-
isters in their community. These emissaries would spread
the new faith among other bands of their tribe. Finally, the
Prophet warned that all the tribesmen should follow his
directives closely. "Those villages which do not listen to
this talk and send me two deputies, will be cut off from the
face of the Earth."[25]

In mid-December Tenskwatawa and his Shawnee followers returned to Greenville. Meanwhile, many of the Indians

who had assembled at Wapakoneta rode back to their homes. Although some were skeptical of the new Prophet's sincerity, many saw in him a religious deliverance from the problems that beset them. Had the holy man not risen from the dead? Had he not spoken with the great powers of the universe? Did he not promise to cure the sick and bring back the departed? Would he not restore the game to the forests? Perhaps even the hated Long Knives would be driven into the eastern sea. Inspired with the zeal of new converts, the returning warriors spread the word of the remarkable new religion to their neighbors. Among the Delawares, Moravian missionaries labored mightily to limit growth of this new "heathenism," but most of their efforts were in vain. Discouraged, one of the Moravians recorded that the new faith was being received "with great favor" among the tribes of Ohio and Indiana.[26]

Chapter Three

Black Suns
and Witches

In the following months, the new religion spread like wild-
fire among the Delawares in Indiana. Uprooted and forced
west several times since early in the eighteenth century, the
Delawares were particularly susceptible to Tenskwatawa's
teachings. Several Delawares had listened to the Prophet's
exhortations at Wapakoneta, and when they carried word of
his doctrines back to their villages, many of their kinsmen
readily subscribed to the new faith. Following the Prophet's
teachings, Delaware pilgrims journeyed to Greenville, met
with the holy man, then returned to their villages to enlist
other tribesmen in the rapidly growing religious movement.
Like new converts everywhere, the Delawares were zealous
in their efforts to adhere to the new creed and were particularly concerned with Tenskwatawa's admonitions against
witchcraft. Searching within their society, they probed for
those who appeared to be servants of the Evil Spirit.[1]

They soon found several tribesmen who seemed to fit the
role. Immediately suspect were those Delawares most closely
associated with the children of the Great Serpent, the Americans. Moravian missionaries had labored for decades among
the Delawares, and, although their ministry recently had
declined, several Delawares in Indiana still professed Christianity and maintained ties with the white community. Believing that such tribesmen opposed Tenskwatawa and

therefore were in league with the Great Serpent, the Prophet's disciples turned on these kinsmen and accused them of witchcraft. Not only were these Delawares guilty of spreading chaos in the world, they also were charged with using their evil medicine to poison other tribe members.

In early March 1806, the Prophet's converts among the Delawares assembled near Woapikamunk, a tribal village on the White River. Meeting in secret, the conspirators made plans to seize all Delawares suspected of witchcraft and to confine them in the nearby village. Each of the accused would then be "brought before their grandfather—that is, fire—and if he would surrender his poison and give up his bad art, he should be pardoned. But if he should refuse, he should be killed by tomahawk and have his body thrown into the fire." Meanwhile, messengers were dispatched to Greenville, asking Tenskwatawa to journey to Woapikamunk to assist his disciples in ridding their people of such evil. If the Prophet could converse with the Master of Life, surely he could identify witches among the Delawares. Hopefully, he could assist them in ferreting out those sorcerers wily enough to escape their notice.[2]

The Prophet arrived at Woapikamunk on March 15 to find about one dozen Delawares confined in the village. Most were former Christians or tribesmen with important ties to the white community. Some were elderly chiefs, men who had led their tribe for decades and who had developed powerful enemies. Fearful for their lives, most disavowed any connection with withcraft and asked only to be released.[3]

After discussing the charges against each Delaware, Tenskwatawa requested that the prisoners be seated in a circle facing each other. Then, with "a great many ceremonies," he passed before each of the captives, staring into their faces and declaring their guilt or innocence. The first prisoner whom the Prophet condemned was Caritas, or Anne Charity, an old woman and an avowed Christian. She had been raised among the Moravians in Ohio, survived the Ameri-

44

can Revolution, and had adopted white modes of dress and manners. Described by Moravian missionaries as "an active, industrious woman, and admired for her cleanliness," her very adherence to white ways made her all the more suspect to the Prophet and his followers.[4]

Declaring the old woman to be a witch and a poisoner, the Delawares led her to the center of the village where a large campfire was burning. Binding their victim securely, they suspended her over the fire, exhorting her to confess her guilt and to reveal where she had hidden her poison and medicine bundle. At first she resisted their torture, but at last, screaming with pain, she admitted that she had given her bundle to her grandson. After burning the old woman to death, the Delawares searched for her grandson, whom they eventually found hunting in the forest. They carried him to Woapikamunk, where the frightened young man readily admitted that he once had borrowed his grandmother's medicine bundle, and that it did indeed possess great power. Using such medicine, he claimed to have flown through the air like a bird, crossing the Ohio River into Kentucky, then turning west to the Mississippi before returning to his village on the White River. Not only had the bundle enabled him to fly, it also allowed him to complete this lengthy journey within the space of a few hours. Yet the young Delaware declared that the power of the bundle had so frightened him that he had returned it to his grandmother.[5]

Surprised by the youth's unabashed testimony, Tenskwatawa ordered him released. But Caritas's torture-induced confession and her grandson's corroboration did not bode well for the remaining Delaware captives. The admission of guilt, even under such questionable circumstances, only strengthened the Delawares' suspicion that sorcery was rampant among their people, and they continued the witch hunt with a vengeance. The second victim was Tetepachsit, an old chief and former Moravian convert. Seized and tortured before the Prophet's arrival, Tetepachsit had confessed to spreading poison throughout the tribe, and had named several of the other captives as coconspirators. Although he later retracted his testimony, the old chief's fate was sealed. Since he earlier had confessed to hiding his poison in the Moravian village, a party of Delawares, their faces painted black, carried him to the mission, where they searched for his medicine bundle. When the bundle was not found, they ordered the old man to build a fire, tomahawked their victim, and threw him into the flames. Forcing the horrified missionaries to watch, the Delawares awaited until Tetepachsit's body was charred, then demanded food and tobacco from the Moravians before returning to Woapikamunk. Meanwhile, the fire spread to the nearby forest, filling the mission with smoke and adding dramatic impact to the scene.[6]

Joshua, a Mohican among the Moravians who had served the missionaries as an organist, carpenter, and interpreter, suffered a similar fate. He had been named by Tetepachsit as a poisoner and had been seized by the Delawares on March 13. Tetepachsit later denied that the Mohican was guilty and when Joshua was brought before the Prophet the Shawnee also declared that the man had not spread poison among the Delawares. But Joshua earlier had admitted to having a vision in which an enormous bird appeared, informing him, "I am a man-eater, and if you wish to feed me, you need but point out to me some one, and then I will put him out of the way." To Tenskwatawa, such an admission was tantamount to sorcery. Declaring the man to be possessed by the Evil Spirit, the Shawnee condemned him to the stake. Although the Moravians desperately attempted to intercede in his behalf, their pleas only confirmed the Delawares' suspicions. On March 17, 1806, Joshua was first tomahawked, then burned.[7]

Although the Prophet returned to Greenville, the witch hunt among the Delawares continued. About two weeks after Joshua's death, two more prisoners, the widow and nephew of Tetepachsit, were brought into the Delaware council house. The young man, Billy Patterson, was a skilled gunsmith and a devout Christian. When told to confess his sorcery, he defiantly refused. Taunting his captors, Patterson declared himself innocent and vowed to die as "a christian and a warrior," rather than be intimidated. He was led to the stake, where he stood praying, until killed by the fire.[8]

Tetepachsit's widow suffered a kinder fate. Also condemned to death, she watched as the flames consumed her nephew and preparations were made for another fire. But before the wood could be lighted, her brother, a young warrior in his early twenties, interceded, stepping forward and leading her away from the center of the village. He then returned to the council house, defying anyone to again seize his sister and declaring that the Prophet was an evil spirit who caused the Delawares to destroy one another. Surprised by the opposition, the Prophet's followers allowed the woman to remain free. Other Delawares, encouraged by the young man's actions, then intervened in behalf of the other captives, and the remaining prisoners including Hockingpomsga, a chief prominent in land cessions to the United States, were released. Most tribesmen seemed relieved. They had burned enough of their kinsmen. By mid-April 1806, the witch hunt among the Delawares was over.[9]

It was just starting among the Wyandot villages along the Sandusky River. Many Wyandots had listened to the Prophet at Wapakoneta in November 1805 and, like the Delawares, they too feared the power of witches in their midst. Learning that Tenskwatawa had assisted the Delawares in exposing the sorcerers, young Wyandots from villages near Upper Sandusky sent riders to Greenville asking the Shawnee to come to northern Ohio. In early May, Tenskwatawa journeyed to the Wyandot villages, where he conducted a series of purges resembling those in Indiana. By mid-May, four women had been accused of witchcraft and preparations were made for their execution. Once again, the captives were "of the best women in the nation," acculturated Wyandots who had adopted much of the white lifestyle. But unlike the Delawares, among these Wyandots the Prophet's followers, although vocal, were limited in number, and the Wyandot villages in the region were dominated by Tarhe ("the Crane"), a staunch friend of the Americans. Viewing the Shawnee religious leader and his followers as threats to his authority, Tarhe interceded, using his influence to free the captives. Angered, Tenskwatawa returned to Greenville.[10]

While the Prophet was seeking sorcerers among the Wyandots, news of the Delaware witch hunts slowly filtered back to white settlements in Ohio and Indiana. At Vincennes, Harrison was shocked by reports of the executions and immediately attempted to stop the burnings. In mid-April he wrote to the Delawares:

My heart is filled with grief, and my eyes are dissolved in tears, at the news which has reached me. You have been celebrated for your wisdom above all the tribes of red people. . . . I charge you to stop your bloody career. . . . Let your poor old men and women sleep in quietness, and banish from their minds the dreadful idea of being burnt alive by their own friends and countrymen.

Denouncing Tenskwatawa as a "pretended prophet" and "imposter," Harrison admonished the Delawares: "Drive him from your town, and let peace and harmony once more prevail amongst you." The Prophet, he added, had deluded the Delawares and led them down a "dark, crooked, and thorny road" to "endless woe and misery." Why would the Great Spirit have selected such a charlatan to deliver his message to his Indian children? The Delawares should demand that the Shawnee prove his powers by performing miracles: "If he is really a prophet, ask of him to cause the sun to stand still—the moon to alter is course—the rivers to cease to flow—or the dead to rise from their graves. If he does these things, you may then believe that he has been sent from God."[11]

But the Delawares received Harrison's message with "poor grace" and "indifference." When asked why they had executed their kinsmen, tribal spokesmen replied, "You white people also try your criminals, and when they are found guilty, you hang them or kill them, and we do the same among ourselves." The Delawares burned no more witches, but they remained under the Prophet's influence.[12]

Ironically, Harrison's demands that Tenskwatawa produce a miracle eventually played into the Shawnee's hands. Throughout the spring of 1806 several teams of astronomers and other scientists had traveled over Indiana, Kentucky, and Illinois establishing observation stations to study an eclipse of the sun scheduled to occur on June 16. Although Harrison must have been aware of such preparations, he evidently had forgotten about the upcoming eclipse when he wrote to the Delawares in April. In the meantime, Delaware messengers brought copies of Harrison's speech to Greenville, where the Prophet considered the governor's challenge. Like Harrison, Tenskwatawa also was aware of the scientists' activities. Moreover, he knew that among the Shawnees such an eclipse was called Mukutaaweethee Keesohtoa, a Black Sun; an event surrounded with dread, and supposedly warning of future warfare.[13]

If doubters needed proof of his medicine, the Prophet would give it to them. In early June Tenskwatawa assembled his followers at Greenville and astonished even his most devout disciples by declaring that he would use his power to darken the sun at midday. Instructing his audience to spread word of the upcoming miracle, the Shawnee directed them to reassemble at Greenville on June 16, when the Master of Life would send a Black Sun as mute testimony of the Prophet's authority.

By mid-June, Indians from many tribes had assembled in the Shawnee village. Realizing that the upcoming event would undoubtedly increase his influence, Tenskwatawa enhanced the drama by remaining in his lodge throughout the morning of June 16. Then, as the noon sun faded into an eerie twilight, the Shawnee holy man appeared among his frightened followers, shouting, "Did I not speak the truth? See, the sun is dark!" The Prophet then assured his frightened audience that just as he had darkened the sun, so he also would restore its former radiance, and as the eclipse ended, the Indians were much relieved. They also were convinced of the great power of Tenskwatawa's medicine. Even the doubters who could not forget that the new holy man once had been Lalawethika, the drunken loudmouth, now seemed satisfied of his sincerity. The Prophet was indeed favored by the Master of Life.[14]

While Tenskwatawa was winning converts through his "miracles," federal Indian policy continued to push other tribesmen into his camp. Anxious to acquire as much Indian land as possible, between 1804 and 1807 Harrison and other officials conducted seven separate treaties with the Delawares, Sacs and Foxes, Miamis, Wyandots, Ottawas, and other tribes. Negotiated by old "government chiefs" friendly to federal agents, these agreements ceded millions of acres to the United States. In return, the Indians received small annuities, usually doled out through those chiefs who cooperated with the government. The land cessions angered many members of the tribes, alienating the younger warriors from their leaders. Convinced that the friendly chiefs were selling their birthright, the young firebrands denounced the transactions as illegal and refused to give up their claims to the territories. During 1806 and 1807, white agents among the tribes reported that resentment against the United States seemed to be growing and warned their superiors that steps should be taken to defuse the hostility. But the government made plans for future cessions, and Indian bitterness continued unabated.[15]

Such discontent fed the new religion, which soon spread to other tribes. It found willing recipients among the Kickapoos. Always a conservative people, the Kickapoos re-

sented white settlement along the Wabash Valley and opposed the northern advance of American homesteads into
the fertile prairies of central Illinois. During the summer of
1806 Kickapoos from the headwaters of the Sangamon River
journeyed to Greenville, where they received the Prophet's
blessing, then carried the new faith back to their villages.
Warned that Tenskwatawa's influence was expanding westward, Harrison dispatched messengers to the Kickapoo towns
to caution them against "the advice of those who would
lead [them] to destruction." Although the Kickapoos along
the Vermillion River seemed receptive to the governor's admonition, their kinsmen on the Sangamon ignored the
warning and deposed those chiefs who spoke out against the
new doctrine. Throughout the following months they refused all offers of American reconciliation and by the summer of 1807 the Kickapoo villages on the Sangamon had
become seedbeds for the Prophet's influence in Illinois.[16]

Tenskwatawa's teachings also found a fertile ground among
the tribes near Lake Michigan. During early 1807 numerous
Potawatomi warriors journeyed to Greenville, meeting with
the Prophet and listening to his exhortations. Scattered in a
wide arc from Detroit to the Illinois River Valley, the Potawatomis disagreed among themselves over accepting the new
faith. Chiefs from villages near Detroit and Fort Wayne who
were leaders dependent on the American annuity system
rejected the doctrine and discouraged their young men from
visiting the Shawnee holy man. But Potawatomis from
western Michigan, Illinois, and Wisconsin were eager for
the new deliverance, and when the spring grass was high
enough to feed their horses, they rode in large parties across
Indiana toward Greenville. Entranced with Tenskwatawa,
many remained for several weeks, preparing to carry the
religion back to their people. They also hoped to proselytize
other western tribes, inviting the Sacs, Winnebagos, and
Menominees to meet with them at Crow Prairie, on the
Illinois River, in June 1807.[17]

The Prophet also found disciples among the Ottawas and Chippewas. During the spring of 1807 many Ottawas from Michigan traveled to the Prophet's village to question him about his revelations. Among the Ottawa pilgrims was Le Maigouis ("the Trout"), a prominent warrior from L'Arbre Croche, a village on the western shores of Lake Michigan, between Michilimackinac and Little Traverse Bay. Impressed with the Ottawa warrior, the Prophet singled him out for special attention, informing Le Maigouis that he should become "the Herald of this new Religion" to both his people and the Chippewas. Inspired by such distinction, Le Maigouis returned to Michigan, then journeyed to Ottawa villages on the Grand River and at Saginaw Bay, urging his kinsmen to accept the Shawnee's promises.[18]

At Michilimackinac, Captain Josiah Dunham, the American military commander, attempted to intercept Le Maigouis, but the Ottawa eluded capture and spoke to an assemblage of his kinsmen within the shadow of the very walls of the American fortress. Holding a wampum belt given to him by Tenskwatawa, Le Maigouis assured his listeners that the Prophet spoke with the voice of the Great Spirit, adding, "Those villages which do not listen to this Talk . . . will be cut off from the face of the Earth." He then explained the new religion, informing them that they should send delegates to Greenville to meet with the Shawnee. He also instructed the Ottawas to keep the new faith secret from the Americans. "You must not speak of this Talk to the Whites— It must be hidden from them," for the world would soon end, and only the Indians were worthy of salvation.[19]

Angered at the Ottawa's audacity, Dunham again ordered his troops to arrest Le Maigouis, but several Ottawa chiefs interceded and Dunham reluctantly agreed to his release. Hoping to minimize Le Maigouis's efforts, the officer sent a speech to the neighboring Ottawas and Chippewas denouncing Le Maigouis as a "Dog" who "has taken great pains to avoid me, by creeping round behind the island . . .

as if he were guilty of some mischief." Dunham also condemned the Prophet as a "great Imposter" who had nothing good to offer, but only "mischief in his heart." Yet Dunham's warnings fell on deaf ears, for during the summer of 1807 wampum belts symbolizing acceptance of the new doctrine passed among all the Ottawa villages. Traders near Michilimackinac and L'Arbre Croche complained that the Indians now refused to accept their whiskey and reported that the chiefs from the Grand River and Saginaw Bay had left their villages to visit the Prophet at Greenville.[20] When the chiefs returned they still professed friendship to the United States, but they refused to discuss further cession of Indian lands in Michigan. Only Kawachawan ("the Eddy"), an elderly chief residing near Detroit, seemed genuinely loyal to the Americans, and by early autumn his influence was diminishing.[21]

Following his release, Le Maigouis crossed over to Sault Ste. Marie and then journeyed westward along the southern shores of Lake Superior. There he found that word of the Prophet's religion had preceded him and that the Chippewas were eager to learn more of the new doctrine. At Whitefish Point he met a party of Chippewas from Keweenaw Bay carrying pelts to Michilimackinac. La Maigouis called the Chippewas into council and explained the Shawnee's teachings. He added, for dramatic effect, that the world was in its final days and soon would be ending. Eternal night would encompass the earth, and the Master of Life would provide light only for Tenskwatawa and his true believers at the village near Greenville.[22]

Dumbfounded, the Chippewas returned to their homes, then sent messengers to their kinsmen scattered in villages across Wisconsin and Minnesota. At Chequamegon Bay, Chippewas gathered just opposite Madeline Island to "dance the dances and sing the songs" of the new deliverance. Subscribing to the Prophet's teachings, they threw their medicine bags into Lake Superior and made preparations to visit the holy man in Ohio. Other Chippewa villages experienced

similar conversions, and within twelve months the Shawnee religion had spread westward through the Chippewas to
the Crees and Assiniboins. In 1808 almost the entire population of a Chippewa village at Lac Court Oreilles, in northern Wisconsin, carried a dead child to Lake Superior, hoping
to transport the body to Greenville where the Prophet mi-
raculously would restore the child to life. Although the be-
reaved tribesmen eventually turned back, so many other Indians abandoned their villages for the trek to Greenville that
during the summer of 1808 white traders found most of the
Chippewa towns along the southern shore of Lake Superior
deserted.[23] Many of these travelers failed to complete their
pilgrimage, but during the summers of 1807 and 1808 so
many Chippewas passed through American posts enroute to
the Prophet's village that federal officials became much
alarmed.[24]

The officials also were alarmed over the spread of the
Shawnee's doctrine to other tribes in Wisconsin. Although
the Menominee chief Tomah evidently rejected Tenskwatawa's teachings, young warriors from his village on the
shores of Green Bay listened attentively to the Prophet's
spokesmen. Menominee leaders refused to attend a multitribal council held at Crow Prairie, on the Illinois River, but
younger tribesmen danced the new dances, and during the
summer of 1807 they joined with the Chippewas and traveled to the Prophet's village.[25]

At Greenville, Tenskwatawa also received a delegation of
Winnebagos. Residing in villages across southern Wisconsin, the Winnebagos first learned of the new religion from
Potawatomi neighbors to the south. Intrigued by sketchy
reports of the Shawnee's teachings, the Winnebagos conferred among themselves before sending a small party of
warriors to investigate the doctrine. Finally, eleven young
men led by Smoke Walker and Dog Head, an old medicine
man, first journeyed to the Potawatomi towns on the St.
Joseph River in Michigan, then traveled on to Ohio. There

the Prophet greeted them warmly, calling them his "younger brothers" and explaining his religious experiences to them.[26]

The Winnebagos found the Prophet's camp crowded with Indians. In addition to Shawnees, Delawares, Wyandots, and Indians from the Great Lakes, they encountered Sacs from the Rock River and Miamis from the Wabash Valley.[27] They also learned that messengers had been sent to the Senecas, soliciting converts among the Iroquois Confederacy, but there the Shawnee's efforts had been opposed by both tribal leaders and the Seneca prophet, Handsome Lake.[28]

The village at Greenville hummed with activity. Smoke Walker, Dog Head, and the other Winnebagos found that over sixty cabins and wigwams were clustered around a large frame council-house, whose dimensions measure 150 by 34 feet. Most of the buildings lay within a belt of timber bordering Greenville Creek, while to the south and east a broad prairie stretched off into the distance. The Prophet's disciples had planted corn, beans, and other Indian crops in small patches, but since the vegetables had not yet matured, the village was short of provisions. Undeterred, the Indians continued to fell trees and saplings, constructing shelters for the burgeoning population. Meanwhile, Tenskwatawa kept them in a state of religious exhilaration. On almost every evening they assembled in the council house to listen to the Prophet's new revelations and to dance and sing in celebration of their deliverance. Whites complained that the drums and accompanying uproar could be heard for miles, but since most frontiersmen gave the village a wide berth, such claims are probably much exaggerated. Nevertheless, most federal officials agreed that the Prophet's encampment had become a new mecca for the religious fervor sweeping through the tribes of the Old Northwest.[29]

Although the religious activity at Greenville alarmed the Moravians, it aroused the curiosity of some other frontier Christians. In the fall of 1806 Tenskwatawa entertained John Simpson, a Quaker missionary who passed through the village en route to Dayton. The Shawnee provided him with food and shelter, and Simpson left the Indian camp assured of the Prophet's good intentions. His impressions were echoed by a delegation of Shakers who visited Greenville during the following spring. Arriving on March 27, 1807, David Darrow, Richard McNemar, and Benjamin Youngs found the Indians busily collecting sap for maple sugar. Although the Prophet was ill, he met with the Shakers and patiently explained his doctrines to them. They also talked with Tecumseh and Kumskaukau, who both resided in the village. The visitors spent four days at Greenville, sharing the tribesmen's meager provisions and observing the religious celebrations. Tenskwatawa labored mightily to persuade them of his "righteousness" and the Shakers returned home convinced "that God, in very deed, was mightily at work among the Indians."[30]

In fact, however, the Prophet was hard at work among the Shakers. He earlier had forbidden the use of white foods, but since his village could not feed the large numbers of new converts descending on it, he needed provisions regardless of their source. Therefore, during June he sent twenty warriors to the Shaker settlement near modern Union, Ohio, where they "worshiped every evening . . . and behaved with order and decorum." They also persuaded the gentle "Believers" to furnish them with twenty-seven pack horses loaded with foodstuffs, which they took back to Greenville. Two months later the same Shakers provided additional supplies to a similar delegation. The congregation at Union expressed shock at charges that they were supporting the Prophet and encouraging him to make war, but when militiamen from nearby communities threatened them "with being put to the sword's point," their relationship with the Shawnee holy man ended.[31]

The threats against the Shakers reflected the growing apprehension among frontier settlements in Ohio and Indiana. Alarmed over the large numbers of Indians at Greenville, white citizens in western Ohio petitioned Governor Edward Tiffin to investigate the Prophet and his followers. In February 1806 Tiffin sent a message to Greenville, asking the Indians to explain the purpose of their assembly. In reply, the Prophet assured him of their peaceful intentions and declared that any reports to the contrary were nothing more than "foolish lies."[32] But in May 1806, after a white farmer was killed by Indians on the Mad River, panic struck the settlements and Tiffin ordered another investigation. He dispatched Simon Kenton (a renowned Indian fighter), Isaac Zane, and five other frontiersmen to Greenville to question the Indians about the murder. Speaking for the Prophet, Tecumseh disclaimed any responsibility for the crime, suggesting instead that Black Hoof's people at Wapakoneta were responsible. Both Kenton and Tiffin remained suspicious, but the Indians asserted that their only purpose was "to follow the Prophet" and "to live quietly with their women and children."[33]

Tecumseh's relationship to the Prophet and his movement during this period remains somewhat a mystery. Some contemporary sources argue that Tecumseh was a true believer and that he wholeheartedly subscribed to the new religion. Others assert that he was skeptical of Tenskwatawa and never accepted his faith. Yet regardless of Tecumseh's conversion, he remained in close association with the Prophet, and when Tenskwatawa established the new village at Greenville, Tecumseh was in his retinue. In retrospect, it seems that although Tecumseh at first may have questioned the sincerity of his brother's revelations, he certainly did not oppose the new religion, but seemed to accept it as a welcome change from the degradation that recently had plagued the tribes. Undoubtedly, Tenskwatawa's promotion of many traditional Shawnee values appealed to the war chief, and he also was attracted by the anti-American themes inherent in his brother's teachings. Tecumseh, therefore, assisted his brother in the latter's relationship with federal officials, and although the Prophet dominated the new movement, Tecumseh, Blue Jacket, and others served as his advisers.[34]

Throughout the fall of 1806 Tenskwatawa continued to welcome visiting Indians into his camp, and although the winter snows discouraged some pilgrims, by the spring of 1807 trails leading to Greenville again were full of tribesmen. At Fort Wayne, Indian agent William Wells reported that hundreds of warriors were passing his post and all efforts to divert them had failed. He warned both Harrison and Secretary of War Henry Dearborn that the Prophet constituted a serious threat to American authority in the region and recommended that the Shawnee and his followers be ordered to leave Greenville.[35]

White frontiersmen were not the only residents of Ohio anxious to be rid of the Prophet. At Wapakoneta, Black Hoof and his followers continued to follow the government's assimilation program, erecting permanent log cabins and planting fields like their white neighbors. But the white man's road was hard, and the Shawnees at Wapakoneta resented the criticism leveled at them by the religious upstart at Greenville. They still remembered him as Lalawethika, the "Noisemaker," and refused to believe that he was blessed by the Master of Life. Moreover, their adherence to white ways made them, like the Moravian Delawares, susceptible to charges of witchcraft. Black Hoof complained to the Americans that his people were accused of depredations committed by the Prophet's followers, and that the Shawnees at Greenville were renegades and should not share in the Shawnee annuities. By the spring of 1807 relations between the two groups of Shawnees had deteriorated so badly that when two of Black Hoof's kinsmen were found murdered in the forest, he immediately accused Tenskwatawa. Missionary William Kirk tried to mediate between the two sides, but the Prophet considered him an ally of Black Hoof and refused any reconciliation.[36]

William Wells, meanwhile, was taking steps to force the Shawnee holy man from Ohio. In April 1807, he dispatched Anthony Shane, a Shawnee half-blood, to Greenville demanding that Tenskwatawa, Tecumseh, and several other Shawnees come to Fort Wayne to hear a message sent by the president. When Shane arrived in Ohio he received an icy reception. Not only did the Prophet refuse the government summons, but Tecumseh also lashed out at the messenger, informing him that the Shawnees had no intention of going to Fort Wayne. If Wells wished to meet with them, let him come to Greenville.[37]

Shane returned to Fort Wayne, but six days later Wells sent him back to the Shawnee camp with a letter, which was read to the assembled Indians. Wells reminded the Prophet that he was camped on ground ceded to the United States by the Treaty of Greenville. According to Wells, just as "the Great Chief of the Seventeen Fires loves his red children and will not suffer his white children to interrupt his red ones, . . . neither can he suffer his red children to come on the lands of the United States." The Prophet's intrusion was upsetting his "white brothers"; therefore, the Indians must immediately "move from that place and off the land of the United States."[38]

Shane's audience was angered by the message. Tecumseh replied that the lands in Ohio had been given to the Shawnees by the Master of Life; the Indians no longer recognized white men's boundary lines. The Prophet then rose and faced his followers. He was incensed that Wells had refused to come to Greenville. After all, was he not the Prophet, a holy man acclaimed throughout all the western tribes? Why should he suffer insults from Wells, a Miami squaw-man? Speaking slowly, he asked Shane, "Why does not the president send to us the greatest man in his nation?" He, Tenskwatawa, would talk with him. "I can bring darkness between him and me—nay more, I can bring the sun under my feet, and what white man can do this?" Afraid to reply, Shane left the camp and the council ended.[39]

Except for his ties with the Shakers, relations between the Prophet and his white neighbors deteriorated during the spring and summer of 1807. At Fort Wayne, Wells wrote letter after letter condemning the Shawnee as a British agent, and recommended that the government send troops to drive "the villain and his insolent band" beyond the white frontier.[40] In the meantime, several settlers were murdered in western Ohio and frontiersmen began to desert their farms, retreating toward the safety of the settlements or crossing over into Kentucky. In May, after the Wyandot leader Roundhead brought his followers from Sandusky to settle permanently at Greenville, frightened citizens at nearby Staunton petitioned the government to remove the Indians from Ohio.[41]

Alarmed, Governor Edward Tiffin mobilized the state militia and sent messengers to both Greenville and Wapakoneta, demanding that the Prophet and Black Hoof surrender any Indians responsible for the recent deaths. Both denied that their followers had any part in the murders, so Tiffin requested that they meet in council with state officials at Springfield, a frontier village on the Mad River. The council took place in June 1807 and reflected the growing bitterness between the Shawnee camps. Although both the Prophet and Black Hoof professed friendship toward whites, they accused each other of the recent depredations. Recrimination between the two groups almost spilled over into bloodshed, but white officials at Springfield had wisely insisted that the warriors attend the conference unarmed, and violence was prevented. Through close examination it finally was ascertained that the recent murders had been committed by a few straggling Potawatomis, but the conference at Springfield did little to alleviate the apprehensions of white settlers in Ohio.[42]

The large numbers of western tribesmen who flocked to Greenville during the summer of 1807 intensified the frontiersmen's suspicions. They also added to the Prophet's logistics problem. The small fields at Greenville scarcely produced adequate crops for the permanent residents and most new converts arrived after a long journey. They were hungry and their food supply was exhausted. The provisions donated by the Shakers brought some relief, but in August, Tenskwatawa sent Blue Jacket and several other Shawnees to Detroit, where they persuaded General William Hull that the Prophet "was a friend to the United States, and had ever advised all the Nations to be friendly." The wily Blue Jacket so beguiled Hull that the officer finally gave him over half of all the Shawnee annuities. Hull boasted that he had convinced Blue Jacket and his party that "their safety, happiness and even existence depends on their fidelity to the United States," but Blue Jacket and the Prophet had the last laugh, and the annuities helped to feed the Indians at Greenville.[43]

Just before Blue Jacket left for Detroit, news reached Ohio that British warships had fired on the *Chesapeake*, an American frigate out of Norfolk, Virginia. Assuming that their country was on the brink of war with Great Britain, American officials were afraid that the Prophet and his followers would side with the British and spread destruction across the frontier. To forestall such an alliance, Governor Thomas Kirker of Ohio dispatched Thomas Worthington and Duncan MacArthur to Greenville. They were ordered to meet with the Prophet and to inquire about his intentions. The two commissioners were accompanied by Stephen Ruddell, a former white captive among the Shawnees, who served as their interpreter.[44]

Tenskwatawa received them warmly. On September 12, 1807, he summoned the many tribesmen crowding his camp to a general council at which the commissioners first read a message from Kirker, then addressed the Indians themselves. On the following day the Prophet and his converts gave their formal reply. First Blue Jacket, recently returned from Detroit, assured the Americans that the Prophet and his followers wanted no alliance with the British. Reminding his audience that the Redcoats had refused to assist the warriors following the Battle of Fallen Timbers, Blue Jacket promised that if war erupted between the British and the Long Knives, the Indians would not interfere. Indeed, the tribesmen had assembled at Greenville only "to seek for that which [should] be [their] eternal welfare, and unite [themselves] in a band of perpetual brotherhood."[45]

The Prophet then spoke. When asked why he had chosen to settle on lands claimed by the United States, he replied: "(He) did not remove to this place because it was a pretty place, or very valuable, for it was neither; but because it was revealed to him that the place was a proper one to establish his doctrines; that he meant to adhere to them while he lived; they were not his own, nor were they taught him by man, but by the Supreme Ruler of the universe." He then explained his revelations to the commissioners and denounced Black Hoof and the Shawnees at Wapakoneta, whom he accused of spreading malicious rumors and poisoning the minds of white men toward him. To prove his good will, Tenskwatawa offered to send a delegation of his "chiefs" to meet with Governor Kirker at Chillicothe. Convinced of his sincerity, the commissioners accepted the offer and in late September, Tecumseh, Blue Jacket, Roundhead, and one other warrior rode with them back to the capital. There Kirker also was persuaded that the Prophet and his followers posed no immediate threat to settlers in Ohio, and plans to mobilize the militia were abandoned.[46]

The Prophet did not accompany the party of Indians that journeyed to Chillicothe. During September his village continued to receive a steady flow of new converts from the Great Lakes, tribesmen who had traveled long distances to meet with him, and he felt obligated to minister to them. He also received another message from the Americans. At Vincennes, William Henry Harrison remained alarmed about the village at Greenville and, like Wells and Kirker, he saw the specter of British intrigue behind many of the Prophet's activities. Yet Harrison could not even accept that Tenskwatawa was the dominant Indian figure in the movement, and still believed that the Shawnee holy man was controlled by more traditional leaders within the tribe. Therefore, in early September he sent John Connor with a message to "the chiefs and head men of the Shawanese tribe of Indians," rebuking them for listening "to a fool who [spoke] not the words of the Great Spirit but those of the devil, and of British Agents." They should, he said, send Tenskwatawa beyond the Great Lakes, where he could "hear the British more distinctly."[47]

To Connor's dismay, on reaching Greenville he found that Tenskwatawa *was* the "chief and head man" of the Indians in the village. He was, in fact, the only leader present since Tecumseh, Blue Jacket, and Roundhead had gone to Chillicothe. Although he was angered by Harrison's accusations, the Prophet was surprisingly temperate in his response. Choosing his words carefully, he asked Connor to write down his reply:

Father, I am very sorry that you listen to the advice of bad birds. You have impeached me with having correspondence with the British; and with calling and sending for the Indians from the most distant parts of the country, "to listen to a fool that speaks not the words of the Great Spirit; but the words of the devil." Father, these impeachments I deny, and say they are not true. I never had a word with the British, and I never sent for the Indians. They came here themselves to listen and hear the words of the Great Spirit. Father, I wish you would not listen any more to the voice of bad birds; you may rest assured it is the least of our idea to make disturbances, and we will rather try to stop such proceedings than encourage them.

Relieved that the conference was over, Connor hurriedly left the village and returned to Vincennes.[48]

Wells's and Harrison's accusations that the Prophet was a British agent reflected their ignorance about the nature of his influence. Unable to comprehend the widespread frustration among the tribes, American officials refused to concede that Tenskwatawa's movement was an indigenous uprising, born of desperation. If they admitted that many of the Indian grievances were valid, they would be forced to address those most responsible for such injustice: themselves. Of course they were unwilling to do so and therefore they sought external causes for their domestic crisis. Not surprisingly, they focused their suspicion on the British. After all, hadn't the British sent the Indians against the American frontier during the revolution? Didn't the Redcoats supply the warriors with arms and encouragement during the border wars of the 1790s? And finally, weren't British agents still meeting with tribesmen who continually journeyed to Amherstburg, in Upper Canada? Obviously, then, the British were behind the Prophet's conspiracy. The Shawnee was the tool of the British Indian Department.[49]

Ironically, British Indian agents were almost as confused about the Prophet as the Americans were. Because they believed that war with the United States was imminent during the summer of 1807, the British admitted they were not "entirely inactive in preparing the Indians for the probable results." Yet they remained suspicious of Tenskwatawa and warned other tribesmen to avoid him. In November, Colonel William Claus, the deputy superintendent of Indian affairs in Upper Canada, accused "that rascal, the Prophet" of being a French agent but advised his superiors that they should curry the Shawnee's favor.[50] During the following months the British sent presents, which Tenskwatawa accepted, but he steadily refused their invitations to come to Amherstburg. Frustrated, in February 1808 Claus reported that he had dispatched a personal messenger to bring Tenskwatawa to Canada, but since the Shawnee would not come, the man and his motives remained a mystery.[51]

The Prophet was reluctant to leave Greenville during the fall of 1807 because he was meeting with the most influential Indian in Illinois and Wisconsin: Main Poc of the Potawatomis. Like Tenskwatawa, Main Poc also held powerful medicine, which he used for both spiritual and political pur-

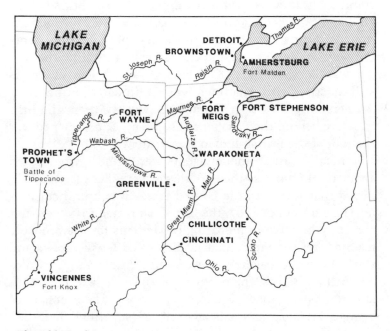

The Old Northwest, 1805–15

poses. Born without a thumb or fingers on his left hand, Main Poc declared that the deformity was a special sign of favor from the Great Spirit, and through guile and perseverance he had attained the role of *wabeno*, or "firehandler," a shaman much feared among the Potawatomis. An eloquent speaker, Main Poc also held great influence over the Sacs, Winnebagos, and part of the Chippewas. He was active in intertribal warfare, leading large war parties from Illinois and Wisconsin against the Osages, and his medicine was so strong that many of his followers believed him invulnerable to any arrow or bullet fashioned by mortal man.[52]

Main Poc arrived in Ohio late in October and remained with Tenskwatawa for almost two months. Their conversations were not recorded, but the two men were congenial and the Prophet undoubtedly explained his revelations to his guest. A "holy man" himself, Main Poc evidently accepted part of Tenskwatawa's teachings, but rejected others. He agreed that the Americans were the spawn of the Great Serpent, but he was unwilling to renounce their firewater. He also refused to give up his warfare against the Osages, declaring that "the Great Spirit often told him that if he ever refrained from going to war and drinking spirituous liquor he would become a common man." Although the Potawatomi was willing to cooperate with the Prophet's movement, he refused to subjugate himself to the Shawnees. Still, Tenskwatawa seemed pleased by Main Poc's pilgrimage to Greenville and regarded him as a welcome ally in the spread of the new religion throughout the northwest.[53]

In late December 1807, Main Poc and a small party of Potawatomis left Greenville and traveled back toward Illinois. En route, they passed through Fort Wayne, where Wells tried his best to wean them from the Prophet's influence. Wells reported that Main Poc was "the pivot on which the minds of all the western Indians turned," and the Indian agent spent over eight hundred dollars "to secure his influence and attach him to the United States." Exploiting this opportunity, the wily old Potawatomi remained at Fort Wayne till spring, well fed from the government's larder and milking Wells for arms and ammunition. Wells boasted that he had convinced Main Poc to become an ally of the United States, but on April 12, when the chief left Fort Wayne, he ignored Wells's pleas that he visit Harrison in Vincennes, announcing instead that he intended to return to Illinois to recruit a war party against the Osages. Both Main Poc and the Prophet knew that he also intended to promote the new religion among the western tribes.[54]

Self-satisfied, Wells smugly reported to his superiors that Tenskwatawa's influence was declining. Not only was Main Poc now alienated from the Shawnee, but Miami and Delaware leaders in the Fort Wayne region denounced the Prophet as a liar and openly plotted his death. Little Turtle of the Miamis brought Wells the welcome news "that all [the Prophet's] plans are defeated." He no longer could feed those Indians who remained at Greenville. Encouraged, Wells believed that the government could use the offer of foodstuffs to lure many of the starving tribesmen away from the Shawnee's camp. But before any of these plans could be implemented, word reached the Indian agent that Tenskwatawa and his followers had abandoned the village at Greenville, and were moving west.[55]

Chapter Four

Prophetstown

The spring of 1808 brought a welcome melting of the snow
that lay drifted across the forests and prairies of northern
Indiana. By early April green patches of new grass had appeared on protected, southern slopes, while along the streams
willows were in full bud, milking the warm sunshine before
bursting forth in foliage. Many of the smaller rivers were
full, spilling their waters into the Wabash, which in turn
poured over its banks and flooded the wooded bottomlands
that followed the river as it curved southwestward toward
the Ohio. On the upper reaches of the Mississinewa, an important tributary flowing into the Wabash from eastern Indiana, a bedraggled band of warriors were camped in temporary shelters along the river bank. Their numbers were
not large, probably no more than sixty, although a few were
accompanied by their wives and children. Most of the Indians were thin, for their deerskin bags held little corn, and
game had not been plentiful. A small herd of horses, perhaps
thirty, grazed nearby, far too few to carry all the Indians and
their possessions. En route to a new home, the tribesmen
busily constructed rafts and canoes, planning to descend the
Mississinewa to the Wabash and then paddle westward, following the larger river to the mouth of the Tippecanoe.[1]

The winter months had not been easy for the Prophet and
his followers. Tenskwatawa had been hard pressed to feed

his disciples during the summer of 1807, but by fall the multitudes of new converts descending on his village had completely exhausted his provisions. Afraid of white retribution, the Shakers no longer dared to supply him with foodstuffs, and the meager harvest of corn from the few fields at Greenville was almost gone. Indeed, by December the Shawnee holy man could barely feed Main Poc and his party, so the Potawatomi had withdrawn to Fort Wayne to dine at the Long Knives' table. Other devotees also scattered from his village, some also seeking food from the Americans while others, near starvation, straggled back to their earlier homes.[2]

December 1807 had been a month of soul-searching for Tenskwatawa. It was obvious that growing white hostility soon would force him from Ohio. Although the Master of Life had informed him that the village near Greenville "was a proper one to establish his doctrines," it was too near the onrushing white frontier and vulnerable to American military forces. Moreover, the village was too far from the majority of his converts, the tribes of Michigan, Illinois, and Wisconsin. Disciples from these western peoples had been forced to travel great distances to seek his revelations, and therefore could not contribute food or other resources to the holy assemblage. To make matters worse, most of the tribesmen living in the region, Black Hoof's Shawnees, Tarhe's Wyandots, Little Turtle's Miamis, and some Potawatomis led by Five Medals were dominated by federal Indian agents and still opposed the new religion. In November, Main Poc had suggested that Tenskwatawa take his followers to the west, inviting him to settle on lands claimed by the Potawatomis near the juncture of the Tippecanoe and Wabash rivers. There, according to the Potawatomi leader, the Prophet would be much nearer to his disciples, and they in turn could provide him with assistance. The new village might soon outshine Greenville and become a mecca for all the tribes as far west as the Great Plains.[3]

In January 1808, Tenskwatawa decided to accept Main Poc's

offer, but he was afraid to break camp before the winter ended. Although the Master of Life frowned on such sustenance, during February and March the Prophet and his people slaughtered "stray" hogs and cattle that they "found" wandering in the nearby forest. In late March the Master of Life provided them with about twenty head of horses that also had been "lost" from the white settlements, and during the first week in April the Shawnee leader and his flock abandoned Greenville and traveled west, following the Mississinewa until it became navigable.[4]

The Prophet's withdrawal from Ohio pleased American Indian agents, but it caused much alarm among those tribesmen still loyal to the government. Traditional chiefs such as Little Turtle and Five Medals did not want the Shawnee holy man establishing a new town in close proximity to their villages. In early April "government chiefs" among the Miamis, Delawares, Shawnees, and Potawatomis met in hurried council, then dispatched Little Turtle and several other delegates to the Mississinewa, where they encountered Tenskwatawa and his people building canoes. Convinced that the Prophet's influence was waning, Little Turtle forbade him to settle on the Wabash, warning the holy man that if he continued to the Tippecanoe, the government chiefs and their warriors would "cut him off." His scalp would hang in their lodges.[5]

If Little Turtle believed that the Prophet would be intimidated by his warning, he was sorely mistaken. Tenskwatawa's followers had dwindled, but they still outnumbered the small party accompanying Little Turtle. The Prophet rebuked the Miami chief, informing him that he intended to proceed on to the Wabash and that it "was not in the power of man" to stop him. His journey had been sanctioned by the Master of Life, who wanted all Indians to assemble at the mouth of the Tippecanoe. There, at a new village, Prophetstown, "they would be able to watch the Boundry Line between the Indians and white people—and if a white man put his foot over it that the warriors could easily put him back." When the corn became ripe, "every nation from the west" would be united and the government no longer would be able to cheat them out of their lands. Following the meeting Little Turtle returned to Fort Wayne. The Prophet and his followers descended the Mississinewa-Wabash waterway to Prophetstown.[6]

Tenskwatawa's speech on the Mississinewa marked his first recorded reference to the problem of defining the boundaries between Indian and white lands. It also indicated a shift away from an entirely spiritual solution to white aggression, toward a more political response. For the first time the Prophet spoke of large numbers of warriors "united" in a common political or military cause. Of course he still claimed that the Master of Life guided his movement and had instructed him to move to the Tippecanoe, but the hard realities of providing food and other supplies for the multitude at Greenville seemed to have tempered his belief that all of the Indians' problems could be solved by divine intervention. Although his spiritual leadership still provided the magnet that attracted disciples from throughout the west, he now would be forced to devote more of his efforts to secular necessities.

To obtain such assistance, the Prophet turned to the British. Although he earlier had seemed indifferent to British overtures, soon after arriving at Prophetstown Tenskwatawa met with Frederick Fisher, a British agent who long had traded among the Shawnees. In previous conversations with Fisher the Prophet often had denounced the United States (he once had "discharged wind loudly, clasped his hand to his backsides and exclaimed he cared no more for [the Americans] than that"), but he had refrained from openly vowing his friendship toward the Redcoats. Now, in late April 1808, he informed Fisher that he wished to journey to Canada to meet with British Indian agents.[7]

Fisher carried the message to William Claus, the deputy

superintendent of Indian affairs at Amherstburg, who was delighted with the request. In reply Claus sent a Fox warrior to Prophetstown to inform Tenskwatawa: "I will be very glad to take you by the hand and as there will be several Nations with you, I will be glad to take some of their young men by the hand also." But the Prophet remained in Indiana. By mid-May parties of western Indians already were arriving at Prophetstown, and he hesitated to make the long journey to Canada.[8]

Instead, he sent Tecumseh. Accompanied by five warriors, the Shawnee chief arrived at Amherstburg on June 8. He met repeatedly with British officials, including Lieutenant Governor Francis Gore, and remained in Canada until mid-July. The British listened attentively to Tecumseh's pleas for food and other assistance, provided the Shawnee and his party with gifts, and seemed receptive to the Prophet's movement. In response, Tecumseh informed his hosts of Tenskwatawa's activities:

[The Prophet is] endeavoring to collect the different nations to form one settlement on the Wabash 300 miles south of Amherstburg in order to preserve their country from all encroachments. That their intention at the moment is not to take part in the quarrels of white people; that if the Americans encroach upon them they are resolved to strike—but he added that if their father the King should be in earnest and appear in sufficient force they would hold fast by him.[9]

Tecumseh returned to the Tippecanoe in late June. His mission had been successful. At Montreal, Governor General James Craig recommended to his superiors that the Crown expand the British Indian Department. He complained that British indifference had "driven the Indians into the arms of the Americans," and "though they would be of little use as friends, it [was] an object of infinite consequence to prevent them from being [British] enemies."[10]

While Tecumseh was in Canada, Tenskwatawa supervised the construction of Prophetstown. The settlement was laid out with a symmetry atypical of most Indian villages. Bark wigwams were arranged in orderly rows along the north-west bank of the Wabash, just below the mouth of the Tip-pecanoe, and extended up from the river bottoms onto the adjacent prairie. Near the river the Indians erected a large structure called the "House of the Stranger" to shelter pilgrims visiting in the village. On the prairie, at the opposite end of the town, were two other buildings: a long council house and the Prophet's medicine lodge, where the holy man secluded himself to converse with the Master of Life.[11]

Faced with some of the same problems that had plagued him in Ohio, Tenskwatawa worked to consolidate his position at Prophetstown. By June 1808, warriors from the western tribes were flocking into his camp, more than doubling the original population of the village. Runners from the Winnebagos, Chippewas, and Potawatomis reported that hundreds of their kinsmen were also making preparations to travel to the Tippecanoe. The women had planted their cornfields, but food was so short that most of his followers were reduced to a diet of roots and what little game they could find in the forests. Although his brother was meeting with the Redcoats, help from that quarter would not soon be forthcoming. Therefore, the Prophet decided to solicit provisions from the Long Knives. After all, hadn't the Shakers supplied him in the past? Perhaps he could get similar assistance from Harrison.[12]

Since converts continued to arrive from the west, Ten-skwatawa remained at Prophetstown, but in mid-June he sent a small party of envoys to Vincennes. The identity of this delegation remains unknown. Perhaps Blue Jacket, who had so successfully beguiled Hull at Detroit, was included, for the warriors were remarkably effective in presenting the Prophet's case to Harrison. Through his emissaries, Ten-skwatawa assured the governor, "It never was my intention to lift up my hand against the Americans." On the contrary, the Master of Life had advised him to "live in peace with you and your people," for "we are all his children . . . although we differ a little in colour." According to the Prophet, he had brought his women and children to Prophetstown to reside near Harrison; and "in consequence of our removal we are in great distress. We hope that you will assist our women and children with a little corn. We are now planting and hope to have a plenty when it is ripe." Then, promised Tenskwatawa, he would visit Harrison and personally "remove every bad impression you have received of me."[13]

In reply, the governor informed the delegation of warriors that he had been suspicious of the Prophet and his religion in the past, but he added, "The solemn assurance which you now give me that you will have no other object but that of making your people happy . . . have in a great measure removed my prejudice and if your subsequent conduct agrees with your present professions you may rest satisfied that you will continue to enjoy the favor and protection of the 17 fires." Yet he warned the warriors not to listen to the British, who had deceived them in the past. If the Indians ever again dared to "lift up the tomahawk" against the United States, the Americans would never rest until the tribesmen were all dead or driven beyond the Great Lakes.[14]

Following the conference Harrison provided the delegation with corn, some hoes, and a plough. After packing the grain on their horses, the Indians thanked him for the implements, obsequiously stating, "Father, you can give us nothing that will be more acceptable." Pleased with their duplicity, the delegation hurried back to Prophetstown. In turn, Harrison smugly informed his superiors that Tenskwatawa obviously had been much "misconstrued." He boasted that the Shawnee's "character and intentions" were now under his control, and he would make the Prophet a "useful instrument in affecting a radical and salutary change in the manners and habits of the Indians."[15]

At Prophetstown, Tenskwatawa was elated. Not only had Tecumseh returned with promises of British assistance, but

William Henry Harrison, the chief of the Long Knives, also seemed willing to support the Shawnee's movement. Harrison, who only recently had denounced him as a "fool" and an "imposter," had been hoodwinked into believing that the new religion was favorable to the Americans. If the Prophet's credibility among his starving followers had lately diminished, it now flowed forward like the mighty Wabash. Flushed with his coup, Tenskwatawa made plans to visit Harrison, intending to bring many of his followers to Vincennes with him. Not only would the large retinue impress the governor, but the Americans would be forced to feed them. The small supply of food at Prophetstown could be used for other purposes.

Tenskwatawa and his disciples arrived in the frontier village in mid-August. For the next two weeks he met intermittently with Harrison. Aware that the governor disliked William Wells, the Prophet endeavored to increase the differences between them. He chided the governor, telling him, "Father, I was told that you intended to hang me," but admitted that Wells had supplied such information and suggested that perhaps Wells was a liar. He acknowledged that "white people and some Indians were against me . . . but I defy them to say I have done anything amiss." Indeed, his sole purpose was to bring happiness to his Indian brothers, for the Master of Life "told [him] to tell the Indians, that he had made them and the world—that he had placed them on it to do good and not evil." Both Indians and white men were brothers, but they should follow their separate customs. Indians, especially, should not drink the white man's firewater. Tenskwatawa assured Harrison that his followers would plant their corn, mind their own business, and "never take up the tomahawk, should it be offered by the British, or the Long Knives." They only wished "to live in peace with [their] father and his people forever."[16]

While in Vincennes the Prophet met daily with his followers, publicly haranguing them on the evils of alcohol and warfare. Harrison, like many of the other residents of the frontier village, was astonished at the "considerable talent of art and address" with which he seemed to mesmerize his disciples. The governor, as expected, fed the Indians (whom he estimated at "some hundreds") and when Tenskwatawa left Vincennes he provided the Shawnee with corn, more utensils, and a small store of powder. Harrison may still have had some lingering doubts about the Prophet's ties with the British, but he assured Secretary of War Henry Dearborn, "The influence which the Prophet has acquired will prove advantageous rather than otherwise to the United States."[17]

That "influence" continued to attract large numbers of western Indians into the Prophet's camp. Throughout the summer and fall of 1808 tribesmen from Michigan, Illinois, and Wisconsin flocked to Prophetstown, where they listened to Tenskwatawa's religious revelations and to his new pleas for political unity and a halt to further land cessions. Although Harrison now considered the Prophet a friend of the United States, government chiefs from Fort Wayne did not share the governor's optimism. They were frightened by the large assemblage of western tribesmen and by the Prophet's new doctrine of political unity. Any consolidation of political power by the Prophet threatened their influence, and they urged the government to drive the holy man away from the Tippecanoe. During the summer such chiefs among the Miamis and Delawares sent a delegation of warriors to Prophetstown to demand that Tenskwatawa dismiss his followers, but he refused to meet with them. Instead, Tecumseh intercepted the delegation and denounced them in such terms that they fled back to their villages in "terror and apprehension."[18]

But once again logistics proved to be the Prophet's downfall. When Harrison had met with Tenskwatawa and his followers in Vincennes, he had described them as "the most miserable set of Starved wretches my eyes ever beheld," and

although he sent a small supply of corn back to Prophetstown, it was insufficient to feed all the Indians. Meanwhile,
the expected harvest of corn from fields along the Tippecanoe failed to materialize. The Indians were so swept up in
their religious and political movements that they failed to
tend their gardens. Main Poc had promised assistance, but
in the autumn of 1808 he had succumbed to American invitations to visit Washington, and remained in the east until
the following February, so when the winter snows blew down
from the north, Tenskwatawa still could not feed his disciples.[19]

This time the suffering was intense. The winter of 1808–
9 was especially severe and snow that fell three feet deep in
November blanketed the ground until April. At Prophetstown the meager supplies of corn were soon exhausted. By
December the Indians were eating their dogs and horses.
And then, disaster struck. Weakened by their lack of food,
the tribesmen fell prey to another of the white man's nameless diseases that entered their camp and infected their lodges.
This time the coughing sickness seemed selective, often
passing over the Shawnees, Kickapoos, and Wyandots, but
taking a heavy toll among the tribesmen from the north.
During the winter almost 160 Ottawas and Chippewas succumbed, but the Master of Life took only 5 Shawnees. By
spring, those northern Indians able to travel fled from the
Tippecanoe. Many nurtured doubts about the Prophet's di-
vinity. Others harbored suspicions about the deaths of their
kinsmen.[20]

When the northern Indians straggled back to their home
villages, their resentment erupted into angry accusations
that their dead relatives had been poisoned. Why else would
only the Ottawas and Chippewas have died? Perhaps the
Prophet had not been chosen by the Master of Life. Maybe
he was a false prophet, as the Long Knives charged. Or even
worse, perhaps he was in league with the Great Serpent. Did
not witches and other servants of this dark power use poi-

son against their victims? Their suspicions aroused, Ottawas and Chippewas from villages near the eastern shores of
Lake Michigan vowed to test the Prophet's authority. He
had warned them that no violence must be committed in
his village, or the Master of Life would destroy the perpetrators. Well, let blood be spilled! Then they would see if Tenskwatawa really could turn the Master of Life against them.[21]

In mid-April 1809, a small war party of Ottawas and Chippewas journeyed to Prophetstown, which they entered late
at night, surprising a Shawnee woman and her child near
the edge of the village. Striking quickly, they tomahawked
the two Shawnees, then fled to their temporary camp about
thirty miles distant. When no great calamity befell them,
they rode confidently back to Michigan, spreading word of
Tenskwatawa's vulnerability. On their return, warriors from
several villages of Ottawas and Chippewas assembled, making plans to attack the Prophet's village.[22]

At Prophetstown, Tenskwatawa attempted to defend both
his credibility and his life. The woman and child had not
been killed by his enemies, he declared, but had recently
died of natural causes, from the white man's illness. Indeed,
their bodies had been mutilated by tomahawks, but the war
party had only butchered corpses. His village remained in-
violate. Meanwhile, to repel any war parties from the north,
Tenskwatawa appealed to the tribes of Illinois, soliciting
warriors from the Sacs, Kickapoos, and Potawatomis.[23]

Ironically, federal officials intervened in the Prophet's behalf. At Detroit, General William Hull learned of the Ottawa and Chippewa plans and sent messages to their villages forbidding them to move against the Shawnees. Blindly
following the government position that intertribal conflict
should be avoided at all costs, he reminded the Ottawas and
Chippewas that "the Shawanoese were under the protection
of the United States, and we should consider hostilities
against them, the same as against us." If the Shawnee Prophet
had injured them, "they must represent it to their Great

Father ... and he would take measures for their satisfaction." Surprised at Hull's admonition, the northern tribesmen relinquished their campaign against Prophetstown. Under government auspices, they met with Black Hoof and his followers to assure them that they harbored no ill will toward other members of the Shawnee tribe.[24]

Tenskwatawa's pleas for assistance to the tribes in Illinois reflected Tecumseh's efforts in that region. During the spring of 1809 Tecumseh had journeyed west, meeting with Sac and Winnebago converts in villages along the Rock and Mississippi rivers. Building on the Prophet's religious success, Tecumseh espoused the political goals of the movement, urging the Sacs and Winnebagos to guard their lands against white encroachment. His pleas struck a responsive chord. Late in 1808 the federal government had erected Fort Madison near the confluence of the Des Moines and Mississippi rivers, and many Sacs and Winnebagos resented the intrusion. British traders who long had dominated the fur trade on the upper Mississippi also used their influence among the Indians to denounce the post. By May 1809, Indian resentment toward the fort reached such peaks that Tecumseh was hard pressed to keep the Sacs and Winnebagos from attacking the installation. News of the Sac and Winnebago hostility reached officials in St. Louis, who informed Harrison of their problems. Already concerned over rumors that the Prophet again was fomenting a widespread conspiracy, Harrison called out his militia.[25]

Once more, Tenskwatawa took steps to allay the Americans' suspicions. In early May, John Johnston, who had succeeded Wells as Indian agent at Fort Wayne, sent messengers to the Tippecanoe inviting the Prophet to come to the post for a conference. Envisioning the invitation as an opportunity to ingratiate himself with the new agent, Tenskwatawa accepted. He arrived at Fort Wayne on May 25, accompanied by a delegation of eleven warriors. Anxious to persuade Johnston of his good intentions, the Prophet returned two horses that he admitted had been stolen by some of his young men in western Ohio. He spent the next four days in council with the agent, denying "in the most solemn manner, having any views inimical to [the American] peace or welfare." Aware that Johnston disliked Wells, Tenskwatawa asserted that all charges against his religious movement had resulted from the "personal and private motives" of Wells and Little Turtle. According to Johnston, "The Prophet related to me all that passed between them, and put the right construction on Wells' motives." To allegations that Tenskwatawa remained hostile, Johnston reported, "I have taken much pains and have not been able to find that there existed any grounds for the alarm." Satisfied that Johnston was convinced of their friendship, on May 29 the Prophet and his delegation returned to their village.[26]

If Tenskwatawa was able to beguile the inexperienced Johnston, he was less successful with Harrison. The governor had been duped by the smooth-talking holy man during the previous summer, but continued reports of hostile Indians on the Tippecanoe caused him to reassess his opinion of the movement. During the spring of 1809 he sent two spies, disguised as traders, to Prophetstown, and they confirmed his suspicions that Tenskwatawa's willage remained a center for anti-American activity. Therefore, in late June when the Prophet and a delegation of forty warriors appeared in Vincennes, they received a cool reception.[27]

Tenskwatawa again pleaded friendship to the United States. When Harrison asked why he had met with large numbers of unfriendly Indians at his village, the Prophet had a ready answer. Of course the tribesmen were hostile. Indeed, according to Tenskwatawa, nine tribes had joined together to attack the frontier, and only his intercession had saved the Americans. Playing on the governor's suspicions, he declared that the conspiracy had been instigated by the British. But now, through his efforts, the danger had dissipated. Yet when queried why he neglected to report the conspiracy to U.S. officials, the Prophet had no answer. He remained in Vincennes for about ten days, unsuccessfully trying to convince Harrison that he intended the Americans no harm. But this time his ruse failed. The governor reported to his superiors that he now believed Tenskwatawa to be a "great scoundrel": "Suspicions of his guilt have been strengthened rather than diminished in every interview I have had with him since his arrival."[28]

Although Harrison now was convinced of the Prophet's hostility, he did believe that the influence of the holy man had waned. Since the Ottawas and Chippewas near Lake Michigan had defected, and since the Prophet still could not feed his followers, Harrison assumed that the Shawnee's star was falling and that he could muster no effective opposition to further land cessions. Meanwhile, white settlers continued to pour into the woodlands northeast of Vincennes. As a result, in the summer of 1809 the governor made plans to meet with the Miamis, Potawatomis, and Delawares to purchase a tract of land along the Wabash and a smaller region in eastern Indiana. Assuring officials in Washington that "the time [had] arrived when the purchase [could] be attempted with a considerable prospect of success," he instructed Johnston at Fort Wayne to meet individually with government chiefs among the three tribes and to "assure them that their interests would be attended to" if they persuaded their tribesmen to sell the land.[29]

Harrison's careful preparations ensured his success. During September and October he conferred with spokesmen for the Miamis, Delawares, and part of the Potawatomis at Fort Wayne. On September 30, 1809, the Indians signed a treaty ceding over three million acres in Indiana and Illinois to the United States. In return, the three tribes received an increase in their annuities, ranging from $250 to $500, and a gift of trade goods worth $5,200, which was distributed on the treaty grounds. Both the Delawares and the Miamis had legitimate claims to the ceded region, but the Potawatomis had never extended their villages into the area and hunted there only occasionally. Especially significant were the names of those Indians signing the document for their tribes: Anderson and Beaver for the Delawares; Winamac and Five Medals for the Potawatomis; and Little Turtle and Pecan for the Miamis. These and almost all the other treaty signatories were government chiefs. They shared in the government annuities, but they were despised by more militant members of their tribes.[30]

Since it illustrated that the Prophet still was powerless to keep the government chiefs from signing away their people's lands, the Treaty of Fort Wayne was a temporary victory for Harrison. But it had a larger impact that worked in the Shawnees' favor. Tenskwatawa and Tecumseh had warned the tribesmen that, regardless of Harrison's protestations, the government intended to purchase all of the Indian lands. The lands along the upper Wabash still remained under tribal control, but reflective people in Indian villages across northern Ohio and Indiana now gave more credence to the Prophet's warnings. Miami warriors long faithful to Little Turtle now questioned his leadership in ceding their lands to the United States. Although the Wyandots held no claim to the ceded territories, they long had envisioned the territory north of the Wabash as the "land of promise," a potential homesite if they were forced from Michigan and Ohio. And even some Senecas, hard pressed in their villages in New York, cast wistful glances toward the region. Perhaps the Shawnee brothers were right. Perhaps the Long Knives did intend to push the original people into the Great Lakes.[31]

At Prophetstown, Tenskwatawa was incensed over the treaty. Both he and Tecumseh denounced the transaction as illegal and argued that the ceded territories belonged to all Indians and not just to those tribes signing the agreement. Declaring that the treaty chiefs had betrayed their people, the Shawnee brothers threatened to kill those chiefs who had dared to place their marks on the white man's document. The Prophet was especially bitter in his condemnation of Winamac, a Potawatomi spokesman who had assisted Harrison in negotiating the land cession. He also warned both the Weas and the Kickapoos who signed supplementary treaties relinquishing any minor claims to the ceded territories against accepting payment for their cooperation. Finally, both the Prophet and Tecumseh vowed that the lands in question would neither be surveyed nor settled by white men. In defiance, Tenskwatawa now openly expressed his hostility to the Americans. He sent a message to Harrison asserting "that his people should not come any nearer to him, that they should not settle on the Vermillion river—he smelt them too strongly already."[32]

The Shawnee holy man also redoubled his efforts to regain influence among the tribes of Michigan and northern Indiana. During the spring of 1810 he again sent messages to the Ottawas, Potawatomis, and Chippewas living along the eastern shores of Lake Michigan warning them that the Treaty of Fort Wayne was an omen of things to come, and asking them to rejoin his movement. The recent treaty had engendered some resentment in their villages, so in May these northern people announced they would send delegates to the Potawatomi villages on the St. Joseph River to consider the Prophet's invitation. When the government chiefs from those tribes who had signed the treaty learned of the council, they rushed to the St. Joseph to urge continued peace with the Long Knives. Especially persuasive was a delegation of Delawares who carried a speech from Harrison urging the northern tribes to reject any association with the holy man. Also influential was Winamac, who reminded his kinsmen from Michigan that only two winters ago many of their number had died at Prophetstown. The speeches of the government chiefs had the desired effect. The Ottawas, Chippewas, and Potawatomis acknowledged that Tenskwatawa had sent them the "Tomahawk," but they chose to bury it rather than grip it by the shaft.[33]

Although the council on the St. Joseph proved to be a disappointment, the Prophet received good news from other quarters. Large numbers of western tribesmen, Sacs, Foxes, Winnebagos, Kickapoos, and Iowas still visited his village and seemed loyal to his cause. And for the first time he was able to provide them with adequate food and shelter. During the spring British supplies reached his village in such quantities that his followers refused to purchase goods from American traders.[34] British officials also were generous to any of his disciples who continued on to meet with His Majesty's Indian Department in Canada. Travelers in the Detroit region reported that the British recently had been "very liberal and indulgent," and that "the Indians were loaded with silver ornaments." In June, over 240 Sacs and Foxes passed from Prophetstown through Fort Wayne to Malden, where Matthew Elliott treated them royally, furnishing them with large quantities of arms and ammunition. The Sacs assured the British Indian agent that they were anxious to attack the Long Knives. Elliott encouraged them to remain prepared, but cautioned them against any premature attacks. Still, most tribesmen interpreted British generosity towards the Prophet's followers as a de facto endorsement of the holy man and his movement.[35]

While the Sacs were at Malden, Tecumseh and other emissaries labored mightily among those tribes remaining in Ohio. In June the Shawnee warrior traveled to Black Hoof's people on the Auglaize River, attempting to win them away from the Americans. Although Black Hoof and the other government chiefs refused to meet with him, Tecumseh warned the younger warriors that they were being duped by the Americans, and he invited them to join the Prophet on the Wabash. When shown a letter Harrison had recently sent to the Ohio Shawnees, Tecumseh angrily threw it into the council fire, declaring that if the governor were present, he would treat him in a similar manner. Fearful that Black Hoof's people might be wavering, federal Indian agents rushed in to neutralize Tecumseh's influence. Soon after the Shawnee warrior left the Auglaize, John Johnston spent two days with Black Hoof and his followers. Johnston reported that he had been forced to be "more liberal than usual" in dispersing bribes and presents, but he believed he had countered Tecumseh's arguments.[36]

Other emissaries were more successful among the Wyandots. Shortly before Tecumseh arrived among the Shawnees, messengers from Prophetstown had again been active in the Wyandot villages along the Sandusky River. Although Tarhe and other government chiefs still opposed the Prophet, by the summer of 1810 their influence was declining. Many Wyandots were concerned over the recent land cessions at the Treaty of Fort Wayne, and even Tarhe had complained about the growing number of white settlers spilling onto Wyandot lands in Ohio. Moreover, the government had recently failed to provide certain payments in both specie and gunpowder that the Wyandots believed were due them. Grumbling among themselves, many Wyandots who earlier had refused to listen to the Prophet now agreed to meet with his messengers.[37]

Tenskwatawa was particularly anxious to win more converts among the Wyandots. Although relatively few in number, they were venerated by many other tribes, who referred to them as their "uncles," and who believed they were especially blessed with wisdom and common sense. Following the Treaty of Greenville, the other tribes had asked the Wyandots to keep the great beaded belt that had signified the unity of the Indians in their earlier attempts to keep the Long Knives from Ohio. Now, through his messengers, the Prophet asked the Wyandots how they, as keepers of the Great Belt, could sit idle while white men stole land from all the Indians. Let them bring the Great Belt to Prophetstown and unite in defense of their homeland. Tarhe refused to attend the meeting, but many of the other Wyandots who assembled around the council fire voiced their approval. Some spoke out, declaring that "everything that had been done since the Treaty of Greenville between the white people and the Indians [was] as good for nothing." Others stated that "they had been driven back until they could go no further and that they had as well die where they were as to be driven upon other Indians." Following the conference a large party of Wyandot warriors escorted the messengers back to Prophetstown. Carrying the Great Belt, they passed through Miami villages along the Mississinewa, where they chided these followers of Little Turtle for their friendship to the Americans.[38]

Other tribesmen friendly to the Americans suffered a crueler fate. The Prophet's expanding influence among the Wyandots also was reflected in the tribe's rekindled interest in witchcraft. During June 1810, the Wyandots near Lower Sandusky killed two old women whom they declared had "injured [them] from time to time by Destroying [their] people." They also turned on Leatherlips, an aged chief outspoken in his criticism of the Prophet and well known for his friendship to the Americans. Leatherlips was seized by six young warriors near a Wyandot camp on the Scioto River. Although several settlers tried to intercede in his behalf, the old man was tomahawked. He did not die immediately, but clung to life for several hours, a phenomenon that only seemed to confirm his murderers' suspicions. Bewildered by the events and apprehensive of the government's reaction, the government chiefs tried to minimize the significance of the assassinations. Eventually, Tarhe and others attempted to claim that Leatherlips had been executed because he *supported* Tenskwatawa.[39]

Delighted by his new converts among the Wyandots, the Prophet also was encouraged by his growing success among other tribes. His efforts at undercutting the traditional chiefs now showed some success. Younger Miami warriors openly expressed their misgivings about the land cessions at Fort Wayne and the ailing Little Turtle no longer could keep his people securely in the American fold. Indeed, U.S. Indian agents reported that many Miamis now found Little Turtle "contemptible beyond description," and pro-American Wea and Piankashaw chiefs were so frightened that they asked Harrison for permission to lead their remaining followers west into Illinois. In June, Tenskwatawa welcomed Main Poc and a large party of Potawatomis from the Illinois River, as well as many Kickapoos, who added their lodges to his village. Although the Kickapoos were scheduled to receive a government annuity payment, paid primarily in salt, they refused. When the barrels of salt were carried up the Wabash by government boat, the Kickapoos, at Tenskwatawa's direction, left the salt on the river bank. The Prophet informed the boatmen that the Indians were undecided about the payment and would wait until Tecumseh returned before making any decision. The crew proceeded on to the Fort Wayne region, but on their return they stopped again at Prophetstown to learn of the Indians' verdict. When the boatmen stepped ashore, Tecumseh demanded that they reload the salt on their vessel. The Shawnee warrior "seized the master and several others by the hair and shook them violently asking whether they were Americans." Much alarmed, the captain and crew loaded the salt and hurriedly sailed down the Wabash.[40]

At Vincennes, Harrison viewed the Prophet's expanding influence with much alarm. During the past five years he had seen the holy man's authority both wax and wane, but now the Shawnee's dominance seemed to be permeating tribes that earlier had resisted him. Estimates of the number of warriors under his control varied from 650 to almost 3,000, and rumors reached the governor that the Prophet and his advisers were making extensive plans to attack the western posts and settlements. The governor's concern was heightened by his inability to receive adequate intelligence about the Prophet's activities. Throughout the spring he had kept a creole from Vincennes as a spy in the Prophet's camp. The Frenchman, Michael Brouillette, had posed as a trader and had regularly provided the governor with information. Both

Brouillette and Harrison assumed that Tenskwatawa was unaware of the trader's true purpose, but late in June the Prophet publicly denounced Brouillette as an "American dog" and drove him from his village. Harrison continued to receive reports from Winamac, but the Potawatomi had become so closely identified with the Americans that he now was forbidden to attend any of the Prophet's councils. Winamac still visited Prophetstown, but he feared for his life and rarely stayed long in the village. Moreover, the Potawatomi was so anxious to ingratiate himself with Harrison that he seemed reluctant to report unfavorable intelligence.[41]

Anxious for an accurate assessment of Tenskwatawa's strength, Harrison sent a messenger to Prophetstown to meet with the Shawnee and to observe the activity in his village. Through the messenger, Toussaint Dubois, Harrison inquired about Tenskwatawa's "hostile preparations and enmity" for the United States. He warned the holy man that the frontier was much alarmed and that "warriors both here and in Kentucky were preparing themselves for service." He also informed him that a reinforcement of regular troops was en route to Vincennes, but only to defend the village and not to attack Prophetstown unless the Shawnee's "disposition to commit hostilities could no longer be doubted." Although Tenskwatawa considered Dubois a spy, he listened politely to Harrison's message. He again asserted that the Master of Life had instructed him to raise a new village on the Wabash and that he was collecting warriors for holy purposes. When pressed by Dubois about his hostility to the government, he replied that the recent treaty had cheated the Indians out of their lands and that "no sale was good unless made by all the Tribes." Dubois suggested that the Shawnee lay his grievances before the governor in Vincennes, but the holy man declined, stating that on his last visit, during the previous summer, he had been treated disrespectfully.[42]

Dubois reported back to Harrison that the Prophet's influence was declining. Not only had the holy man been intimidated by the message, but his followers were much alarmed over the announcement of the American military mobilizations. Yet other reports continued to cause the governor considerable apprehension. During July warriors from Prophetstown stole horses from white settlements along the Wabash. Others, hoping that angry Americans would retaliate indiscriminately against friendly Delawares, slaughtered the livestock belonging to farmers who recently had settled along the White River. Harrison received other intelligence of growing British influence among the tribes of northern Indiana. If the Prophet's power was waning, why the upsurge in depredations? Gambling, Harrison decided to invite the holy man to visit Washington. Perhaps a trip to the capital would so impress the Shawnee with the power and population of the United States that he no longer would dare to challenge the government.[43]

In late July, Harrison sent Joseph Barron, an interpreter, to Prophetstown with an invitation for Tenskwatawa to visit the capital. Barron was not well received. Unnerved by Harrison's earlier warning that "warriors both here and in Kentucky were preparing themselves for service," many Indians mistook the messenger for a scout in advance of an American military expedition against Prophetstown. When he rode into their camp, they panicked. Tenskwatawa and his advisers were able to restore order, but when the American messenger was brought before him, the Shawnee was infuriated. He had tolerated Brouillette in his camp as an American agent, and he had treated Dubois cordially, even when the envoy had pressed him about his attitude toward the United States. But Barron's abrupt and unannounced entrance was too much. When the messenger was brought before him, the Prophet sat in silence for several minutes, staring at the man. Then, before allowing Barron to deliver Harrison's message, he asked, "For what purpose do you come here? Brouillette was here; he was a spy. Dubois was here; he was a spy. Now you have come. You, too are a spy." Pointing to the ground before the messenger, he exclaimed, "There is your grave, look upon it!" Yet before any harm befell the frightened messenger Tecumseh intervened and assured Barron he would not be harmed.[44]

Barron then delivered Harrison's speech, in which the governor scolded the Prophet for his "folly," but assured him: "There is yet but very little harm done but which may be easily repaired. The chain of friendship which unites the whites with the Indians may be received and be as strong as ever—a great deal of that work depends upon you." The governor warned Tenskwatawa that a confederacy comprising warriors from all the tribes could never stand against the United States: "I know your Warriors are brave, ours are not less so, but what can a few brave Warriors do against the innumerable Warriors of the 17 fires. Our blue coats are more numerous than you can count, and our hunting shirts are like the leaves of the forests or the grains of sands on the Wabash." He concluded the message by assuring the Prophet that if he could prove that the government had taken lands illegally from the Indians, their Great Father, the president, would restore them. If Tenskwatawa and three of his chiefs would like to go to Washington to meet with their Great Father, "everything necessary [would] be prepared for [their] journey and means taken to ensure [their] safe return."[45]

Surprised by the invitation to travel to Washington, the Prophet instructed Barron to remain overnight in the village. A formal reply would be made on the following day. The messenger spent the night in Tecumseh's lodge, but on the next morning Tenskwatawa informed him that he still remained undecided. Within a few days Tecumseh would deliver his message to Harrison in Vincennes. Before leaving Prophetstown Barron noticed that certain Wea chiefs previously thought friendly to the government were present. Yet after quietly talking with them he thought they were still loyal to the United States. Winamac also was present and used the messenger's appearance to denounce the Prophet. Tenskwatawa promptly labeled Winamac a liar, but Barron knew that he was reluctant to have the Potawatomi assassinated. Winamac had strong family ties throughout the Potawatomi villages in Indiana. Any attack on the warrior, regardless of his perfidy, might bring retaliation from his kinsmen. Such a vendetta would destroy any hopes for intertribal unity.[46]

Accompanied by a large party of warriors, Tecumseh arrived in Vincennes on August 12, 1810. He remained in the frontier village for ten days. He met repeatedly with Harrison, carefully explaining his doctrine of land tenure and intertribal political unity. At first things did not go well. Tecumseh readily admitted that he and the Prophet (who remained in Prophetstown) were attempting to unite all the tribes against any further cession of Indian lands to the Americans. He asserted that they planned to execute all the chiefs who had signed the recent Treaty of Fort Wayne and would no longer "suffer any village chiefs to manage the affairs of the Indians." He also cataloged examples of American mistreatment of the Indians (of which Harrison privately admitted, "There are unfortunately too many of them"), including the massacre of the Moravian Delawares of Gnadenhutten during the Revolutionary War. Harrison attempted to refute the allegations, but when the governor's speech was translated Tecumseh sprang to his feet and denounced the governor as a liar. He also heaped invective on the sycophantic Winamac, who was sitting in the grass at Harrison's feet. Fearing for his life, Winamac recharged his pistol, and many of the warriors accompanying Tecumseh seized their tomahawks and prepared to defend themselves. In response, Harrison and his advisers drew their swords, while a small party of soldiers stationed nearby hurried to the council ground, their arms drawn. Fortunately, cooler heads prevailed, and the talks were adjourned until the next morning.[47]

On the next day, August 13, Tecumseh met with the governor and assured him that neither he nor his warriors had intended any attack on the white men. The conference then resumed and continued intermittently for the next eight days. During that period the Shawnee informed the governor that both he and the Prophet would continue to oppose the survey or settlement of the lands ceded at Fort Wayne. He warned Harrison that all the tribes planned to meet soon at the Wyandot village near Detroit to discuss the fate of those chiefs who had signed the treaty. He asked the governor to give up the government's claims to the region: "If you do not it will appear as if you wished me to kill all the chiefs that sold you this land. I tell you so because I am authorized by all the tribes to do so. I am the head of them all. . . . If you do not restore the land you will have a hand in killing them." In contrast, if Harrison returned the lands and promised not to seek any more cessions, there could be peace between the Long Knives and the Indians. Indeed, the tribesmen would then support the United States. Otherwise they would be "compelled to unite with the British." The governor promised he would send Tecumseh's remarks to the president, but admitted "there was no probability of their being agreed to." Tecumseh solemnly replied that he hoped the Master of Life would induce the president to give up the lands. "It is true he is far off; he will not be injured by this war; he may sit still in his town and drink his wine, whilst you and I will have to fight it out."[48]

In conclusion, Tecumseh again warned Harrison to hold no more treaties with the village chiefs, for according to the Shawnee, he was "alone the acknowledged chief of all the Indians." And neither he nor Tenskwatawa would accept Harrison's invitation to visit the president. When Harrison inquired if the Kickapoos and other Indians would still receive their annuities, Tecumseh replied:

Brother. When you speak to me of annuities I look at the land, and pity the women and children. I am authorized to say that they will

92

not receive them. Brother. They want to save that piece of land, we do not wish you to take it. It is small enough for our purposes. If you do take it you must blame yourself as the cause of trouble between us and the Tribes who sold it to you. I want the present boundary line to continue. Should you cross it, I assure you it will be productive of bad consequences.

On the evening of August 21, 1810, the conference ended. Tecumseh and his followers returned to Prophetstown.[49]

The months following the Treaty of Fort Wayne formed a major watershed in the career of the Shawnee Prophet. Before the treaty Tenskwatawa and his emphasis on spiritual renewal had dominated the Indian movement. Of course, as early as 1808 he had spoken against further land cessions, but such secular considerations were only of secondary importance when compared to his doctrine of religious revitalization. The Indian men and women who had flocked first to Greenville, then to Prophetstown had sought a divine deliverance from the problems that beset them. Faith in the medicine of the Shawnee holy man was the catalyst for the Indian movement sweeping through the Old Northwest.

But after the Treaty of Fort Wayne, the nature of the Indian movement changed. Concern over the continued loss of land shifted the focus of Tenskwatawa's followers away from religious solutions toward the more pragmatic leadership of Tecumseh. The Shawnee war chief's emphasis on usurping the power of the village or government chiefs and concentrating it in his own hands may have violated traditional concepts of political structure, but it appealed to many young warriors. The Treaty of Fort Wayne illustrated that the Prophet's medicine could not protect the Indian homelands. Perhaps the new political unity championed by Tecumseh offered a better answer.

And so Tecumseh used the religious movement of his brother as the basis for his attempts to forge a political and military confederacy among the western tribes. By his own admission, he still believed in the Prophet's divine mission, but he evidently questioned Tenskwatawa's ability to provide a religious solution to the crisis now facing the tribes. Since he had traveled widely to recruit followers for the movement, Tecumseh already was well known by many of the Indians, and his close relationship to the Prophet provided him with the influence needed to eclipse Tenskwatawa in the eyes of the warriors at Prophetstown. In many ways Tecumseh's efforts to destroy the position of the village chiefs and to become "alone the acknowledged chief of all the Indians" (as he had boasted to Harrison at Vincennes) was a concept more alien to traditional Indian ways than any of the teachings of the Prophet. But trying times demand innovations, and Tecumseh was willing to challenge the old ways to protect his people's homeland.[50]

At Vincennes, Harrison also was aware of the changing pattern of Indian leadership. He still regarded the Prophet as a powerful adversary, but in August 1810, he reported to his superiors that Tecumseh was "really the efficient man— the Moses of the family. . . . He [was] described by all as a bold, active, sensible man, daring in the extreme and capable of any undertaking."[51]

Temporarily short of miracles, Tenskwatawa remained in his village while Tecumseh went to Vincennes. The Prophet's reaction to the rising influence of his brother remains unknown, but it is doubtful if he regarded Tecumseh's ascendancy with much enthusiasm. The Prophet was a proud man and he obviously enjoyed his position of prominence. Yet his influence was still extensive. The recent assassinations of Leatherlips and the other Wyandots indicated that he still could sway his followers. In the past Harrison's challenges had provided him a Black Sun. Perhaps the Long Knife would again offer him an opportunity to prove his medicine.

Chapter Five

Tippecanoe

The autumn of 1810 found the Wabash Valley basking in apparent tranquility. At Prophetstown, Tenskwatawa's followers harvested their corn and pumpkins in preparation for the upcoming winter. For once, the Shawnee holy man believed that he had amassed enough foodstuffs to last until spring. Many of the warriors residing in his village during the past summer had returned to their own tribes to make ready for winter hunts, and although the Winnebagos had quarreled with the Sacs and Kickapoos, the resulting altercation had taken place en route to their homes and not in his village. In early October he met with Michael Brouillette when the creole brought a message from Harrison, again inquiring about his intentions. Although Tenskwatawa had driven Brouillette from his village during the previous summer, he now treated the courier with "unusual friendship." He assured Brouillette that he and Tecumseh intended the Americans no harm, but reiterated that they would not surrender the lands ceded at Fort Wayne. And let the Long Knives not be mistaken. Many of the warriors had vacated his camp, but they still remained under his control. Brouillette was pleasantly surprised by his warm reception and when he returned to Vincennes he informed Harrison that the holy man seemed less hostile. In turn, the governor reported to other officials that the Prophet's influence was declining.[1]

Harrison also was pleased by the results of two intertribal councils—one at the Wyandot village near Brownstown, Michigan, the other at Fort Wayne. Both the Prophet and Tecumseh had at first planned to attend the Brownstown conference, but it was soon apparent that the meeting would be dominated by village chiefs friendly to the government. None of the tribes from Illinois or Wisconsin (villages controlled by Tenskwatawa's supporters) sent representatives, and the pro-American chiefs even invited Governor William Hull to take part in the proceedings. Convinced that the proposed council would be a charade manipulated by the Long Knives, the Shawnee brothers refused to attend.[2]

On the surface, the conference went much as expected. Pro-American delegates from the Ottawas, Chippewas, Potawatomis, Shawnees (Black Hoof's people), Delawares, Senecas, Onondagas, Oneidas, and a scattering of Mohawks assembled at the Wyandot village in late September. After condemning the British, they pledged never again to take part in any of the white man's wars, and to "attend to agriculture and the domestic arts, and live in peace with their white brothers." Hull attended most of the speeches and supplied the assembled Indians with food and tobacco. He also took special pains to inform the old chiefs that Tecumseh recently had denounced them at Vincennes and had boasted to Harrison that he alone was "the acknowledged chief of all the Indians." Hull's scheme seemed to have the desired effect. The angry tribesmen addressed a speech to the Prophet asking him why he had "forsaken their ancient customs, discarded [his] good old chiefs," and "invited the young men of the old nations to [his] Council and influenced them to measures contrary to the customs of the nations to which they belong[ed]?" If the Prophet wished to live apart from other Indians, they had no objections, but they declared, "You must invite no other Nations. We are willing to forget what is past, provided the same thing does not take place in the future."[3]

The Fort Wayne council produced similar results. In October, John Johnston met with almost eighteen hundred Indians from northern Indiana and western Ohio. For the most part, these tribesmen also seemed friendly and pledged their loyalty to the United States. Like Hull, Johnston was generous in dispensing food and other provisions. He also used the conference to distribute annuity payments to the tribes. Since part of the Potawatomi, Delaware, and Miami annuities constituted compensation for the Fort Wayne treaty lands, the government was anxious for the Indians to accept the money and goods. Most were eager to receive the annuities, but Miamis from villages along the Eel and Mississinewa rivers refused. Led by Pecan, a chief from the Eel River, they declared they now were opposed to the treaty and had signed it only because "the Tomahawk was hung over their necks" by the government. If the Long Knives ever tried to occupy the region, they first would have to "build a bridge across it" (defend it). In reply, Johnston accused them of joining Tenskwatawa and warned that, if necessary, the United States "would build a bridge of warriors with rifles in their hands." He then distributed their annuities to other members of their tribe, and although the dissidents stalked off angrily, Johnston assured his superiors that the council had been "highly satisfactory" to the government. Neither the Prophet nor Tecumseh had dared to attend, but he did admit that two of Tenskwatawa's emissaries had carefully observed the entire proceedings.[4]

The dissension at Fort Wayne was a portent of things to come. Even the conference at Brownstown had not gone as favorably as the government supposed. Beneath the platitudes of friendship ran an undercurrent of suspicion toward the United States. The village chiefs were jealous of the Prophet and his movement, but they had been stirred by his warnings. Unbeknown to Hull, while he was absent from their council they secretly agreed to sell no more land. Moreover, most of the tribesmen who met at Brownstown and dined on Hull's provisions also visited the British at

Malden. If they railed against the Redcoats in Hull's pres-
ence, they complained about the Long Knives to British Indian agent Matthew Elliott. Indeed, Elliott reported to his
superiors that the Prophet's confederacy was so widespread
he was afraid he no longer would be able to restrain them
from attacking settlements in the western states.[5]

At Prophetstown, Tenskwatawa took steps to nullify any
advantages recently gained by the Americans. During the
early fall he sent the Great Belt, given to him by the Wyandots, to the tribes of Wisconsin and Illinois. Accompanying
the belt was a message in which he assured his western
followers that his movement was growing and would "confine the great water and prevent it from overflowing them."
The pro-American speeches of the village chiefs were only
"sweet words, like grass plucked up by the roots, they would
soon wither and come to nothing." Indian agents reported
that the message was well received by tribes along the Mississippi, and that the Winnebagos, especially, "breathed
nothing but war against the United States." Meanwhile, following the conference at Brownstown, the Prophet's disciples among the Wyandots executed four more of their
kinsmen as witches.[6]

While Tenskwatawa was strengthening his ties with the
western tribes, Tecumseh and a group of warriors again journeyed to Malden. In mid-November they met repeatedly with
Matthew Elliott, informing the agent that the confederacy
was growing and that the Indians needed continued British
support. They were, Tecumseh assured him, quite capable
of defending their lands and were eager to do so. They wanted
only provisions, not British troops. Elliott lavished gifts on
the visitors and promised that more arms and ammunition
would be forthcoming. When he questioned Tecumseh about
the extent of the confederacy, the Shawnee answered that
not all the tribes were yet enrolled, but that the movement
was expanding and "the business would be done" before he
visited the British again.[7]

Elliott seemed uncertain over what role the British should

play. His close ties to the Indian community (he had been married to a Shawnee woman and had lived with the tribe) may have prompted him to offer more encouragement than official British policy warranted. He was anxious to retain the loyalty of the Prophet and his followers. Elliott knew that if war erupted between Britain and the United States, British officials in Upper Canada would desperately need the Indians' assistance. Elliott's superiors in the British Indian Department also hoped to maintain the Indians' friendship, but they didn't want to be tied so closely to them that they would be drawn into a war not of their own choosing. Throughout the winter of 1810–11, these agents sent food, arms, and ammunition to Tenskwatawa and his allies, but they also urged restraint. They warned that any premature attack on the Americans would be disastrous to the Indians. Of course, such advice was offered "out of regards to their safety, comfort, and happiness," but under no circumstances were the tribesmen to attack the United States.[8]

During the early months of 1811 the Prophet and Tecumseh seemed to heed the British advice. Although they met repeatedly with small groups of warriors, they urged their followers not to precipitate a war with the Long Knives. Encouraged by the decline in depredations, Harrison reported that the Prophet's influence had deteriorated and that the Shawnee could not "excite the usual disturbance this spring amongst the Indians." The governor took advantage of the apparent calm to begin the survey of the lands ceded at Fort Wayne, hoping to plot the tracts before the tribesmen learned of his efforts. To forestall Miami opposition to the survey, he reappointed William Wells to the Indian service. Harrison still distrusted Wells, but the new agent had powerful friends in Washington. Moreover, the governor believed that Wells's influence among the Indians near Fort Wayne was so extensive that he could "accomplish much" if his efforts were channeled in the government's behalf.[9]

The spring of 1811 brought a resurgence of Indian activity.

It also brought an end to Harrison's optimism. In Illinois, Main Poc made no pretense of friendship and sent his warriors on raids against American settlements near Kaskaskia. Although ostensibly a follower of Tenskwatawa, the old Potawatomi was a powerful shaman himself and had grown jealous of the Shawnee's claim to religious leadership over the tribes. Main Poc exercised such influence among the Sacs and Potawatomis that he refused to be restrained by the Prophet's and Tecumseh's warnings. The wide-ranging attacks created panic in southern Illinois, and settlers deserted their farms and fled toward Kentucky. Governor Ninian Edwards of Illinois appealed for assistance and requested that Harrison use his influence among the government chiefs to force the Potawatomis to surrender those warriors responsible for the recent depredations.[10]

Harrison met with little success. Although the Prophet and Tecumseh still refrained from any overtly hostile actions, they used the spring of 1811 to seek new recruits. Tecumseh again journeyed among the Shawnees and Wyandots in Ohio, then rode north among the tribes in Michigan. Meanwhile, Tenskwatawa dispatched emissaries to Iroquois refugees in Canada who had fled the United States after the American Revolution. The Iroquois were invited to unite with the Prophet's followers and to "participate with them in the Enjoyment of their Territory." Other messengers were sent across the Mississippi to the Iowas and Otoe-Missourias. Although both the Canadian Iroquois and the western tribes generally refused the invitations, a few warriors from these nations did journey to Prophetstown.[11]

Tenskwatawa also entertained more messengers from Harrison. During May he met with William Wells and John Connor, who arrived in his village and asked that he surrender any of his followers who had participated in the recent raids in Illinois. In addition, Wells requested that the Prophet give up all stolen horses in his camp. To Wells's surprise, the Shawnee surrendered four horses, but disclaimed any responsibility for the attacks near Kaskaskia. Both the Prophet and Tecumseh admitted that Potawatomis under their influence had ridden with the war party, but they placed the blame on Main Poc and declared that all the raiders had now joined his camp on the Illinois River. But the raiders' withdrawal from Prophetstown had no bearing on the situation, for if they had remained, Tenskwatawa declared, they would not have been surrendered. The Shawnee brothers treated the messengers politely, but Tecumseh again asserted that they were determined "to resist the encroachments of the white people." When Wells told him that resistance was impossible, Tecumseh icily replied that if Wells was lucky, he "would live to see the contrary."[12]

The surrender of the horses was only a ruse. Many of the animals stolen by the Potawatomis were tethered at Prophetstown, and Tenskwatawa hoped that by giving up four of the animals he could convince Harrison that his village held no others. He also gambled that such minor concessions would placate the Americans and keep them from taking any stronger actions. Unquestionably, by the summer of 1811 both the Prophet and Tecumseh believed that a military confrontation with the Americans was inevitable. Warriors arriving in Prophetstown were now promised a "rich harvest of plunder and scalps," and told that they soon would be provided with an "ample supply of arms, ammunition, and provisions." But the warriors were urged to wait until the time was ripe. Only a well-planned and coordinated attack would bring victory over the Long Knives.[13]

Unfortunately, waiting was not the Indians' strong point. After repeatedly admonishing his followers to be ready to attack the Americans, Tenskwatawa was hard pressed to keep them under control. American travelers on the Wabash were repeatedly waylaid and their property stolen. Even the Weas, closely tied to the government through annuities, seemed infected with a new militancy. When Harrison's surveyors entered their lands, Wea warriors seized the men, stripped them of their possessions, and threatened them so violently that several members of the survey party fled to Cincinnati. And the Prophet's own actions added to the growing crisis. Although he advised the warriors to be cautious, he was anxious to reassert his position of leadership. In June, while Tecumseh was absent from Prophetstown, Tenskwatawa seized a boatload of annuity salt sent up the Wabash by Harrison. When the boat crew complained, he boasted that the shipment was needed, for he soon would have over two thousand warriors assembled at his village.[14]

Harrison took the boast seriously. He cautioned William Clark at St. Louis, "All the information that I receive from the Indian country confirms the rooted enmity of the Prophet and his determination to commence hostilities. From the uncommon insolence which he and his party have lately manifested, I am inclined to believe that a crisis is fast approaching." Afraid that Tecumseh might descend the Wabash with "six or eight hundred men," the governor wrote to officials in Washington to ask for reinforcements. In late June, when fifteen warriors from Prophetstown arrived in Vincennes on a trading mission, he ordered local blacksmiths not to repair any of their weapons. As soon as the Indians departed, Harrison sent a message to the Tippecanoe forbidding the Shawnee brothers to approach Vincennes with a large party of their followers. He warned them that the Kentucky militia, "as numerous as the musquitos on the shores of the Wabash," would "intercept their return, should they descend that river with hostile intentions."[15]

At Prophetstown, Harrison's message was received with some misgivings. Most of the northwestern tribes had been brought into the confederacy, but Tecumseh now was eager to spread his political movement to the Five Southern Tribes. The governor's warnings indicated that the Americans were alarmed, and the Shawnee war chief did not want a confrontation with the Long Knives before his plans reached fruition. Both Tecumseh and the Prophet seemed uncertain of what policies to follow. If they gave in to Harrison's demands, wouldn't the Americans interpret their acquiescence as a sign of weakness and push for further advantages? And what would their young warriors do if their spiritual and military leaders submitted to the Long Knives? On the other hand, any open defiance of the United States might bring on the war they temporarily wished to avoid. They finally decided for a middle position. Tecumseh would go to Vincennes to assure Harrison of their peaceful intentions, but to impress him with their strength, he would be accompanied by a large party of his followers. On July 4, 1811, Tecumseh answered Harrison's message, informing the governor, "I will be with you myself in eighteen days . . . to wash away all these bad stories that have been circulated. When I come to Vincennes and see you, all will be settled in peace and happiness." He did not tell the governor he was bringing hundreds of warriors.[16]

Harrison was alarmed by the Shawnee reply. For months rumors had circulated up and down the Wabash that Vincennes would be the first target in any general Indian uprising, and the governor feared that Tecumseh's visit might be a Trojan horse for such an attack. Although the messenger bringing Tecumseh's answer had assured him that the Shawnee chief would be accompanied by only a few warriors, Harrison dispatched scouts up the Wabash to monitor the Indians' approach. Their report caused a near panic in Vincennes. Tecumseh and over fifty canoes full of warriors were descending the river toward the settlements. Moreover, other Indians were traveling to Vincennes on horseback. American observers estimated the number of warriors at about three hundred, and, surprisingly, they were accompanied by about thirty women and children. Stranger still, subsequent reports indicated the entire party had traveled no farther than a site about seventy miles upstream from Vincennes, when they stopped and camped on the river bank for a week. Reflecting public sentiment, the *Vincennes Sun* reported that the Indians planned "to sack and burn this town and murder its inhabitants." Harrison called up all the federal troops at his disposal and mustered militiamen from throughout the lower Wabash Valley. By late July he had almost eight hundred men under arms. In the interim, he sent Captain Walter Wilson up the river to demand an explanation from Tecumseh.[17]

Wilson encountered Tecumseh and his entourage descending the Wabash about twenty miles north of Vincennes. In reply to Harrison, the Shawnee stated that he had asked only twenty-four warriors to accompany him; the rest had come of their own accord. As soon as he arrived in Vincennes, "everything would be explained to [Harrison's] satisfaction." Aware that the size of his party would alarm the Americans, Tecumseh had spent almost two weeks enroute from Prophetstown, hoping that his slow pace and the inclusion of the women and children would convince Harrison that he came in peace. The fleet of canoes landed at Vincennes on July 27. On the following day those Indians traveling overland arrived. Although Harrison wanted an immediate conference, the Indians did not assemble in council until July 30, three days after their arrival in Vincennes.[18]

The conference followed predictable lines. Harrison again questioned Tecumseh's and the Prophet's motives, demanded to know why Tenskwatawa had seized the annuity salt, ordered the Indians to surrender all warriors guilty of depredations, and refused to discuss the return of any lands ceded at Fort Wayne. In contrast, Tecumseh was much more conciliatory than in his previous meetings with the Americans. He assured him that "the White people were unnecessarily alarmed." Tenskwatawa and he "meant nothing but peace." Indeed, "the United States had set him the example of forming a strict union amongst all the fires that compose their confederacy. That the Indians did not complain of it— nor should his white brothers complain of him for doing the same with the Indian Tribes." The seizure of the annuity salt was a minor issue that should be forgotten, and the raiders demanded by Harrison were not residents of Prophetstown. Since "a great number of Indians were coming to settle at his Town this fall," they would need the ceded lands for hunting, and he hoped whites would not move onto them. He would soon visit the southern tribes, and on his return would "go and see the President and settle everything with him." After five days the conference ended. Tecumseh and twenty warriors left Vincennes to visit the southern tribes. The remainder of the Indians returned to Prophetstown.[19]

For the Prophet and his followers, Tecumseh's conference with Harrison was disastrous. Far from postponing any confrontation, the meeting just strengthened the governor's conviction that military force was the only answer to the "Indian problem." Influenced by rumors that Tecumseh originally had planned to murder him, Harrison was convinced that only the assembled troops had prevented disaster. For months he and other frontier officials had demanded that the federal government establish a new fort near Prophetstown and provide adequate military forces to disperse the Prophet and his people. Shortly after the Indians left Vincennes, Harrison received word that his request had been granted. Secretary of War William Eustis informed him that the Fourth Infantry Regiment and an additional company of riflemen had been dispatched to Vincennes from Pittsburgh. In addition, the governor was authorized to call for volunteers from Kentucky. Peace, if possible, was to be maintained, but Eustis also declared, "If the prophet should commence, or seriously threaten hostilities he ought to be attacked; provided the force under your command is sufficient to ensure success."[20]

Harrison was anxious to march on Prophetstown while Tecumseh was in the South. He also took pains to ensure that his army met Eustis's expectations. By mid-September he had assembled a force of over one thousand men, including regular infantry, large numbers of Indiana militia, and two companies of Kentucky volunteers.[21] Hoping to isolate the Prophet from any last minute support, he sent messages to the Weas and Miamis warning them not to travel to Prophetstown. The governors of Illinois and Michigan sent similar warnings to the tribes within their territories.[22]

At Prophetstown, Harrison's activities did not go unnoticed. Before Tecumseh had left for the South, he and Tenskwatawa had discussed the possibility of an American military expedition, and had agreed that the Prophet should do all in his power to avoid a confrontation. But by September, Tenskwatawa was having second thoughts. During the past year his brother had slowly eclipsed his position of leadership. Tecumseh, not Tenskwatawa, had gone to Vincennes. Tecumseh, not Tenskwatawa, had met with Harrison. And even now his brother was traveling through the South offering the southern tribes a political, not religious, alliance. Perhaps the Long Knives would again afford him an opportunity to prove his medicine. In mid-September he sent a delegation of warriors to Vincennes to reassure Harrison that "his heart was warm" toward the United States. But he also dispatched messengers to the Kickapoos, Potawatomis, and Miamis, asking them to send their warriors to his village. Other envoys met with British agents, seeking additional stores of arms and ammunition. If Harrison could be stopped with promises, all would be well; but if the Long Knives came to Prophetstown, Tenskwatawa would be ready for them.[23]

Harrison had heard such promises before. Moreover, during late September several small parties of warriors from Prophetstown infested the lower Wabash Valley, stealing horses and killing livestock. Convinced that the Prophet's "hostility and determined aggression" now demanded "some energetic measure," Harrison prepared to march. First, he sent a delegation of Delawares up the Wabash to warn friendly Indians of his approach. On September 26, 1811, the governor and his army started north from Vincennes. During the next week they proceeded along the east bank of the Wabash until they reached the site of modern Terre Haute. There they halted and began construction of a log stockade, known as Fort Harrison.[24]

For Tenskwatawa the die was cast. Harrison was marching toward Prophetstown, and the Long Knives were building a new fort inside the treaty lands. If he agreed to Harrison's demands, or if he retreated, he would lose face. Moreover, if the Americans captured Prophetstown he would be forced to surrender the large stores of food and ammunition he finally had been able to accumulate. Tecumseh's preparations were unfinished, and he had urged caution, but the Prophet was determined to make a stand. Scouts were sent out to monitor the American advance. Other warriors rode west into Illinois to seek additional assistance from the Potawatomis. While he waited, Tenskwatawa conversed with the Master of Life, assuring his followers of victory.[25]

Scouts riding south to spy on the Americans intercepted the Delawares Harrison had sent to the friendly tribes. Surrounding the Delawares, the scouts exuded optimism, declaring that the Prophet had promised them success. They demanded whether the Delawares "would or would not join them in the war against the United States—that they had taken up the Tomahawk and that they would lay it down only with their lives." Proceeding on to Prophetstown, the bewildered Delawares tried to persuade Tenskwatawa to agree to the American demands. They received a scathing reply. The Shawnee denounced them for their friendship to Harrison and warned of dire consequences for those tribesmen refusing to join his cause. Sending them from his camp with "the most contemptuous remarks," he boasted that he would burn the first four American prisoners that fell into his hands.[26]

If Tenskwatawa earlier had used his religious exhortations to bolster the confidence of his warriors, he now seemed caught up in his own success. Like the most fanatic of his followers he seemed to welcome the impending confrontation with Harrison. After all, weren't large numbers of Potawatomis arriving daily from Illinois? And hadn't the British furnished his warriors with new muskets and powder? Twice before Harrison had played into his hands. The governor had challenged him to produce a miracle and the Master of Life had provided a Black Sun. And in 1808 the governor had naïvely supplied him with food until his crops could be harvested. Perhaps the Master of Life was again leading the Long Knife into his hands. If such was the case, then Harrison must be goaded onward. Any peaceful solution was now out of the question.

Hoping to taunt the Americans into action, in mid-October Tenskwatawa dispatched a small war party to Fort Harrison. They were instructed to remain quietly in the vicinity of the post and to ambush any soldiers who wandered into the woods. Since most of Harrison's men were busy constructing the stockade and the others remained within the clearing holding the post, the war party was unsuccessful. Frustrated, on the evening of October 10 they fired on the sentries, wounding only one soldier but spreading alarm throughout the camp. Although the Indians fled, they had accomplished their purpose. Harrison reported to his superiors that he had always believed "the Prophet was a rash and presumptuous man, but he has exceeded my expectations. He has not contented himself with throwing the gauntlet, but has absolutely commenced the war."[27]

Yet Harrison made one final, futile attempt at negotiation. By the end of October the fort had been completed and garrisoned, and the army prepared to depart. But before leaving camp, Harrison sent another party of friendly Miamis to Prophetstown. They were to inform the Prophet that if he would send all the Potawatomis, Kickapoos, and Winnebagos from his camp; return all stolen horses; and promise to surrender all warriors guilty of depredations against the

United States, the Americans would not attack his village. On October 29 the American army marched north from Fort Harrison. Two days later they crossed over to the west bank of the Wabash, then paused near the mouth of the Vermillion to construct a small blockhouse (Fort Boyd) to serve as a supply post for the final leg of the expedition. On November 3 they resumed their march and the following day forded Pine Creek, where Harrison took special precautions against an expected ambush. By November 5 they were within twelve miles of Prophetstown.[28]

Scouts brought Tenskwatawa reports of the American advance, but the holy man seemed uncertain of his response. He had expected Harrison to continue up the southeast side of the Wabash, which eventually would have brought the army to a point facing his village, but on the *opposite* bank of the river. Since additional warriors were en route from Michigan and Illinois, he had hoped to stall the governor until they arrived. Therefore, he had met with the delegation of Miamis, instructing them to return down the opposite bank of the Wabash and to inform Harrison that he wanted to meet with him to discuss the Americans' demands. But when the governor and his army crossed over to the northwestern bank of the river, the Prophet's plans went awry. The Long Knives were now marching toward his village and the Wabash no longer protected him. Though committed to war, he still remained a religious leader, not a war chief. He could inflame his followers to a fever pitch, but he had never led warriors in battle. When messengers brought news that a small party of Potawatomis had attacked an American supply boat, his village seethed with excitement. Many of his followers now urged him to attack Harrison's column as it forded Pine Creek. But the Prophet still hesitated. Perhaps more warriors would arrive. Perhaps his medicine would again provide him with the power to overcome his enemies.[29]

Harrison's arrival ended Tenskwatawa's indecision. At

midafternoon on November 6, 1811, scouts reported that Harrison's army, marching in battle formation, had emerged from the forest less than one mile west of Prophetstown. Small parties of warriors had followed his progress throughout the day, and although the Americans had repeatedly attempted to meet with the Indians, the warriors had refused all offers of negotiations. Indeed, on several occasions they had attempted to surround a party of American scouts who had preceded the main body of soldiers, but the Leathershirts had retreated when the tribesmen had tried to cut them off. Now the Long Knives were about to enter the Prophet's village. Unless they could be hoodwinked into stopping, he and his warriors would have to meet them in the open fields that surrounded his settlement, a prospect that neither the Prophet nor his followers found appealing. In desperation, Tenskwatawa sent a small party of warriors forward under a flag of truce. Meeting with Harrison, they feigned surprise that he was advancing on their village since (they claimed) the Prophet had sent a message of accommodation through Winamac and the Miamis. Unfortunately, according to the warriors, the governor must have missed the Miami delegation because it had returned down river along the southeastern bank of the Wabash. The Indians assured Harrison that Tenskwatawa sincerely wanted to avoid bloodshed, and proposed that both sides meet on the following day to discuss the American demands.[30]

Much to his officers' dismay, Harrison accepted the offer. Although he doubted that their differences could be settled peacefully, he believed that Eustis's orders still obligated him to negotiate. Both sides agreed to meet on the following day. They also agreed to remain at peace, at least until the negotiations were completed. After some confusion over locating a suitable campsite, the Indians suggested that the Americans camp along Burnett's Creek, a small stream emptying into the Wabash about two miles downstream from Prophetstown. Harrison eventually selected a triangular neck of land overlooking the prairie. On the east side, toward Prophetstown, the hill rose about ten feet above a grassy marsh that stretched off toward the Indian village. On the west the slope fell off sharply—almost twenty feet—to a small willow-choked ravine carved by the creek along the skirts of the escarpment. The campground was covered by an open oak forest, the trees now leafless in the autumn. Harrison stationed his men in a hollow, unevenly shaped trapezoid, about 150 yards long and 50 to 75 yards in width. The soldiers were ordered to sleep at their posts, weapons primed and ready. Meanwhile, sentries were sent out in all directions to guard against a surprise attack.[31]

Although Harrison took all necessary precautions, he doubted that the Indians would attack his camp. Since they had not tried to ambush him en route to Fort Harrison, he believed that the Prophet and his followers were too intimidated to strike the first blow. He assumed too that the Indians would not choose to fight at night because the warriors feared the darkness might assist a well-disciplined and highly trained body of troops. He did not expect the next day's negotiations to go well, and if the Prophet refused to meet his demands, the governor planned an attack of his own. Tomorrow night, when the conference had ended and the Indians had retreated into their village, Harrison intended to launch a surprise attack. He would treat the Indians to American "bayonets and buckshot," and then burn Prophetstown.[32]

Tenskwatawa made plans of his own. While Harrison's army bedded down for the night, the holy man rallied his warriors. Wearing a necklace of deer hoofs and carrying strings of his sacred beans, he exhorted his followers to attack the Americans. Assuring them that the Master of Life had provided him with medicine to gain a great victory over their enemies, the Prophet promised he would make them invulnerable to the Long Knives. He would send rain and hail to dampen the Americans' powder, but the weapons of his warriors would not be affected. His followers must strike

the Long Knives before dawn, for in the darkness his medicine would spread confusion in the American ranks and many
would fall to the ground in a stupor. The same darkness
would hide the warriors and blind the soldiers, while he
would provide light "like the noon-tide sun" to guide the
Indians. But Tenskwatawa warned the warriors that they
must kill Harrison. The Master of Life had demanded that
the governor should die, for if he lived, the Long Knives
could never be defeated. Therefore, the initial attack must
penetrate as far as the governor's tent, in the center of the
American camp. When Harrison fell, the surviving soldiers
"would run and hide in the grass like young quails." Then
they could be captured and forced to serve as slaves for the
women of Prophetstown.[33]

Assured of victory, the Prophet's followers decided to attack the Americans approximately two hours before dawn.
They planned to encircle the entire camp while a special
party of about one hundred hand-picked warriors would
penetrate the American lines on the northwestern perimeter and kill Harrison. If the infiltrators were discovered, they
were to give the war cry, which would be answered by all
the warriors surrounding the American position, and a general assault would take place. Tenskwatawa assured them
that the Long Knives would panic in the darkness and that
his followers would "have possession of the camp and all its
equipage, and [the warriors could] shoot the men with their
own guns from every tree." As the warriors took their positions in the predawn darkness, their medicine seemed strong.
A cold rain began to fall, heralding one of the Prophet's pre-
dictions. Meanwhile, they found that the Americans had
built large bonfires within their lines, impeding their ability
to see into the darkness, but silhouetting the camp and its
inhabitants to the surrounding Indians. Although the fires
hardly glowed "like the noon-tide sun," they would show
the warriors their enemy. Tenskwatawa was keeping his
promises.[34]

Harrison arose at 4:15 A.M. on November 7 and was putting on his boots when he heard a rifle shot from the northwestern corner of his camp. As the Indians attempted to infiltrate the American lines, they were discovered by a sentry standing picket duty near Burnett's Creek. Frightened, the soldier fired his weapon, then fled back toward the bivouac. Other sentries, alarmed by the shot, also retreated toward the American position. Many of the warriors already had penetrated the northwestern picket lines, and when another sentry fired, they sprang up and sounded the war cry. Instantly the shout was echoed by the other Indians who had surrounded the camp and who began to fire upon the soldiers. Realizing they were discovered, the party of warriors assigned to kill Harrison charged into the hastily forming American lines, killing some soldiers before they could reach their positions. A few of the Indians penetrated to the interior of the camp and attempted to attack the officers in their tents, but most were shot down by American troops rushing forward to reinforce their comrades.[35]

Now fully dressed, Harrison shouted for his servant to bring his horse, a light gray mare that the governor had ridden the previous day and which was still saddled in preparation for such an emergency. But in the confusion, the animal had broken loose and the governor was forced to mount a dark stallion belonging to one of his aides, Major Waller Taylor. Accompanied by Colonel Abraham Owen, Harrison rode to the northwestern perimeter, where he ordered reinforcements to strengthen the American lines that had buckled dangerously from the Indian onslaught. Inside the American camp, two warriors who had escaped notice desperately searched for Harrison. As the two mounted officers rushed forward in the darkness, the warriors mistook Owen, who was riding a white horse, for the governor. One of the Indians fired, instantly killing Owen. Harrison passed on in safety, believing his companion hit by enemy fire from outside the American lines. The two warriors were soon killed by American soldiers.[36]

The attack now became general. The Indians continued to pour a deadly fire on the Americans. Harrison ordered all the bonfires extinguished, but Indian marksmen still took a heavy toll. To the southeast, a party of warriors occupied a small clump of trees only twenty paces from the American lines, firing into the very faces of a company of regulars opposite them. The Americans attempted a sortie, but the warriors drove them back, mortally wounding Major Joseph H. Davies and killing several of his men. A subsequent attack dislodged the warriors, and the focus of the battle now shifted to the southwest corner of the perimeter, where Indians firing from the brush along Burnett's Creek had killed or wounded most of the officers in that sector. Again Harrison reinforced his lines and again the Americans bent, but were not broken. Convinced that victory would soon be theirs, the Indians fought with a dogged tenacity, and the battle raged on. But as dawn broke over the Wabash, they began to withdraw. In response, Harrison rallied his forces and ordered bayonet charges against those warriors still remaining opposite his flanks. As the Americans advanced, the warriors retreated into the marshes. The Battle of Tippecanoe was over.[37]

Tenskwatawa took no part in the action. During the battle he stationed himself on a small hill near Prophetstown, across the marshy prairie from Harrison's camp. Out of range of American bullets, he spent the early morning in incantations, asking the Master of Life to protect his warriors and give them victory over the Long Knives. But his medicine was barren. As dawn broke and the Indians retreated, the Prophet also fled to his village, where he was confronted by angry warriors. Especially incensed were the Winnebagos, long among the most devoted of his followers, who had lost many kinsmen in the battle. Seizing the holy man and brandishing their war clubs over his head, the Winnebagos threatened him with death and demanded to know why he had misled them into believing "that the white people were dead or crazy when they were all in their senses and fought like the Devil." Frightened for his life, Tenskwatawa declared that the fault was not his. The blame, he told them, should be placed on his wife, for she had failed to inform him that she was having her menstrual period. Of course all the warriors knew that during her menstrual period a woman was unclean and should not handle sacred things. But the foolish woman had not told him, and he had allowed her to assist him in his incantations and to handle his sacred strings of beans. If the Winnebagos and the other warriors would regroup, Tenskwatawa would cleanse his sacraments and again make medicine, this time pledging that his followers would win over the Long Knives. But too many warriors had already fallen. His followers now scoffed at his claims, and although they spared his life, they hurried to abandon Prophetstown.[38]

Following the Indian retreat, Harrison and his men spent the day caring for their wounded and fortifying their camp. The volunteers and militiamen also searched the area surrounding the American perimeter for fallen warriors left behind by their kinsmen. They discovered thirty-six bodies, which they promptly stripped, scalped, and mutilated. Two Indians were found alive. One was killed as he attempted to flee, but the other, a mortally wounded Potawatomi, was carried into camp, where his wounds were dressed and he was questioned. On the following morning a company of dragoons rode to Prophetstown and found it deserted. Only one old woman, too infirm to travel, remained in the town. The soldiers confiscated large amounts of abandoned household items and foodstuffs, then burned over five thousand bushels of corn and beans. They also set fire to most of the wigwams. On November 9, Harrison broke camp and marched back down the Wabash. He placed the dying Potawatomi in the care of the old woman, instructing him to inform any returning tribesmen that if they now would abandon the Prophet, the government would treat them as friends.[39]

Harrison described the battle as a "complete and decisive" American victory, and three decades later he would gain the presidency as "Old Tippecanoe," a military hero who had soundly beaten the Indians on the Wabash. But a closer examination of the battle and its outcome indicates that Harrison's claims were exaggerated. Both white and Indian losses were much the same. The American force numbered close to 1,000 officers and men. They suffered 188 casualties, of which at least 62 were fatal. The number of Indians engaged in the contest is much more difficult to ascertain, but there were probably between 600 and 700 warriors. Reports of Indian casualties also vary widely, but probably at least fifty were killed and seventy to eighty were wounded.[40]

Although the destruction of Prophetstown dispersed the hostile warriors and brought a temporary respite to the lower Wabash Valley, these Indians now scattered across the Old Northwest, infesting the frontier in other areas. Anxious for revenge, Winnebago warriors returning from Prophetstown fired on the garrison at Fort Madison in Iowa, fatally wounding soldiers assigned to hunting and wood-cutting details. Meanwhile, wandering bands of "vagabond" Indians committed depredations across Michigan and Ohio, killing settlers and stealing livestock. Other survivors of Harrison's "victory" set ambushes near the mouth of the Ohio, waylaying American travelers as they floated downstream. If Vincennes was finally safe from Indian attacks, knowledge of that town's security brought little comfort to solitary frontiersmen in other parts of the Northwest. Barricaded in their cabins, they now faced the former residents of Prophetstown.[41]

In retrospect, the Battle of Tippecanoe was less an American victory than a personal defeat for Tenskwatawa. He had committed his warriors to battle with assurances of their personal safety. Now many lay dead on the field. His medicine was broken. No longer would he play a major role in the struggle against the Long Knives. No longer would Indians flock to his camp from throughout the Old Northwest. No longer would his enemies fear his allegations of witchcraft. Now Tecumseh would completely dominate the Indian resistance movement. In the years ahead the Prophet would become an outcast, a fallen pontiff clinging to his brother's coattails. The Great Serpent had triumphed. The medicine days were over; the bitter days were just beginning.

Tens-qua-ta-wa or *The One that Opens the Door / Shawnese Prophet*, by J. O. Lewis. Although this painting is dated 1823, documentary evidence indicates that it was painted in December 1824. (Courtesy Amon Carter Museum, Fort Worth, Texas)

TENS - QUA - TA - WA

or THE ONE THAT OPENS THE DOOR

Shawnese Prophet

Brother of Tecumthe

Painted for Gov. Lewis Cass by J. O. Lewis at Detroit 1823.

This portrait of Tecumseh is
from B. J. Lossing's *Pictorial Field-
Book of the War of 1812*, and is
based on a pencil sketch made by
Pierre Le Dru, a trader at Vincennes, during the War of 1812.

This portrait of William Henry
Harrison was based on a painting of
the governor completed in 1814.
Harrison is wearing a military uni-
form from the War of 1812. (Courtesy Indiana Division, Indiana State
Library)

This scene depicts the confrontation between Tecumseh and Harrison at Vincennes in August 1810. (Courtesy Cincinnati Historical Society)

The Battle of Tippecanoe, fought
on November 7, 1811, was hardly
the military victory that Harrison
claimed, yet the Indian retreat had
a devastating impact on the influence of the Shawnee Prophet.
(Courtesy Indiana Historical Society Library)

A View of Amherstburg, 1813,
by Margaret Reynolds. Amherstburg, the site of Fort Malden, was
the most important center of British influence among the northwestern tribes. (Courtesy Fort Malden
National Historic Park)

Established by William Henry
Harrison is 1811 as he was en route
to the Tippecanoe, Fort Harrison
was attacked by the Prophet's followers in September 1812. (Courtesy Indiana Division, Indiana State
Library)

This scene depicts Tecumseh's attempts to stop the killing of prisoners following Dudley's Defeat, at Fort Meigs, in May 1813. (Courtesy Cincinnati Historical Society)

General Henry Procter, by
J. C. H. Forster. Procter, who succeeded General Brock, was generally disliked by the Indians. He
commanded the British forces that
fled at the Battle of the Thames, in
October 1813. (Courtesy Fort Malden National Historic Park)

The Battle of the Thames, by B. Rawdon. This scene depicts American horsemen charging the British and Indians at the Battle of the Thames October 1813. (Courtesy Public Archives of Canada, 7763)

Ca-ta-he-cas-sa-Black Hoof, Principal Chief of the Shawanoes. An active opponent of the Shawnee Prophet and Tecumseh, Black Hoof led the pro-American Shawnees at Wapakoneta during the first third of the nineteenth century. This portrait was included in the McKenney-Hall portfolio. (Courtesy Amon Carter Museum, Fort Worth, Texas)

William Clark, by George Catlin. Superintendent of Indian affairs at St. Louis, Clark assisted the Shawnee Prophet and other Indians in their removals west. (Courtesy National Portrait Gallery, Smithsonian Institution)

Chapter Six

The War of 1812

The onrushing winter seemed to complement the Prophet's misfortunes. Chilling rains that had fallen at Tippecanoe changed to snow in December, and leaden skies promised that the cold months had permanence. For Tenskwatawa, the bleak winter of 1811–12 marked the nadir of his influence. At least he remained alive. Still angry over their fallen kinsmen, the Winnebagos had bound him with rope and had forced him to accompany them to a temporary camp on Wildcat Creek, about twenty miles east of Prophetstown. There they had taunted him again before abandoning the campsite to return to the west. Several Wyandots and a handful of Shawnees still lingered near Prophetstown, and these refugees gave him food and shelter, but it was obvious they no longer venerated him as their leader. Other tribesmen shunned him and when Tenskwatawa asked the Kickapoos of the Prairie if he could withdraw to their town on the headwaters of the Sangamon, they adamantly refused.[1]

There were other portents of even greater calamity. In mid-December a severe earthquake shook the Mississippi and Ohio valleys. Other tremors continued until the following spring. Although the Prophet argued that he had summoned the earthquakes to destroy the Long Knives, his detractors declared the Master of Life had shaken the ground because the Shawnee was an imposter.[2] His old enemies, the government chiefs, plotted against him. Anxious to ingratiate themselves with Harrison, they met in council near Fort Wayne and planned his assassination. Fortunately for Tenskwatawa, their plot became entangled in a bitter feud between Indian agent John Johnston and William Wells and their schemes never materialized. Still, the Shawnee feared for his life.[3]

Tecumseh returned from the South in mid-January 1812. His journey had achieved only limited success. Since August he had visited the Chickasaws, Choctaws, and Creeks, soliciting new recruits for his spreading confederacy. But in the South Tecumseh encountered a new kind of Indian: a tribesman who was rapidly acculturating toward the white man's value system. During September he met with the Chickasaws, hoping to enlist their support against the United States. He was sorely disappointed. Dominated by the highly acculturated Colbert family, the Chickasaws listened politely to his entreaties, but refused to give him their allegiance. After leaving the Chickasaws, Tecumseh and his party rode south to the Choctaws, where they met with a similar reception. There the persuasive Choctaw chief Pushmataha, a steadfast ally of the Americans, worked diligently to minimize the Shawnee's influence. Like the Chickasaws, the Choctaws listened attentively to Tecumseh's pleas, but they remained tied to the government.[4]

Only among the Creeks did Tecumseh's efforts reap any harvest. Unlike the Chickasaws and Choctaws, the Creeks had recently quarreled with the Americans, and they resented white encroachment on their lands in western Georgia and the Yazoo strip. Moreover, the Shawnees, and especially Tecumseh, had close ties with the Creek confederacy. Here the northern Indians spent several weeks, visiting the scattered Creek villages and recruiting warriors to serve against the Long Knives. Not all Creeks were receptive to Tecumseh's plans, but many of the younger warriors listened attentively, and vowed to ride north to assist their brothers at Prophetstown. Others promised that if war erupted between the British and Americans, they too would lift their hatchets against the Long Knives. Unaware that Harrison and Tenskwatawa had clashed near Prophetstown, Tecumseh left Alabama in December and rode back to Indiana.[5]

Tecumseh's arrival on the Tippecanoe brought the Prophet a mixed blessing. Undoubtedly, the beleaguered holy man felt more secure with Tecumseh's return, for threats against his life soon diminished, but he was well aware that the war chief had instructed him not to fight the Long Knives, and he feared his brother's anger. His fear was justified. Chagrined that his followers were scattered and his movement was in disarray, Tecumseh demanded to know why his brother had attacked Harrison before their confederacy was completed. Tenskwatawa attempted to defend his actions, but his excuses only increased Tecumseh's anger. Infuriated, he seized the Prophet by the hair and shook him, denouncing him as a child. Although he released his brother, Tecumseh remained incensed and threatened him with death if he again disrupted their plans for a political and military confederation. Subdued, the Prophet did not resist his brother's onslaught. He had lost his position of leadership and would follow his brother's counsel.[6]

Tecumseh immediately began to rebuild the faltering confederacy. Riders were sent to Potawatomi and Kickapoo villages in Illinois and to the Winnebagos, asking them to reassemble on the Wabash in the spring and be ready for war. Meanwhile, he erected a temporary village on Wildcat Creek, east of the Wabash, where he consolidated the Shawnee and Wyandot refugees. Since Harrison's men had destroyed most of their food, hunting parties were sent as far east as the Mississinewa, seeking game for their cooking pots.[7]

Tecumseh also sought assistance from the British. Shortly after returning from the South, the Shawnee war chief welcomed two Delawares whom British agents in Canada had sent to his camp. Both Tecumseh and the Prophet informed the messengers that their people desperately needed provisions. The Delawares returned to Amherstburg, and in late February Indians from the new village on Wildcat Creek met with British agents near Sandusky Bay, where the British supplied them with a small quantity of lead and powder. Three weeks later a delegation of twenty-four warriors traveled to Canada seeking food and clothing. Although the British had little food to spare, they did provide the party with clothing and ammunition.[8]

Tecumseh next sought a temporary respite from the Americans. This time the Long Knives played into his hands. Aware that war with the British was imminent, federal officials again held out the olive branch to the tribes. Convinced that the Prophet no longer posed a military threat, in January 1812, Secretary of War William Eustis instructed Harrison to invite the Prophet, Tecumseh, and other western chiefs to Washington. Harrison had serious misgivings about the proposal, but sent a messenger up the Wabash offering amnesty to the holy man if he and his brother would accept the government's invitation. They would not, however, be permitted to serve as spokesmen for the western tribes, but only as members of the delegation. Envisioning acceptance of the offer as a means of placating the Long Knives, Tecumseh replied that they would visit their Great Father during the summer.[9]

The Shawnee chief took great pains to create an illusion of cooperation with the Americans. In March he sent a mixed delegation of Kickapoos and Winnebagos to Vincennes to assure Harrison that these former adherents of the Prophet were eager for peace. The Kickapoos and Winnebagos played their role as penitents to the hilt. They blamed the Prophet for their past mistakes and when Harrison inquired why some Winnebagos recently had attacked the garrison at Fort Madison, they replied that their kinsmen were unaware that the Indians and the Long Knives had "buried the tomahawk." They volunteered, however, to ride to the Mississippi and bring the warfare to an end. Harrison was so impressed by their sincerity that he offered them horses with which to make the journey. He also invited them to visit Washington with the Prophet, Tecumseh, and other western chiefs, and suggested that the Indians assemble at Fort Wayne to prepare for the expedition. Convinced that the tribes now were "sincere in their professions of friendship and their desire for peace," Harrison sent a message to Wildcat Creek to pardon the recalcitrant Shawnees and Wyandots and "even to forgive the Prophet." He also instructed Tenskwatawa and Tecumseh to meet with the others at Fort Wayne in anticipation of their trip to Washington.[10]

The journey never materialized. Harrison also invited delegates from the Miamis, Potawatomis, Eel Rivers, and Delawares to accompany the other Indians, but in mid-April, when the tribesmen were to assemble at Fort Wayne, most were absent. Although Tecumseh and the Prophet originally had accepted a belt of wampum symbolizing their approval of the journey, they returned the wampum to Fort Wayne and remained in their village. The Kickapoos and Winnebagos, recently so cooperative, also failed to make an appearance. The Delawares refused to participate and the Miamis, Potawatomis, and Eel Rivers, although in attendance, were so intimidated that they refused to leave Indiana. Embarrassed, Harrison admitted that he again had been duped: "The hopes . . . entertained of our being able to avoid a war with the Indians are entirely dissipated."[11]

In contrast, British influence on the Wabash increased. British officials also believed that war was close at hand and made plans to warn the tribesmen. They hoped to prepare their Indian allies, but did not want the Indians to precipitate the conflict. Fearing that messengers to Tecumseh and the Prophet might be intercepted by the Americans, British officials devised a scheme through which messages could be delivered, even with the Americans' blessing. Supposedly neutral Wyandots were sent to territorial officials in Michigan to suggest that "some of their most respectable young Men should visit the Prophet and his party and forbid them to make any further depridation [*sic*] on the Americans." Convinced of the Wyandots' sincerity, Reuben Attwater, secretary to Governor William Hull, approved the mission and even furnished the Wyandots with provisions and letters of introduction for the journey.[12]

Unknown to Attwater, the "most respectable young men" were led by Isadore Chaine, a mixed-blood Wyandot long in the British service. Chaine was instructed to assume the role of a peacemaker, but to secretly inform Tecumseh and the Prophet to prepare for war. He openly carried a belt of white wampum given him by the Americans, but his saddlebags concealed black wampum from the British, wampum signifying war. In late February, Chaine arrived at Fort Wayne, where he spent two months ingratiating himself with pro-American chiefs such as Little Turtle of the Miamis and Five Medals of the Potawatomis. With their assistance he organized a multitribal council, held on the Mississinewa River during mid-May. Since many tribes were invited, the conference was attended by almost six hundred Indians.[13]

On the surface, the council appeared to go in the Americans' favor. The Prophet, Tecumseh, and several of their followers were present, but they seemed to be on the defensive. Although Tenskwatawa vowed that his heart now was "inclined for peace," he became the scapegoat for the other Indians' problems. When the Potawatomis were asked why their warriors recently had attacked some settlements, they replied that their "foolish young men" had been led astray "by this pretended prophet, who [they knew had] taken great pains to detach them from their own chiefs and attach them to himself." The Delawares charged that "both the red and white people had felt the bad effect of [Tenskwatawa's] counsels," and even Tecumseh declared that his brother's attack on Harrison's army had been a foolish blunder, adding, "Had I been at home, there would have been no blood shed at that time." [14]

Speaking in open council, Chaine urged the tribesmen to remain at peace. He instructed them to put away their weapons, informing them that even the British had "advised all the red people to be quiet and not meddle in quarrels that may take place between the white people." All the Indians seemed in agreement, and when Tecumseh replied that Winamac and those chiefs who had sold Indian land were the major troublemakers, the Delawares interrupted him, telling the Shawnee, "We have not met at this place to listen to such words." Both the Miamis and the Kickapoos pleaded for peace and urged the Potawatomis to surrender any of their young warriors guilty of the recent depredations. When the council ended, Chaine and the pro-American village chiefs returned to Fort Wayne, where the latter informed government officials that the conference was a success. [15]

In reality, it was the British who reaped the greatest rewards on the Mississinewa. Unknown to the village chiefs, Chaine met privately with Tecumseh and the Prophet and instructed them to again unite the tribes and prepare for war. They were to keep their warriors quiet, but Tecumseh was invited to Canada to meet with Matthew Elliott, who would inform him of British plans and provide his followers with a large quantity of arms and ammunition. The Shawnees agreed to the British proposal, but Tecumseh warned that if the Long Knives again marched on their village, the Indians would defend themselves: "And if we hear of any of our people having been killed, We will immediately send to all the Nations on or towards the Mississippi, and all this Island will rise as one man—Then Father and Brothers it will be impossible for either of You to restore peace between us." [16]

American officials eventually learned of Chaine's schemes, but by that time his mission had been accomplished. Meanwhile, Tecumseh and the Prophet were hard pressed to keep their followers from attacking the Americans. Much of the difficulty originated with the Potawatomis. Although supposedly followers of the Prophet, many Potawatomis actually were loyal to Main Poc, and Tecumseh's efforts to restrain them met with little success. In April and May Potawatomi war parties swept south across the prairies, attacking isolated settlements from the Mississippi to the Wabash. Panic-stricken frontiersmen abandoned their farms and fled toward Kentucky, while American efforts to intercept the raiders ended in frustration. Ominously, when officers at Fort Harrison sought assistance from the Weas in apprehending the hostiles, the Weas laughed in their faces and chided them to be careful lest the Shawnees feed them to the crows. Harrison reported that it was impossible to exaggerate "the alarm and distress which these murders [had] produced," and predicted that the lower Wabash Valley would soon be depopulated unless the attacks ended.[17]

Not all the hostile Indians were raiding in Illinois. Many had returned to the Prophet's village. Early in the spring, part of the Winnebagos who previously had threatened Tenskwatawa's life came back to the Wabash and erected a small village on Wildcat Creek. In the meantime, the Prophet and Tecumseh moved their camp back across the Wabash to the site of the original Prophetstown. There they were joined by many Kickapoos and some Miamis, who established another village on the northwest bank of the Wabash, just below the mouth of the Tippecanoe. By mid-May over three hundred warriors again were encamped in the immediate vicinity of Prophetstown, and their numbers increased daily. Not surprisingly, the same old logistical problems that earlier had plagued the Prophet reappeared. Since Harrison had burned Tenskwatawa's storehouses, he was desperately short of provisions. And ironically, the large numbers of warriors who increased the Shawnee brothers' military power also depleted their supplies of British powder. By early summer Tecumseh and the Prophet no longer could feed all their followers.[18]

To obtain additional stores of lead and powder, Tecumseh again turned to the British. At the Mississinewa council Chaine had informed him that Elliott wished to meet with him in Canada. Moreover, Chaine had promised that the British would be generous with their ammunition. Leaving the Prophet in charge of their followers on the Wabash, in mid-June, Tecumseh and ten warriors set out for Malden. They passed through Fort Wayne, where Indian agent Benjamin Stickney tried to dissuade them from their journey, and continued on to Canada, where they arrived on July 1, 1812.[19]

Tecumseh and his party were not the only group of armed men advancing toward the Canadian-American frontier. Aware that war was imminent, the Americans moved rapidly to strengthen their forces across the river from Malden. During the spring Governor William Hull (recently appointed to the rank of brigadier-general) raised an army in Ohio and in June marched north toward Michigan. Accompanied by about two thousand men, Hull reached Detroit on July 6, 1812. Four days earlier he had received notification that the United States had declared war on Great Britain.[20]

News of the war reached the Wabash on July 6, but at first the message had little impact. Following Tecumseh's instructions, the Prophet took pains to keep his followers quiet until he received further word from his brother. He sent messengers to the tribes in Illinois, informing them that the Redcoats and Long Knives had gone to war, but since food was so scarce on the Wabash, he did not encourage them to assemble at Prophetstown. Instead, Tenskwatawa sent each of the western tribes a pipe and a belt of wampum, charging them to wait until late in the summer, when they were "to join him at his village when the corn is made, so [they all could] agree when and where to strike on the Americans." At that time, according to the holy man, the British would furnish them with clothing, guns, and powder.[21]

Meanwhile, the Prophet took care not to alarm the Americans. Still haunted by memories of Tippecanoe, he was determined to prevent any new expeditions against his village. Since Tecumseh had passed safely through Fort Wayne enroute to Malden, Tenskwatawa decided to visit the post and assure government Indian agents that his followers would remain at peace. His chicanery had worked in the past. At least it might forestall open warfare until his brother returned from Canada.[22]

Tenskwatawa arrived at Fort Wayne on July 12, 1812, accompanied by over ninety warriors. He remained at the post for ten days, using all his persuasion on the Americans. Making "strong professions of friendship," the Prophet loudly complained that the British considered the Indians "as dogs, who would run at their call and bite at any thing they directed." Of course the British had asked them "to take up the tomahawk" and had promised them large quantities of guns and powder, but he and his followers "were determined not to listen to them." Indeed, the three nations now lodged near Prophetstown—the Shawnees, Kickapoos, and Winnebagos—had prepared a great wampum belt, which Tenskwatawa presented to Stickney. According to the holy man, the belt represented the Wabash Valley from Fort Wayne to Vincennes, and the white color of the wampum was indicative of the peace that now would reign over the region. To prove their sincerity, he and his followers would give up their claims to the lands ceded at the Treaty of Fort Wayne. Those lands, however, would be relinquished to Stickney, not Harrison, for "their Great Father's mouth talked good things and straight, at Detroit, at Fort Wayne, and every other place except Vincennes: and there it talked crooked and very bad." Therefore, the Prophet and his followers were determined "to give themselves up" to Stickney's "care and protection."[23]

Stickney obviously was suspicious of Tenskwatawa's motives, but he encouraged the Shawnee's peaceful pretensions. He informed the holy man that the government planned to hold a major conference with all the tribes of Ohio, Indiana, and Michigan at Piqua, Ohio, in August, and asked him to attend. The Shawnee agreed, and even promised to send to Canada for Tecumseh so that his brother could "stand by his side" at the council. He then requested that the agent supply his followers with food and ammunition, but Stickney had little of either to spare and agreed to give ammunition only to some friendly Delawares who would provide the Prophet's followers with just enough lead and powder for hunting. Stickney furnished some of the Kickapoos with horses to make the journey to Piqua, however, and the agent seemed optimistic about keeping the tribes at peace.[24]

His optimism was unwarranted. While Tenskwatawa was still encamped at Fort Wayne, he received a messenger bringing important dispatches from Malden. The rider carried a huge red wampum belt, three feet wide and six feet long, sent by the British to all the western tribes. Signifying British arms, the belt was named "the King's Great Broad Axe" and supposedly possessed medicine "to cut down all before it." The messenger also brought instructions from Tecumseh. Since Hull had just invaded Canada and the British seemed on the defensive, the war chief urged his brother to muster their warriors at Prophetstown, but to send all their women and children west into Illinois, where they would be safe from American military expeditions. The Prophet and his followers should then attack Vincennes, and afterward follow their women and children into the West before the Americans could retaliate. If Tecumseh survived the American invasion of Canada, he would join them in the land of the Winnebagos, where they could continue their war on the Long Knives.[25]

In late July the Prophet returned to his village, but the plans to attack the Americans were soon altered. Tecumseh had assumed that the British would remain on the defensive, but in August 1812, the tide of warfare in the West changed markedly. British and Indian forces defeated the Americans at the Battle of Brownstown and inflicted heavy casualties on American units at the Battle of Monguagon. Another party of British and Indians captured Fort Michili-mackinac, and on August 15 the Potawatomis attacked and killed most of the garrison that had just abandoned Fort Dearborn. Convinced that he no longer could hold Detroit against his enemies, on August 16 Hull surrendered the American fort at that location. The shifting fortunes of war were not lost on the Indians. Wyandot and Potawatomi warriors near Detroit who previously had pledged their loyalty to the United States now joined Tecumseh. American plans for the grand council at Piqua, Ohio, suffered accordingly. In late August, when the conference finally was held, it was attended by only 250 Indians.[26]

At Prophetstown, news of the American defeats was greeted with jubilation. By late August the fields were full of corn, and warriors from the western tribes again flocked to the village. Although he no longer reigned as the Indian messiah, the Prophet still exercised considerable influence, and while his brother remained in Canada, the holy man again assumed a role of leadership. Most of the tribesmen in northern Indiana now rallied to the British cause. At the headwaters of the Maumee hostile Potawatomis gathered to attack Fort Wayne, while on the Tippecanoe the Prophet and his followers plotted against Fort Harrison. If both forts fell, the entire Wabash Valley would be open to Indian domination. The Long Knives, not the Indians, would be forced to abandon their settlements. Tenskwatawa and his followers need not flee to the Winnebagos. The Prophet's contribution to this change in Indian plans remains unknown. He certainly did not play the dominant role he had assumed before the Battle of Tippecanoe, but the assault on Fort Harrison was planned in his village, and most of the attackers were Kickapoos, warriors long faithful to the Shawnee's cause.[27]

Once again the Prophet and his followers relied on subterfuge. In early September scouts were sent to reconnoiter Fort Harrison and to warn Wea tribesmen living nearby that an attack was imminent. The Weas were told that they must either join in the attack or withdraw from the vicinity. Although the Indians at Prophetstown naïvely assumed that their message would remain secret, some of the Weas informed Captain Zachary Taylor, the commander of the post. Several young braves in the scouting party were eager for war honors, and on the evening of September 3 they ambushed two farmers cutting hay about a quarter mile north of the stockade. The Long Knives lost their scalps, but all hopes for a surprise attack were shattered.[28]

Yet the charade continued. On the following evening about forty Indians from Prophetstown, including a dozen women and children, approached the fort and informed a sentry that they wished to enter the stockade and meet with Taylor. When Taylor refused to admit them, Joseph Reynard, an old Kickapoo, replied that they were starving and would return for provisions in the morning. Meanwhile the other Indians milled about the walls of the stockade in apparent boredom. The tribesmen then withdrew, but the wary Taylor expected trouble, mustered his men, and doubled the guards for the night.[29]

He was not disappointed. Unknown to the Americans, the Indians noticed that some of the chinking had fallen away from the logs at the base of one of the blockhouses that formed part of the stockade wall. Late in the evening Pakoisheecan, a Kickapoo war chief from the village near Prophetstown, crept up to the blockhouse, carrying a blanket full of dried grass and wood shavings. Concealing his efforts under the blanket, he pushed the combustible materials through the openings between the logs and then ignited them with his flint and steel. The fire was soon discovered, but the base of the blockhouse served as a warehouse for the government contractor and the door was securely bolted. Since the contractor was absent, neither Taylor nor his men could gain access to the structure and the fire quickly spread to the walls and roof of the blockhouse. While Taylor fought the blaze, a large war party of Kickapoos and Winnebagos from Prophetstown who had been concealed nearby opened fire on the fort and advanced toward the burning blockhouse. Although Taylor's men at first were panic-stricken over the attack, he rallied them and prevented the fire from spreading beyond the blockhouse. While part of the garrison repulsed the Indians, others erected a temporary log barrier behind the burning blockhouse, which kept Pakoisheecan and his warriors from entering the fort. The Indians kept up a steady fire throughout the early morning hours, but shortly after dawn they withdrew. Part of the war party remained in the region for several days, burning abandoned cabins and slaughtering livestock. Others rode southeast, where they vented their frustration on the small settlement at Pigeon Roost, twenty-five miles north of Louisville. Here they killed over twenty settlers before fleeing toward Prophetstown. Still, their plans had gone awry. The attack on Fort Harrison had ended in failure.[30]

Indian attempts to capture Fort Wayne suffered a similar fate. In early September, Potawatomis from northern Indiana besieged the post but were forced to withdraw when the fort was relieved by Harrison and an American army. Incensed over the recent attacks, the governor sent military expeditions against nearby Potawatomi and Miami villages. In mid-September, American forces cut a wide swath across northeastern Indiana, burning wigwams and destroying cornfields. Prophetstown remained unscathed, but the American advance caused considerable alarm among Tenskwatawa and his followers. Although he had remained at Prophetstown during the abortive attempt on Fort Harrison, the Shawnee had given the attack his blessing and its subsequent failure did little to enhance his bid to reassert leadership. Disgusted with their lack of success, in October most of the Winnebagos left their village on Wildcat Creek and withdrew to their homeland. Part of the Kickapoos also scattered to towns in Illinois. Abandoned by most of his followers, Tenskwatawa feared that Prophetstown was again exposed to American military forces. In late October he withdrew from the village and retreated up the Tippecanoe. There his diminished following established a temporary camp and awaited further instructions from Tecumseh.[31]

The Prophet's withdrawal proved more timely than he at first realized. While his warriors were leaving their villages, the Americans mounted two campaigns against Prophetstown. In mid-October Major General Samuel Hopkins and four thousand Kentucky militia marched up the Wabash Valley, intending to attack Prophetstown and several Kickapoo villages in Illinois. Plagued by desertions, Hopkins and his men became lost on the prairies west of the Wabash before abandoning their expedition and returning to Fort Harrison. Undaunted, the Kentuckian organized another campaign, and in November led over twelve hundred men up the east bank of the Wabash to Prophetstown. The Americans first destroyed the deserted Winnebago camp on Wildcat Creek, then crossed the Wabash to burn Prophetstown and the abandoned Kickapoo village. Scouts brought news of the invasion to Tenskwatawa, but he had neither the warriors nor the inclination to oppose the Long Knives. A war party from his village was sent to harass the expedition, and on November 22 they ambushed a mounted patrol, killing eighteen Americans. Hopkins mounted a cumbersome counterattack, but the warriors eluded their enemy. An early blizzard precluded a retaliatory attack up the Tippecanoe, and on November 25 the Americans struck camp and marched back down the Wabash.[32]

Hopkins's expedition did not bode well for Tenskwatawa. Although the Long Knives had been unable to ascend the Tippecanoe, they had proven that they could march at will along the Wabash Valley. Moreover, the Americans again had struck at the Prophet's greatest weakness—his inability to feed his followers. Although the Indians had taken some provisions when they retreated up the Tippecanoe, they did not have the means to transport most of their recently harvested corn crop. Much of the corn was left behind, poorly hidden in caches near the village. Not surprisingly, Hopkins and his men discovered most of the repositories and either confiscated or destroyed the foodstuffs. Again faced with shortages, Tenskwatawa and his followers now anticipated another long, cold winter. They could remain in Indiana and go hungry, or they could turn to what must have seemed a veritable cornucopia. Hadn't their British father promised to supply all his red children who supported him? Why should they starve on the Tippecanoe while their kinsmen sat before full cooking pots at Malden? In mid-December messengers brought news that another American expedition had attacked the Miami and Delaware towns along the Mississinewa. The die was cast. A few days later the Prophet and most of his remaining followers fled to Canada.[33]

It must have been a bittersweet journey. Tenskwatawa now was assured of adequate food and shelter, but the flight to Canada was symbolic of his declining fortunes. Prophetstown again had fallen to the Long Knives, and he was forced to flee from the Tippecanoe and Wabash valleys. His enemies remained at Fort Harrison, while his followers, at least the Kickapoos and Winnebagos, again had abandoned him. Even worse, the British now recognized Tecumseh as the spokesman for the western tribes. In retreating to Canada, the Prophet was placing himself under his brother's hegemony. He was tacitly admitting that his attempt to reassert leadership had failed.

His arrival in Canada produced some unpleasant surprises. He learned that Tecumseh had been shot in the leg at the Battle of Monguagon. Although the wound was not serious, it had been slow in healing and Tecumseh only recently had regained his health. Meanwhile, the British were making every effort to rally the western tribes for a spring offensive. Tecumseh was eager to return to Indiana to re-cruit warriors for the campaign and he urged Tenskwatawa to accompany him. It seems doubtful that the Prophet would have relished an immediate return to the Wabash Valley, but he reluctantly agreed. Between January and April 1813, they traveled among the Indian villages north of the Wabash, urging their scattered followers to assist the British. Because they were absent from Michigan during these months, neither the Prophet nor Tecumseh took part in the Battle of Frenchtown.[34]

Their efforts in Indiana produced results. After meeting with the Shawnee brothers, delegations of Kickapoos, Potawatomis, Delawares, Winnebagos, and Weas journeyed to Malden, where they assured the British that they would send their warriors in the spring. By late March large numbers of western tribesmen were already assembling at Detroit, while others gathered north of the Wabash, waiting for Tecumseh and the Prophet to lead them to Canada. In April the Shawnees collected their remaining followers and rode east. They arrived at Malden on April 16, 1813.[35]

The Americans also mustered their forces. While the Prophet and Tecumseh were in Indiana, Harrison constructed a new post, Fort Meigs, at the rapids of the Maumee River. He envisioned the fort as a base of operations for the recapture of Detroit and the invasion of Canada. In contrast, Brigadier General Henry Procter, the British commander at Malden, was determined to attack the post before the Americans could launch offensive operations. On April 24, one week after the Prophet and Tecumseh reached Canada, Procter ordered a march against Fort Meigs. While ships transported the British regulars, militia, and artillery across Lake Erie, Tecumseh and the Prophet led almost twelve hundred Indians overland to the mouth of the Maumee. On April 27 the two forces rendezvoused on Swan Creek, where Procter held a council with the Shawnees and explained his plans for attacking the fort. The Indians were to surround the stockade, harass the garrison with their fire, and attempt to cut off any retreat by the American forces. Meanwhile, the British would use their artillery to destroy the fort and inflict heavy casualties on its occupants. If the attack was successful and the Americans surrendered, the Prophet and his followers could claim Michigan Territory as a new homeland. Harrison, if captured alive, would be given to Tecumseh.[36]

But their plans went amiss. Although the British artillery shelled the fort, the Americans were so well entrenched that the bombardment did little damage. The Indians surrounded the post, but their small-arms fire also proved ineffectual. Harrison and his comrades held on, knowing that reinforcements were close at hand. Brigadier General Green Clay and over twelve hundred militia had marched north from Kentucky, and just before midnight on May 4 Harrison received word that Clay and his men had descended the Maumee to the head of the rapids, only two hours above Fort Meigs. Since the Kentuckians were floating down the river in boats, they had gone ashore to await daybreak before negotiating the white water between their camp and the fort. Harrison immediately dispatched a messenger to Clay, ordering him to descend the river in the morning. Before entering the fort some of his men were to surprise the British batteries across the river, spike their cannon, and then flee to the safety of Fort Meigs before the British and Indians could mount a counterattack.[37]

This time the American plans miscarried. Almost 800 Kentuckians, led by Lieutenant Colonel William Dudley, landed and spiked the British cannon, but instead of retreating they pressed forward toward the British and Indian camp and soon were surrounded. About 150 militia escaped, but the rest of Dudley's force was either killed or captured. Flushed with their victory, the Indians forced many of the captives to run the gantlet, then began to kill the bedraggled survivors. Although Tecumseh interceded to stop the slaughter, about forty prisoners died before the killing ended. Ironically, however, the triumph over Dudley's forces proved costly to the British. Most of the warriors believed the victory ended any American threat to Michigan or Canada. Burdened with captured clothing and weapons, they lost all interest in continuing the siege and deserted the British camp by the hundreds. Tecumseh, the Prophet, and a small party remained with Procter, but by May 6, the day following Dudley's defeat, almost all the other Indians were gone. The Canadian militia also petitioned Procter to return to their homes. On May 9 the British commander lifted the siege, loaded the remaining men and artillery aboard his ships, and sailed for Canada. The first Battle of Fort Meigs was over.[38]

The Prophet accompanied Procter back to Malden. Although he had remained at Fort Meigs throughout the entire siege, he took no part in the proceedings. Never a warrior, he refused to risk his life and remained in camp, safely beyond the range of the American artillery. On his return to Canada, the holy man crossed over into Michigan and established a small village on the Huron River, about twenty miles south of Detroit. There he remained through the summer of 1813, refusing to participate in any further campaigns against the Long Knives, but complaining loudly about the lack of British supplies.[39]

Supply shortages were only one of Procter's problems. In early July, Robert Dickson arrived from Michilimackinac with over six hundred western warriors. In addition to further depleting British Indian stores, the tribesmen were so eager for action against the Americans that Procter feared they "must be immediately employed" or they would become dissatisfied and return to their homes. Although Procter preferred to march on American posts along the Sandusky, Tecumseh and other Indian leaders wanted another attack on Fort Meigs. Procter's naval forces were absent, carrying goods on Lake Erie, and he had no means of transporting his siege guns to Fort Meigs, but he reluctantly agreed to the Indian demands. On July 21, 1813, the British and Indians arrived on the Maumee to find Fort Meigs stronger than ever. During June the Americans had both reinforced and resupplied the garrison. Tecumseh and the Indians attempted to lure the defenders from the fort by a sham battle between themselves and an imaginary relief column, but the garrison was not fooled by the ruse. On July 28 Procter raised the siege and the British and Indians departed.[40]

Procter's army next attacked Fort Stephenson, a small post on the Sandusky River. On August 2, when his light cannon proved ineffectual in breaching the stockade, Procter ordered his troops forward in a frontal assault. The Americans, commanded by Major George Croghan, held their fire until their enemies were within pointblank range, then opened a devastating volley on the attackers. The Indians quickly dispersed, but the British regulars were caught in the moat surrounding the walls and were cut down like cordwood. The British finally withdrew, and in the evening Procter abandoned the attack and retreated toward Canada. The Americans suffered one killed and seven wounded. The British and Indians sustained over one hundred casualties. Disheartened, many of the western warriors now deserted the British and returned to their homes.[41]

The departure of the western Indians partially alleviated the shortage of British provisions, but it also diminished the number of Indians left to oppose the Americans. Meanwhile, the Long Knives made every effort to seduce those who remained. In late August, Harrison dispatched a delegation of friendly Wyandots to the Wyandot village at Brownstown, hoping to win them over to the American cause. On the surface, the mission seemed a failure. To the visitors' chagrin, Tecumseh, the Prophet, and even British Indian agents Matthew Elliott and Alexander McKee attended the council. The American Wyandots offered white wampum and reminded their kinsmen that the British had failed to capture the American forts in Ohio. In addition, they warned that the Long Knives had completed the construction of a new navy that would soon sweep the Redcoats from Lake Erie. But the pro-British Wyandots, led by Roundhead, pointedly rejected the peace proposal. After consulting with the Shawnees, Roundhead derisively replied that they had failed to capture the forts because the Americans had buried themselves like animals behind the walls. Now they were pleased to learn that Harrison was planning to come "out of his hole as he [had] been like a ground hog under the ground and [it would] save [the Indians] much trouble in traveling to meet him." Roundhead advised them to return to Ohio and "take no part in the war." The delegation prepared to depart, but before leaving they received a secret message from Walk-in-the-Water, another prominent Wyandot who also was ostensibly pro-British. Walk-in-the-Water informed them that many of his people were hungry and had grown tired of Procter's empty promises. If the Americans advanced toward Canada, he would abandon the British and use his influence to keep his kinsmen neutral.[42]

Although Tenskwatawa did not know of Walk-in-the-Water's duplicity, he was aware that the British now seemed on the defensive. The Wyandots' warning about the new American navy was particularly significant. In July shipwrights had completed the construction of an American fleet at Presque Isle. Instead of attacking the vessels while they still were under construction, the British had hesitated, and by August the American ships, commanded by Lieutenant Oliver Perry, were loose on Lake Erie. The American fleet seriously threatened Procter's supply and communication lines, and on September 10, 1813, the British fleet, commanded by Captain Robert Barclay, challenged Perry's squadron off Put-in-Bay. After a three-hour battle the Americans were victorious. The British fleet was destroyed, and control of Lake Erie passed into American hands.[43]

Neither Tenskwatawa nor any of the other Indians realized the significance of the American victory. They knew the British fleet had gone out to meet the Americans, but they remained ignorant of the outcome. On September 12, however, Procter learned of the disaster and immediately made plans to abandon Fort Malden. His forces now were outnumbered by the rapidly growing American army, and with Perry's fleet in control of Lake Erie, he was in danger of being cut off from lower Canada. He had, moreover, dismantled most of his cannon and placed them aboard Barclay's fleet for the recent battle. Now they lay at the bottom of Lake Erie. Keeping news of Perry's victory from the Indians, Procter gathered all his personal possessions and loaded wagons with military stores. He then made preparations to burn Fort Malden.[44]

Procter's activities caused consternation among the Indians. Hadn't their British father pledged that he would never abandon them? Hadn't he vowed that he "would never draw his foot off British ground?" When the war started Matthew Elliott had urged them to take up the hatchet, promising that they would surely win their lands back. Now the Redcoats seemed anxious to flee. On September 18 Tecumseh, the Prophet, and a large party of warriors confronted Procter and demanded that the British at least give battle to Harrison's army. Tecumseh denounced Procter's plans to withdraw as the conduct of "a fat animal, that carries its tail upon its back, but when afrighted, he drops it between his legs and runs." According to Tecumseh, "The Americans have not yet defeated us by land; neither are we sure that they have done so by water; we therefore wish to remain here, and fight our enemy." If the British refused, he demanded that Procter give him arms and ammunition, for the Indians "were determined to defend [their] lands." If the Master of Life willed it, they would leave their bones in the lands of their fathers.[45]

Attempting to mollify his allies, Procter explained that Harrison and a large army were en route from Ohio. Since the British and Indians now were outnumbered, and the

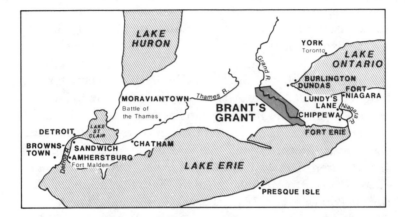

Upper Canada in the War of 1812

American fleet controlled Lake Erie, it was prudent to retreat before they were surrounded. He assured the Indians
he was not fleeing from the Americans, but only withdraw-
ing to the Thames River, where he promised to make a stand.
Following the council Procter sent his sick and wounded,
supply wagons, and personal possessions on toward Chatham.
On September 27, after burning Fort Malden, the British
naval installations, and all remaining supplies, the British
and Indians retreated toward the mouth of the Thames
River.[46]

Procter's withdrawal produced additional problems for the
Prophet and Tecumseh. Although they urged the Indians to
remain loyal to the British, many warriors correctly interpreted the retreat as proof that the Redcoats were losing the
war. About three thousand Indians, including many women
and children, left Malden with Procter, but many others
crossed over into Michigan. Led by Main Poc, scattered parties of Potawatomis, Winnebagos, Foxes, and some Wyandots plundered farmhouses and intimidated the American
population while waiting for the results of the coming battle
between the British and the Americans. If the British were
victorious, Main Poc intended to fall on the ranks of the
retreating Americans. If Harrison prevailed, then the warriors could flee into the forests of Michigan. Other Indians
concluded that the Long Knives already had gained the upper hand. True to his promise, Walk-in-the-Water abandoned
the Shawnee brothers and offered his services to Harrison.
Large numbers of Ottawas, Chippewas, Miamis, and Delawares also deserted and sought an accommodation with the
Americans. By October 1, when Tenskwatawa and Tecumseh reached the mouth of the Thames, they had lost about
fifteen hundred of their followers. Among those sorely missed
was Roundhead. Ever faithful, the Wyandot had been killed
while scouting Harrison's army.[47]

That army was advancing rapidly. During the late summer Harrison had amassed a force of almost five thousand

regulars and militia. With the assistance of Perry's fleet, the American army landed in Canada on September 27, just hours after Procter had retreated from Sandwich. Unopposed, Harrison occupied the site of the former British fortress, then sent a detachment of seven hundred troops to protect Detroit from Main Poc's warriors. Although he was eager to pursue the enemy, Harrison was desperately short of horses, and he waited four days for Colonel Richard M. Johnson's mounted militia to arrive from Ohio. On October 2 Harrison and three thousand men set out in pursuit of the fleeing British and Indians. Because Procter had failed to destroy many of the bridges in his wake, the Americans soon caught up with him.[48]

Burdened by the British baggage, the Prophet and Tecumseh led their followers slowly up the Thames Valley. Procter had assured them he would make a stand near Chatham, and on October 3 the Indians and part of the British troops were encamped just west of that village. Procter and the rest of the British regulars had proceeded toward Moraviantown, ostensibly to examine alternate sites for resisting the Americans. Tenskwatawa knew that the Long Knives were in pursuit, but both he and Tecumseh were surprised when at midmorning scouts brought reports that the Americans were advancing so rapidly they would reach Chatham on the following day. Tecumseh was eager to fight, but after consulting with several British officers, he ordered his women and children to join Procter at Moraviantown. On October 4, while the Prophet and most of the British and Indians withdrew, Tecumseh and a war party remained behind to burn bridges and harass Harrison's army. They were ineffective. The Americans soon dispersed the warriors (killing ten and wounding several others) and captured the bridges. After marching through the abandoned British camp, Harrison bivouacked that night five miles east of Chatham.[49]

The British and Indians decided to meet the Americans about two miles west of Moraviantown. After sending their women and children on toward Burlington, the Indians occupied a swampy thicket to the left of the road that led from Chatham. The British troops, directly opposing any American advance, formed two ranks across the highway and an adjacent open field. On the right, opposite the Indians, stretched the Thames, protecting the British left flank and funneling the Americans toward their enemies. Although he had no intention of risking his life in the battle, Tenskwatawa spent the morning of October 5 boosting Indian morale. Mounted, he rode back and forth before the Indian position, urging the eight hundred remaining warriors to kill the Long Knives.[50]

The battle began at midafternoon. From his vantage point behind the British lines Tenskwatawa saw the American force advance and then hesitate while Harrison formed his mounted militia units into two columns, which he sent against the British center. The British regulars fired two volleys, then disintegrated as the Americans swept through their ranks. Procter's six-pounder, positioned within the British lines, was abandoned before it even could be fired. On the American left the Indians fought valiantly, first repulsing the Long Knives, then fighting hand-to-hand as the Americans swarmed into the thicket. Although the warriors resisted for some time, the Prophet did not witness their struggle. Accompanying Procter, he fled on horseback after the initial American charge. Only later did he learn the grave consequences of the catastrophe. Almost all the British soldiers had been killed or captured, and the Indians finally had scattered through the forests. And most important, Tecumseh was dead, shot down while rallying his warriors. Once again the Prophet's medicine had failed. He remained alive, but this time his movement had ended.[51]

Chapter Seven

Exile

The Prophet's flight following the Battle of the Thames was almost his last, Accompanied by Procter, a few other Indians, and about forty British dragoons, the Shawnee was forced to gallop his horse pell-mell down the road toward the east to keep from being captured. It was a narrow escape. The pursuing Americans advanced so quickly that they overran the British baggage wagons and seized all of Procter's personal property, including his correspondence. They also fell upon the rear ranks of the fleeing Indian women and children, inflicting unnecessary casualties on these unfortunate souls. Tenskwatawa did not stop his flight until he reached Delaware, Ontario, about forty miles northeast of the recent battle.[1]

In the next few days the extent of the British and Indian defeat became apparent. As straggling parties of tribesmen arrived from the west, Tenskwatawa discovered that most of the Indians who still remained loyal to the British were women and children, the families or survivors of those warriors who had fought at the Thames. In late October the bedraggled assemblage moved on to Dundas (near modern Hamilton), where their ranks were swelled with even more refugees. At Dundas the Prophet found 1,062 western Indians eagerly awaiting supplies. Only 374 were warriors; the remaining 688 were women and children. The British were hard pressed to provide the Indians with adequate food and clothing. William Claus purchased flour and pork from nearby farmers, but his funds were insufficient to feed such a large influx of refugees. Additional supplies were sent from Kingston, but much of the food was spoiled or damaged en route and the clothing was "badly assorted" and "not sufficient to clothe one third of the Indians."[2]

The Indians spent a miserable winter of 1813–14 camped together at the western end of Lake Ontario. Although the British provided enough supplies to keep them from starving, the tribesmen were reduced to eating one meal per day and suffered from inadequate clothing. They also remained leaderless. In December 1813, some of the western warriors assisted the British in attacks on Fort George and Niagara, but during the following months their willingness to attack the Long Knives waned. In March a party of Ottawas and Chippewas fought against the Americans at the Battle of Longwood, but they sustained several casualties and seemed reluctant to take up the hatchet again. Aware that spring probably would bring American counterattacks, the British depended on their Indian allies to assist them in the defense of the Niagara frontier. From the British perspective, therefore, it was imperative to rebuild Indian morale.[3]

Attempting to strengthen Indian leadership, in March Sir George Prevost, governor in chief and commander of all British forces in Canada, invited a delegation of leaders from the western tribes to visit him in Quebec. Tenskwatawa was not included. When the Indians assembled for the journey, Pachetha, Tecumseh's adolescent son, accompanied by the aging Tecumpease, represented the Shawnees. The inclusion of Tecumpease particularly rankled the Prophet, for he knew that his older sister continued to mistrust him and sought British support for Tecumseh's son as the new leader of the Shawnees.[4]

Yet the absence of the other leaders might prove to his advantage. Tenskwatawa knew that local officials would have no report of the council with Prevost until the delegation returned from Quebec. If he could reassert himself in the interim, he could achieve a fait accompli. If the tribesmen remaining on Lake Ontario and local British Indian agents would accept his claims to leadership, then he would have to be accorded a position of prominence after the delegation's return. Therefore, in early April, Tenskwatawa assembled his hard-core supporters at Dundas and announced to local Indian agents that the refugee Shawnees had elected him as their war chief. When the war ended, Tecumseh's son might serve as village chief, but until then he, the Prophet, would lead his people. Yet when local officials accepted his claim, the Prophet's ego got the better of him. Never short of audacity, he met with Major General Phineas Riall, who had succeeded Procter, and proclaimed himself "the principal chief of all the Western Nations." Assuming that the Prophet had again unified the western Indians, Riall accepted his claim and presented him with a sword and a brace of pistols. Obviously pleased, Tenskwatawa assured the officer of his full cooperation, pledging that even his "smallest boys capable of bearing arms, [would] be ready at a moment's notice."[5]

Tenskwatawa's bid to reassert his influence was welcomed by John Norton, a Scotsman professing Cherokee ancestry who had assumed a position of leadership among the pro-British Iroquois settled on the Grand River. Norton long had been embroiled in a bitter conflict with British Indian agent William Claus over control of the Indians on the Niagara frontier, but in the spring of 1814 officials in Quebec hoped to mobilize the Iroquois and had commissioned Norton as a captain in the British army and appointed him "Leader of the Five Nations Grand River Indians or Confederates." Since Norton was eager to extend his control over the western tribesmen camped near Lake Ontario, he used his new position to distribute food and clothing to those Indians willing to abandon Claus and settle among the Iroquois. Lured by Norton's generosity, the Prophet attached himself to Norton's camp. The Shawnee then used promises of plentiful provisions to attract most of the refugee Shawnees, Kickapoos, and Wyandots to the Grand River.[6]

Tenskwatawa's defection engendered resentment from both Claus and the Indian leaders who had visited Prevost in Quebec. As dozens of tribesmen moved to the Grand River, Claus and his associates saw their influence diminish. Claus complained that the holy man was "much inclined to be troublesome" and that Norton had encouraged him to foment disharmony among the western tribes. Naiwash, an Ottawa chief who had returned from Quebec, also lamented that the Shawnee was spreading disunity. In response, the Prophet took the offensive. He blamed Claus for all the problems of the past winter and demanded that Thomas McKee, the son of former Indian agent Alexander McKee, be appointed as superintendent of Indian affairs, a post recently vacated by the death of Matthew Elliott. In addition, although he now was supplied by Norton, the Prophet still demanded a share of the trade goods distributed by Claus to the western tribes. And in a significant break with his former religious professions, he requested that the Crown provide his followers on the Grand River with five barrels of rum.[7]

As in the past, it was easier for the Prophet to proclaim leadership than to exercise it. As long as his adherence to Norton provided his people with generous amounts of supplies, they were willing to follow him to the Grand River. But his claims to be a war chief were ludicrous. He had no prowess as a warrior, and his performance at both the Tippecanoe and the Thames did little to inspire his followers. Once again he remained true to form. In early June 1814, Claus met with war leaders from the western tribes at York (modern Toronto) to inform them that the British would transport them to Kingston, where they might raid American forces at Sackets Harbor, New York. The Prophet at-

tended the council but indicated little willingness to participate in the venture. On June 14, when British Indian agent
William Caldwell assembled the western tribesmen at Burlington to give them a "war feast" before their departure,
the Prophet and his followers were notably absent. His earlier professions of assistance forgotten, Tenskwatawa was
reluctant to leave the well-stocked larders on the Grand River
to risk his life at the opposite end of Lake Ontario.[8]

The mission against Sackets Harbor never materialized.
Before Caldwell could transport the warriors to the eastern
end of Lake Ontario, reports reached York that the Americans were planning another invasion across the Niagara River.
The warriors mustered by Caldwell therefore were sent toward Fort George to bolster British defenses. Meanwhile,
messengers rode to the Grand River, asking Norton and his
followers to rush to the Niagara frontier. Norton and the
Iroquois hurried toward the advancing Americans, but the
Prophet moved more slowly. He complained that since his
ascension to "principal chief of all the Western Nations,"
the British had failed to treat him with proper respect and
that his messages to Riall had been disregarded. Only after
Caldwell sent him a personal message did he move forward,
and then he advanced so cautiously that his mixed force of
Shawnees, Kickapoos, Wyandots, and other Indians arrived
at the British lines on July 6, a full day after the Battle of
Chippewa had ended.[9]

Since the British had been unable to dislodge the Ameri-
cans from Canadian soil, the arrival of "the Prophet of the
Shawanons with many of his people and others from the
West . . . rejoiced [the British] not a little." But as John Nor-
ton later recorded, "In this we were greatly disappointed."
Uneasy over the large number of Indian casualties incurred
during the recent battle, Tenskwatawa was more concerned
about safeguarding his rear than carrying the war to the Long
Knives. On the evening of July 7, after remaining in the
British encampment for only one day, the Shawnees noticed

that some of the British had pushed a cannon into the Niagara River and were making preparations to break camp. Although the cannon was being discarded because it was cracked, and the troops were leaving to take up new positions down river, near Lundy's Lane, the Prophet immediately assumed that a general British retreat was imminent. Before British Indian agents could intercede, he loaded his possessions on his horse and encouraged his followers to withdraw toward Lake Ontario. The panic soon spread to the Iroquois, who were dispirited over heavy casualties, and by the following morning fewer than twenty Indians remained in the bivouac.[10]

Tenskwatawa's retreat did not endear him to the British. Although Indian agents followed in the tribesmen's wake and eventually persuaded large numbers of the warriors to return, the Prophet and part of his retinue continued on to the Grand River. Here they remained, refusing to take any part in the conflict. Yet Tenskwatawa's precipitous retreat damaged the holy man as much as it did the British. Many of the warriors who originally had followed him to the Grand River were embarrassed by the affair and agreed to return and assist the British. These warriors—Shawnees, Kickapoos, and Wyandots—later fought at Lundy's Lane and against Fort Erie. In the autumn, when most of the fighting ceased, many refused to rejoin Tenskwatawa and established new villages near Dundas.[11]

The Prophet did his best to remain out of the fighting. In late October 1814, Brigadier General Duncan MacArthur led a force of over seven hundred mounted riflemen east from Detroit, planning to attack Burlington and then join American forces on the Niagara River. Keeping his mission a secret, MacArthur was able to move rapidly and penetrate as far as the Grand River before he met with any British resistance. There a small force of British troops, assisted by warriors from the Grand River and others, turned the Americans back, but the Prophet took no part in the action. Some of the warriors from his camp fought in the battle, but they were led by the Wyandot Split Log, not Tenskwatawa.[12]

In contrast, the Prophet spent the fall of 1814 complaining about the British Indian Department. Once again the British were short of supplies, and once again Tenskwatawa was adamant in his demands for food and clothing. When even Norton no longer could meet his requests for provisions, tribesmen from the Prophet's camp raided nearby farms for livestock. They also met openly with emissaries from pro-American tribes, listening to their pleas for neutrality. Naiwash and other war leaders denounced such fraternization and urged all the Indians to remain united against the Long Knives, but the Prophet ignored their pleas and countered with charges that the Ottawa chief and his friends had stolen British "presents" originally designated for the Shawnees. His patience worn thin, the aging William Caldwell finally threatened to cut off all supplies to the Prophet and his followers if they refused to cooperate against the Americans.[13]

But Caldwell's threat was an idle one. By late fall the British Indian Department knew that the war with the Americans was almost over. Negotiations had been proceeding for several months, at Ghent, Belgium, and recent British reverses at Baltimore and on Lake Champlain accelerated the Crown's willingness to end the contest. British Indian agents realized that the termination of the war would bring drastic cutbacks in the Indian Department, and individual agents plotted against each other in the hope of retaining their jobs.

The Prophet was included in their plans. Colonel William Caldwell had several sons employed in the British Indian Department and he was anxious to promote their careers. In late November he met with the Prophet, Tecumseh's son, and Isadore Chaine, who had carried messages to the Prophet and Tecumseh at the Mississinewa. Evidently believing that his past quarrels with Tenskwatawa would remove the Shawnee from any suspicions of complicity, Caldwell attempted to enlist the Prophet's support against other Indian agents. After plying the holy man with presents, he suggested that the Prophet go to Quebec and charge certain other agents with stealing Indian goods and using them for their own purposes. In return, Caldwell promised more supplies and agreed to honor Riall's acknowledgment that Tenskwatawa was the leader of all the western Indians.[14]

The conference did not go as Caldwell had expected. Although the Prophet at first seemed amenable to his proposals, the elderly Caldwell evidently had forgotten that one of the agents whom he was trying to incriminate was George Ironside, a former trader now married to one of Tenskwatawa's relatives. When Caldwell mentioned the names of those agents to be accused, the Prophet interrupted him and angrily refused to participate in the scheme. Infuriated, Caldwell then denounced the holy man, warning that he "would cast off the whole of the Shawnees" and never again meet with them in council. He also threatened to "raise up a man of his own, who he would make a great man" in the Prophet's place. But Tenskwatawa was no novice to duplicity, and on leaving the conference he hurried to Ironside and the other agents targeted by Caldwell to inform them of the plot. Not surprisingly, he asked them to provide him with presents and to accord him the status offered by Caldwell in exchange for his information.[15]

Before either faction could gain the upper hand, the war ended. Both Caldwell and his opponents were forced to cooperate to ensure that the British Indian Department retained some influence over the tribesmen. News of the Treaty of Ghent reached Canada early in March, and British officials immediately planned a council to inform the Indians that the Crown had not deserted them. When the conference took place at Burlington in April, the Prophet and his followers were in attendance. After extensive ceremonies to "wipe the tears from the eyes" of those tribesmen who had lost friends and relatives, William Claus informed them, "The Hatchet which you so readily took up to assist your Great

Father should now be laid down and buried that it may not be seen." The king had not forgotten his children: "Your interests were not neglected nor would Peace have been made with [the Americans] had they not consented to include you in the Treaty, which they at first refused to listen to." Indeed, Claus assured his audience that if they stopped their warfare against the Long Knives, they could return to the same status and to the same lands they held before 1812. To prove their good will, Indian agents dispensed over twenty-three hundred pounds to the widows and orphans of warriors fallen in the British cause. They also promised that the western tribesmen would always be welcome at Amherstburg, where the king would continue "to hold [them] fast by the hand and treat [them] with all kindness and generosity which good and obedient children have a right to expect." [16]

In response, the Indians reminded the British of the many warriors they had lost and asked the officials to keep their promises. Tenskwatawa did not speak at the proceedings, but Isadore Chaine represented the western Indians, and several orators spoke for the Iroquois. All the Indians at the council seemed concerned over the British commitments to the western tribesmen, and even the Iroquois badgered the agents to provide adequate assistance to their western brethren as the latter returned to their homes. [17]

Not surprisingly, the British were anxious for such an exodus to commence. As soon as the tribesmen returned to their former villages, the Indian department would be freed from the expense of feeding and clothing them. Caldwell already had made preliminary arrangements for their removal to the west, and on May 1, 1815, he instructed his subordinates to encourage the tribesmen to withdraw toward Amherstburg. Although the Indians still had not made peace with the Americans, the British wanted them near Detroit, where they could cross over to their homes immediately after any peace conference. [18]

During the summer of 1815 most of the western tribesmen returned to the Amherstburg region. The Prophet and his followers left the Grand River in late May and arrived at Sandwich (modern Windsor) in mid-June. Although Naiwash and the Ottawas and Chippewas planted corn on Fighting Island, Tenskwatawa and his people refused to till the soil, arguing that they would return to their homes before their crop could be harvested. Both British and American officials agreed that the pro-British Indians should not reenter the United States until they had met with American Indian agents, but in early June a small party of Shawnees crossed over to Detroit and stole several horses. The Prophet opposed the foray and cooperated with British officials in returning the animals to their owners, but the incident irritated the British and only confirmed the Americans' deep distrust of the holy man and his followers.[19]

Harrison and other American officials were eager to conclude a formal peace. During the spring they had met with many of the hostile Indians in Michigan, Indiana, and Ohio, negotiating a series of cease-fire agreements, but Main Poc and part of the Potawatomis had refused to attend the meetings. As a result, officials planned a large, multitribal conference to be held at Spring Wells (near Detroit) in August. In addition to friendly Indians and the exiles from Canada, the Americans hoped that the conference would attract Main Poc and his followers, who still were hostile to the United States. In June the government appointed Harrison, Duncan McArthur, and John Graham to meet with the Indians. To assure that the peace negotiations proceeded smoothly, the agents were instructed to seek no new land cessions.[20]

The Prophet had serious misgivings about the conference. He was reluctant for the western tribesmen to make peace with the Long Knives and return to their homes. Ironically, by 1815 Tenskwatawa had become what he once had condemned: a village chief whose influence over his people was based on his ability to procure supplies and services from a white man's government. He no longer made any pretensions to religious leadership. He now sought prominence through his negotiations with the British Indian Department. He had become a British counterpart to such American government chiefs as Black Hoof, Five Medals, or Little Turtle. If he returned to the United States, he hoped to establish a separate village where he could serve as a middleman between his followers and the Americans.[21]

He also was concerned for his personal safety. Many American frontiersmen had vowed to shoot him, and frontier newspapers had called for his death. He had planned to attend the peace conference, but in early August rumors reached his village that caused him much consternation. An Ottawa warrior, recently returned from Ohio, brought a warning from Black Hoof that the upcoming conference was a trap. Although the rumor was of doubtful authenticity, on August 4 Tenskwatawa met with other Indian leaders and British agents at Amherstburg and informed them that Black Hoof had warned that the Long Knives were mustering their troops to march to Spring Wells and seize all those tribesmen who had sided with the British. According to Black Hoof, if large numbers of troops were present at the council, "You are going to be attacked. . . . Keep your war clubs in your hands!" British officials discounted the rumor, but the Prophet obviously was shaken, and many of the western Indians remained apprehensive.[22]

The Americans had hoped to begin their negotiations on August 25, but they were forced to postpone the proceedings. In a final effort to bolster their influence among the western tribesmen, British officials met with the exiles on August 26 and again assured them of the Crown's good intentions. Meanwhile, Harrison and his associates held preliminary meetings with Indians from the United States, and sent Tarhe, Five Medals, and other friendly chiefs to the hostiles at Amherstburg, asking them to assemble on August 28. But the Prophet and his followers still remained in Canada. Only after Harrison promised that troops garrisoned at Detroit would be confined to their barracks did the holy man venture across the river, and then with some trepidation.[23]

Tenskwatawa and his people arrived at Spring Wells on August 29, 1815, and the formal proceedings resumed two days later. Events did not bode well for the Prophet. Harrison took great pains to extol Black Hoof's Shawnees, Tarhe's Wyandots, the Senecas, and part of the Delawares—Indians who had remained loyal to the United States. Comparing Tarhe's loyalty to the president "to the fidelity of the great archangel to his Creator," Harrison appointed the aging Wyandot to speak for the government. After Tarhe had officially welcomed the exiles and "wiped the tears from their eyes," Harrison specifically addressed the Prophet and assured him that the Long Knives wanted peace. He explained that although the government expected the Indians to abide by all previous treaties, it would not ask for any new land cessions. He urged all the tribes to make peace among themselves, however, and to return to their former homes under "their wise and judicious leaders."[24]

The treaty proceedings continued for another week, but on September 4 Tenskwatawa made his formal reply. On the surface, the Shawnee seemed pleased. He and his followers would remain at peace, he promised, for "the tomahawk was taken out of their hands, so that they were now so completely deprived of tomahawks that he was apprehensive that their old women could hardly cut wood enough to make a fire." Indeed, "all who came from the other side of the river were pleased with the address of the commissioners, and all took them heartily by the hand." He asked the assembled Indians to remain united and to "adhere to our chiefs, and thank them for what they have done for us." War should be forgotten, and "all future efforts devoted to the care of our families."[25]

But as the negotiations progressed, the Shawnee became more apprehensive. He was willing to make peace with the Long Knives if they would accord him the status to which he was accustomed. He had become a government chief under the British and assumed that he would retain the same position under the Americans. Yet Harrison and other American officials were anxious to destroy any influence still held by the holy man. They were determined that he not be allowed to establish a separate village for his followers. The Prophet was welcome back in the United States not as a chief, but as an ordinary tribesman. As the treaty proceedings drew to a close, he was informed that he could not go back to the Tippecanoe. He must return to the village led by his old rival, Black Hoof. Angered, on September 5 Tenskwatawa and part of his followers withdrew from the conference. The Treaty of Spring Wells was completed on September 8, 1815. The Prophet did not sign it.[26]

Instead, he returned to Amherstburg and complained bitterly about his treatment in Michigan. As the other Indians came back from Spring Wells to meet with the British before returning to their homes, Tenskwatawa spoke to them in council and denounced the Americans. He charged that Harrison was a liar, and advised them not to trust his promises. But the Prophet's warnings made little impression. By the fall of 1815 most of the exiles were eager to return to their homes, and, in the weeks following the conference at Spring Wells, they crossed over into Michigan in great numbers. Even some of the Shawnees who had followed him since before the war now deserted the holy man and accepted the government's offer to join Black Hoof in Ohio.[27]

The Kickapoos were a notable exception. They also intended to return to their villages in Illinois, but in early October, after crossing into Michigan, they were attacked by a party of armed settlers. One Indian was killed and the remaining members of the tribe fled back across the Detroit River to Canada. At the same time American frontiersmen stole part of a Kickapoo horse herd the Indians had picketed on Grosse Ile. The Kickapoo experience seemed to strengthen the Prophet's position, and he was quick to champion their cause. He welcomed the refugees back into his camp and demanded that the British seek retribution for the attacks, reminding officials that during the previous spring he had cooperated in returning the stolen American horses. He also asked for additional rations so that the Kickapoos might be fed until "the present difficulties to [their] going to [their] old homes should be removed."[28]

Tenskwatawa was not the only one who wanted the "present difficulties" to end. For two years the British Indian Department had been hard pressed to feed all the exiles in Canada. After the Treaty of Spring Wells, they had assumed that the vast majority would go back to the United States. Most had returned, but officials did not want the Prophet to discourage the removal or to become a magnet attracting dissidents who would have to be supplied at British expense. In addition to the Shawnees and Kickapoos who still lived in his camp, a few Sacs, Winnebagos, and other tribesmen had recently attached themselves to the holy man and depended on him to provide them with British foodstuffs. To discourage such dependence, Indian agents reduced rations to a daily allowance of six ounces of flour and two and one half ounces of pork. They provided the warriors with lead and powder and instructed them to supplement the provisions through hunting.[29]

The Indian response was predictable. In December Tenskwatawa warned that game was scarce and if the rations were not increased his followers would be forced to scavenge through the countryside, pilfering storehouses and livestock. Lieutenant Colonel William James, the military commander at Amherstberg, blamed William Caldwell for the dissension and eventually dismissed the senile old agent, but the change did little to placate the Indians. They were still hungry, and in early February 1816, the Prophet lamented to William Claus:

Yesterday was the ration day and we received our allowances for ten days, what is so small that one man might eat the whole in the afternoon for a Family in one day. In my own family counting of nine persons, our ten days allowance is but a scanty allowance for two days—when our scanty allowance is consumed we are about the necessity of going about the country to endeavor to procure a little corn for which we give our clothing.[30]

Ten days later he met with officials at Amherstburg, and his frustration was evident. He informed Claus and others that he now spoke as a village chief: "The women look to me as their chief according to ancient usage. I am now put in the place of my Brother Techkumthai who is gone from us, and it is expected I will be listened to as he was!" He again reminded the British that his people had faithfully served the Crown. When Matthew Elliott had asked them to strike the Long Knives, they had gladly accepted the hatchet. But now the Redcoats had forgotten them. "A great many promises were made to my Brother and to our chiefs. We have suffered greatly, Father; we now expect that the promises will be fulfilled."[31]

But the promises were forgotten. The very shortages of which the Prophet complained had become part of a British Indian policy designed to force the refugees back into the United States. The British agents listened to his pleas, but their ambiguous response indicated they had no intention of making any changes. Exasperated, Tenskwatawa turned to a subterfuge of his own. If the British refused to honor their commitments, he would bargain with the Americans. Harrison had denied him permission to return to the Tippecanoe, but Harrison had returned to Indiana. Governor Lewis Cass of Michigan Territory had not taken part in the Treaty of Spring Wells and perhaps he might allow them to cross over into unoccupied territory south of Detroit. There the Shawnee and his people could erect a new village, perhaps draw provisions from the Long Knives, and still tap the diminished generosity of the British. In March 1816, he sent a message to Cass, asking to meet with the governor at Detroit.[32]

Tenskwatawa took great pains to ensure that the conference was successful. Intending to play on the Americans' sympathies, he brought some of his women and children to Detroit. He also went to great lengths to make a favorable personal impression. Over a calico shirt and leather leggings he wore a brown coat, whose right sleeve trailed tassels of painted horsehair. He adorned each arm with a silver clasp and two silver bracelets, while a large silver gorget hung around his neck and heavy silver rings dangled from his earlobes. His face was painted in red and black, and a large crest of painted feathers was attached to his turban.[33]

Attired in such splendor, the Prophet did his best to assure Cass of his peaceful intentions. Since 1811, he said, there had been much misunderstanding. "Bad birds" had spread evil stories. The Battle of Tippecanoe had not been his fault. Harrison had advanced on his village, but he had remained friendly and had given the Long Knives a place to camp: "It is true the Winnebagoes with me at Tippecanoe struck your people. I was opposed to it but could not stop it. If we had come to you, then you might have blamed us, but you came to my village! For this you are angry at me?" Indeed, he had fought in the recent war, but he was "determined no more to listen to the British." He would have signed the Treaty of Spring Wells, but, according to the Prophet, "General Harrison told me he had done with me and I went over the river." If he had known that the Americans had really wanted him to sign the document, he would have returned. Now all he really desired was to take his women and children back to the United States to live in peace. Large numbers of warriors no longer would flock to his village. His lodge would be a "house of peace." But he could not go back to Ohio: "My eye is now upon the place where the sun sets! It is the place which my old chiefs have pointed out, the Wabash; it is there I wish to go." And if the time was not yet right for him to return to Indiana, perhaps Cass would permit him to establish a temporary village south of Detroit. He already had chosen such a place: "It is the River Raisin."[34]

Cass was dumbfounded! The Prophet's selection of the River Raisin, a site near the scene of the recent massacre of American prisoners in 1813, seemed the height of effrontery. Moreover, the lands along the River Raisin already had been set aside as military bounty lands for veterans of the War of 1812. In addition, Cass still considered the holy man to be a British agent and believed that a new village, at either the River Raisin or the Tippecanoe, "would enable him to re-new the Scenes of 1811." He had no intention of allowing the Shawnee to establish a separate village. Accusing Ten-skwatawa of duplicity, Cass summarily refused his request to return to the United States. He agreed, however, to forward the Prophet's petition to the president. But he clearly indicated that he would urge its rejection. Chagrined, the Prophet and his followers returned to Canada.[35]

Tenskwatawa now found that his options were limited. He could remain in Canada, but since the British Indian Department refused to provide adequate rations for all his followers, most would eventually desert him and go back to their homes. In contrast, the Americans would allow him to return only if he joined with Black Hoof's people. But there was one option left that still might serve his purpose. What if his remaining followers went back to the United States in small parties, ostensibly agreeing to return to their own villages, but instead reassembling on the Tippecanoe? The Prophet knew that many of the western tribes still were embittered toward the Long Knives, and he believed that the establishment of a new Prophetstown would again at-tract disaffected warriors from throughout the west. He could then leave Canada in secret, return to the Tippecanoe, and reoccupy a position of prominence. The government would be faced with a fait accompli, and federal officials would have to recognize his leadership.[36]

During the summer of 1816 part of the plan was imple-mented. Many of the Indians who still adhered to the Prophet crossed over into Michigan, supposedly en route to their homes. Since Tenskwatawa was anxious to test the American reaction to their passage, he accompanied them for the first few miles of their journey. All went well, so the Prophet and a small party of warriors withdrew from the migration and quietly made their way back toward Canada. But en route to Malden they met with disaster. While preparing to cross the Detroit River they encountered a British soldier whom they believed to be a deserter. Still hoping to curry favor from the British, Tenskwatawa had the man seized and carried back to Canada. There he learned that the man had not deserted, but had been sent to the United States on legitimate business. If the British were irritated over the episode, the Americans were outraged. Cass declared the incident was an attempt by the Prophet to interfere with the laws of the United States, and he issued a warrant charging Tenskwatawa with kidnapping. For once, the holy man really was innocent, at least in intent. He was unaware that he was breaking American laws, and with the emigration underway, he did not want to anger the Americans. He sent apologies to Cass and asked the British to intercede on his behalf, but all their attempts proved futile. The warrant for kidnapping remained. If Tenskwatawa entered the United States, he would be arrested.[37]

Despite the Prophet's problems, the exodus continued. During the late summer of 1816 most of the Shawnees, Kickapoos, and Sacs who had remained tied to the Prophet left Canada for the Wabash. There they established several small villages near the mouth of the Tippecanoe in preparation for Tenskwatawa's return. When the Miamis protested this intrusion, the new arrivals boasted that in the spring, when the Prophet returned from Canada, they would be joined by eight hundred Menominees, Winnebagos, and Chippewas. Once again the sacred fire would be kindled on the Wabash. "We are determined not to put it out at the risk of our lives. . . . We are determined to possess this country or perish in the attempt."[38]

But the holy man lacked the ardor of his followers. The Indians on the Wabash might be willing to risk their lives, but the Prophet was afraid to cross over into Michigan. He had no intention of being arrested by the Long Knives, and although he repeatedly sent messengers to the villages in Indiana, he remained in Canada. By November, however, most of his followers were gone. His village was reduced to only twenty-seven Indians, and many of these were kinsmen, including his immediate family and Tecumseh's son. And they still suffered from inadequate food and clothing. The summer of 1816 had been unseasonably cold and crops failed throughout the Great Lakes region. The British tried to transport additional provisions to Amherstburg, but in December the schooner carrying the goods was shipwrecked on Lake Erie. British Indian agents eventually provided enough food and clothing to get the tribesmen through the winter, but when the Indians complained, they were told they were lazy and should supplement their provisions through hunting. Disgruntled, the Prophet and his handful of followers withdrew from Amherstburg to pitch their small camp near the shores of Lake Erie.[39]

The summer of 1816 marked another major watershed for Tenskwatawa. Following the war he had not returned to the United States, but his decision to remain in Canada had been his own. He had been unwilling to accept the American condition that he return to Ohio and take up residence in Black Hoof's village. Moreover, because of his ties to the British government, he had continued to exercise some influence over the American tribesmen who remained in Canada. But the incident with the British soldier greatly altered his circumstances. After 1816 he could not return to the United States for fear of imprisonment. Most of his followers were gone, and he now led only a handful of exiles, mostly hungry women and children.

Predictably, his relationship with the British Indian De-

partment deteriorated. The British still felt obligated to provide him with minimal amounts of food and clothing, but
they did not feel obligated to provision him well. Anxious
to cut expenses, British officials periodically reduced their
shipments of Indian goods to Amherstburg in the years following the war, and the Prophet and his handful of followers
suffered accordingly. In 1817 the ship carrying food and
clothing for the Indian department again was sunk in a storm
on Lake Erie, and even the Indian agents complained about
the shortage of necessities. During the next few years the
British again reduced expenditures and William Claus warned
that the shortage of goods was so acute that agents were
hard pressed to maintain any influence among the tribes.
Officials at Amherstburg repeatedly encouraged the Prophet
and his people to supplement their provisions through hunting and trapping, but most privately admitted that game
animals were in very short supply.[40]

Never one to remain silent, the Prophet lashed out angrily
at the British Indian Department, focusing much of his bitterness on John Askin, who had become the Indian agent at
Amherstburg following the war. He charged that Askin was
diverting goods from the Indian department and selling them
to white settlers. In 1819, when Charles Lennox, duke of
Richmond, the newly appointed governor general of Canada, toured the upper posts, Tenskwatawa and other tribesmen met with him and complained loudly of their alleged
mistreatment. Bored by the tirade, the governor abruptly
ended the audience and instructed the Indians to put their
charges in writing and send them to him in Quebec, where
he "should pay every attention to their concerns." Although
rebuffed, the Prophet did forward a long list of grievances to
the capital, but in August 1819, the duke of Richmond died
and the new governor general, Sir Peregrine Maitland, ignored the petition.[41]

On January 1, 1820, John Askin also died and was replaced
at Amherstburg by George Ironside. Since Ironside was mar-

ried to a member of Tenskwatawa's family and since the holy man had warned him about Caldwell's plot, Tenskwatawa erroneously assumed that Ironside would give him preferential treatment at Amherstburg. But he was wrong. Ironside was eager to advance his career within the British Indian Department and continued to adhere to the official policy of frugality. In addition, since the Shawnee was unpopular with his superiors, Ironside shunned his in-law as much as possible. Tenskwatawa was incensed. Not only were his hopes of increased influence shattered, but Ironside had ignored blood ties, an affront that was particularly humiliating. In response, Tenskwatawa redoubled his complaints, charging that Ironside also was stealing Indian goods and trying to undermine the authority of his superiors. Yet his ranting had little effect. Ironside countered with accusations that Tenskwatawa was a coward who had fled from battle during the late war and who now repaid British generosity with "impudence and lies." Of course the Indian Department sided with Ironside, and the deputy superintendent for Indian affairs, William Claus, dismissed the charges, commenting that the Prophet was "most vile . . . and a bad man in every respect."[42]

Meanwhile, the Prophet and other refugee Indians in Canada witnessed a scenario that was depressing in its familiarity. During the decade that followed the Treaty of Ghent, immigrants flowed into upper Canada, and between 1815 and 1825 the white population almost doubled. As the new settlers pressed in on them, the Indians complained to the British government. Attempting to maintain the peace, British officials (like their counterparts in the United States) began to purchase Indian lands so that clear title could be given to the white farmers. But settlement advanced more rapidly than the British were able to acquire lands, and the immigrants squatted on areas still owned by the Indians. Although Tenskwatawa and his handful of followers held no claims to any lands in the region, they resented the stream of settlers pouring in around them. For the Prophet and his people, history seemed to be repeating itself. The sequence of events was painfully reminiscent of conditions in Ohio and Indiana before the War of 1812.[43]

Embittered, Tenskwatawa began to sever his ties with the British Indian Department. He still received British rations, and he occasionally joined with other Indians to press old claims against the British government, but more and more after 1821 he refused to meet with British Indian agents. No longer a man of stature, he was despised by former allies and shunned by former friends. Except for the two dozen kinsmen who lived in his camp, other Indians avoided him. Even worse, the Long Knives, who once had feared his influence, now ignored his existence. And so the Prophet spent his days sulking in his lodge, brooding about the past, uncertain of the future.[44]

Chapter Eight

Removal

Tenskwatawa's alienation from the British Indian Department was offset by a change in his relationship with the United States. In the years following 1817 Americans still held no affection for the aging holy man, but they no longer considered him a threat to their peace and security. His followers who had assembled on the Tippecanoe dispersed during the fall of 1817, and he exercised little influence over them. Rumors of his return periodically reached American officials, but these reports reflected the paranoia of white frontiersmen more than any actual schemes by the Prophet.[1] He occasionally met with American Indians when they visited Canada, but American tribesmen now were dependent on the annuity system and were eager to maintain good relations with the government. They were reluctant to harbor a fugitive still wanted for kidnapping. The visiting Indians refused to offer the Shawnee refuge in their villages, and many, like Kishkanon, a Chippewa from northern Michigan, reported their meetings to American officials. At Detroit, Cass still preferred that Tenskwatawa remain in Canada, but in 1819 he reported to officials in Washington that the Prophet no longer constituted a threat to the United States. The Shawnee, he assured his superiors, was "restless and discontented, but he [had] little chance of reaping anything except disappointment."[2]

During the early 1820s Cass's assessment of the Prophet underwent further change. Since he no longer posed a threat, perhaps the Shawnee could actually serve the government. Cass knew that Tenskwatawa had become alienated from the British and still wanted to return to the United States. By 1824 the governor believed that he might turn such a homecoming to the government's advantage.[3]

Cass's decision was based on his desire to remove Black Hoof's Shawnees from Ohio. In the decade following the War of 1812 they and other friendly Shawnees had continued to occupy their villages along the Auglaize and Miami rivers. During this period the Quakers had renewed their efforts near Black Hoof's village at Wapakoneta, and between 1821 and 1825 part of the Shawnees and some neighboring Senecas and Wyandots had again attempted to walk the white man's road. Although some adopted the agricultural lifestyle espoused by the Quakers, others, although friendly to the government, still followed the ways of their fathers.[4] Many of these more traditional tribesmen had expressed a willingness to remove to lands in the west, and Cass believed that their removal might persuade their more acculturated kinsmen to follow their example.[5]

Cass knew, however, that many of the Shawnees wished to stay in Ohio. Ironically, he had earlier signed two treaties that strengthened the tribe's legal right to remain in the state. On September 29, 1817, Cass and Duncan MacArthur had conducted a treaty with several tribes having claims to lands in northwestern Ohio. In the treaty the Indians had relinquished their overlapping claims to the region in return for specific reservations within the ceded lands. The Shawnees had participated in the treaty and had been awarded three reservations, totaling 173 square miles, surrounding their villages at Wapakoneta, Hog Creek, and Lewistown. The treaty had awarded the reservations "by patent, in fee simple" to the chiefs of the three villages, but such definitive terms of ownership had later engendered opposition from the state of Ohio and from officials eager to remove the Indians to the west. Therefore, in September 1818, Cass and MacArthur had negotiated a supplemental treaty with the same Indians, in which the tribesmen agreed to give up their claims to the reservations "by patent, in fee simple" in exchange for the government's promise that they would hold the lands "in the same manner as Indian reservations [had] been heretofore held," and that the reservations would be "held by them and their heirs forever, unless ceded to the United States." Since the Shawnees seemed reluctant to accede to the new terms, the government increased the size of the reservations by thirty-four square miles—twenty at Wapakoneta and fourteen at Lewistown.[6]

Yet Cass believed that the Shawnees still could be persuaded to go west. He knew that federal officials planned to negotiate with the western Shawnees for their lands in Missouri, offering in exchange a new reservation along the Kansas River where all the bands of the tribe could be consolidated. Since whites continued to crowd upon the Shawnee lands in Ohio, he hoped the attraction of the new western reservation, reputed to be rich in both game and farmland, would lure the Ohio Shawnees across the Mississippi. But first, he needed a catalyst for their removal, a Shawnee spokesman who would urge his kinsmen to go to the west. In the summer of 1824 Cass sent a messenger to Canada, asking Tenskwatawa to meet him at Detroit.[7]

The Prophet readily accepted the invitation. He had recently quarreled with Ironside and was angry that the British government had refused to reimburse him for claims he had just submitted for property destroyed by Harrison's troops following the Battle of Tippecanoe. Of course the British still provided him with sparse rations, but by 1824 Tenskwatawa believed he had been betrayed. He envisioned himself as a former ally, exiled from his country, now maligned and forgotten. Although uncertain of Cass's intentions, he welcomed the opportunity to meet with the governor. At least the invitation indicated that the Americans still regarded him as a man of some status. And the meeting might provide an opportunity for his return to his homeland.[8]

On his arrival in Detroit, Tenskwatawa was pleasantly surprised at the deference accorded him. The old charge of kidnapping was forgotten and he was invited into Cass's private quarters, where the governor spent several days querying him about Shawnee life and culture. Although at first suspicious, the Prophet eventually became convinced that Cass was sincerely interested in his people, and he provided the governor with extensive information regarding Shawnee history and ethnography. He returned to Detroit several times during the following months, openly discussing his role in the emergence of the Indian religious movement and describing Tecumseh's efforts to politically unite all the tribes. In December 1824, he posed for James Otto Lewis, a local artist, who painted his portrait in water colors. The painting was sent to Washington and was used by Charles Bird King as the basis for his oil portrait of the Prophet, painted in 1829.[9]

Cass took great pains to cultivate Tenskwatawa's friendship. He provided the holy man with food, lodging, and cash and presented him with a handsome white gelding, equipped with a new saddle and bridle. Although the exact tenor of their conversation remains unknown, Cass reported to his superiors that Tenskwatawa was "radically cured, if we may credit his own declarations, of his Anglo-mania." Subsequent events illustrate that Cass was able to persuade Tenskwatawa to return to Ohio and champion the government's Indian removal policies. Such persuasion was probably an easy task. From the Prophet's perspective, cooperation with the Americans offered many advantages over continued exile in Canada. Not only could he return to the United States, but he also would be forced to spend only a short time at Wapakoneta, under his old enemy Black Hoof, before leaving for the west. And by acting as a spokesman for removal, he might even undercut Black Hoof's leadership and draw away part of the ancient chief's followers. Moreover, by cooperating with the government in the removal he would again attain some status as a leader, even if only as a government chief. In addition, the move west would bring him closer to the Sacs, Foxes, and Kickapoos, tribes over whom he once had exercised great influence. Finally, the government's rationale for the removal, that the Indians would be given an abundant new land in the west, far from the corrupting influence of evil white men, must have held some attraction for him. He no longer claimed to be a prophet, but a homeland free of whites, where Indians could practice their traditional way of life, had once formed the basis for his religious movement. If Cass wanted a spokesman for removal, he had found the right man.[10]

Unknown to Cass, however, another champion of removal already had emerged among the Shawnees in Ohio. Captain Lewis, or Quitewepea (for whom the village at Lewistown was named), had been awarded reservations by the treaties of 1817 and 1818, but had quarreled with his kinsmen, and in 1820 he had left Ohio to visit the Shawnees in Missouri. Impressed with the lands in the west, Lewis traveled extensively throughout southern Missouri and Arkansas, making friends with the Cherokees and other eastern tribesmen who had immigrated into the region. In 1823 the immigrant Indians had met at the Cherokee settlements in Arkansas, where Lewis had used his influence to solicit an invitation from the Cherokees and others to the Ohio Shawnees to remove west of the Mississippi. Lewis carried the invitation back to Ohio, where it elicited a favorable response, and plans were made to entertain a delegation of western Cherokees at the Shawnee village in Ohio. But warfare with the Osages delayed the Cherokees, and when they failed to appear, the Ohio Shawnees turned on Lewis, accusing him of falsifying the invitation. Bewildered, in the fall of 1824 Lewis journeyed back to St. Louis, where the Cherokee delegation had finally arrived. The Indians discussed their removal plans with Indian agent William Clark, who was so impressed with the proposal that he sent both Lewis and the Cherokees on to Washington to present their project to the president.[11]

The Indians first traveled to Ohio, where they informed Black Hoof's people of their intentions, then rode on to Washington, arriving on February 19, 1825. Both President James Monroe and Secretary of War John C. Calhoun instructed Cass to assemble all the Ohio Shawnees at Wapakoneta in May, when Lewis and the others would return from Washington. At that time the government planned to purchase the remaining Shawnee reserves in Ohio and prepare for the tribe's removal west of the Mississippi.[12]

Both Cass and the Prophet welcomed the news of the approaching conference, and Tenskwatawa immediately agreed to assist the governor at the proceedings. Unfortunately, the proposed council was not so popular in Ohio. Black Hoof and other village chiefs were jealous of Lewis, and resented his attempts to represent the tribe in Washington. In April, when Lewis and the others returned from the capital, Black Hoof used his influence to sabotage the plans for removal. He was assisted by several white men. A small group of frontier merchants traded extensively with the Shawnees and were eager to keep them in Ohio. They warned the Indians that the west was inhabited by hostile tribesmen and informed them that if they crossed the Mississippi they would lose their annuities. In addition, Indian agent John Johnston also opposed the conference. Like Black Hoof, he also seemed resentful that he had not been included in the preparations for the meeting. He denounced Lewis's trip to Washington as "money thrown away" and complained that "there was not a person in the deputation who had the shadow of authority from the Indians in Ohio." He warned Cass that he could not assist him with the proceedings.

Johnston assured Cass that he supported the government's removal policies, but he would not attend the conference, for he had more pressing business. He was obligated to attend a meeting of the Ohio "Canal Commissioners" in Wooster during May. Following the canal meeting he intended to travel on to Zanesville "to attend the convocation of the Episcopal Church ... to fix the location of [their] Theological Seminary, and other matters of importance."[13]

Tenskwatawa and Cass arrived at Wapakoneta in mid-May. Prospects for a successful conference were limited. Although most of the Shawnees had assembled at Wapakoneta, neighboring tribes such as the Wyandots and Senecas boycotted the meeting. Surprisingly, the Prophet was accepted by his old enemies, who no longer saw him as a threat, but his advocacy of removal at first fell on deaf ears. Following Black Hoof's lead, most of the Shawnees were determined to remain in Ohio. On May 18, 1825, Cass presented the government's case for removal, arguing that the Shawnees were being surrounded by whites and that their young men were being victimized by whiskey peddlers. If they would sell their lands in Ohio, the government would give them a fair price and provide them with a much larger reservation in the west. There they could live as their forefathers had, protected from the destructive influence of evil white men.[14]

Following Cass's speech, the Shawnees spent several days conferring among themselves. Only about two dozen younger warriors, led by William Perry, or Pemthata, a minor chief from Wapakoneta, were interested in the government's proposals, and they seemed reluctant to speak in opposition to Black Hoof. Yet Tenskwatawa sensed that many of the Shawnees were more opposed to Captain Lewis than to moving west, and he believed that in the near future a significant number could be persuaded to remove. Therefore, preferring not to alienate his kinsmen, the Prophet sided with Black Hoof against Captain Lewis. If Lewis led only a

small party west, many Shawnees who actually favored removal would be left behind. When the conference ended,
Tenskwatawa could remain in Ohio and organize a large
removal party of his own.[15]

On May 23 the Indians issued their formal reply. Displaying copies of the recent treaties that gave the Shawnees title
to their reservations, Black Hoof informed Cass that the
Indians did not wish to sell their lands. Chiding Lewis, the
old chief stated that if his people had wanted to remove,
they could have done so on their own accord. According to
Black Hoof, "We did not want any other person to do so for
us." At first Perry indicated that he was willing to remove,
but as other Shawnees echoed Black Hoof's sentiments, Perry
backed down and agreed that he too would stay at Wapakoneta. Playing his new role to the hilt, Tenskwatawa announced that he spoke for all his followers, and they also
had decided to remain in Ohio. But he concluded the Indian
speeches with a plea designed both to please Cass and to rid
the Ohio villages of those Indians still loyal to Lewis. Ad-
dressing the assembled tribesmen, the Prophet urged those
who favored Lewis's proposal not to "desert the cause [they
had] espoused, but if [they felt] anxious to go, frankly avow
it." Yet neither Perry nor any of the others stepped forward.
The conference ended, and although Lewis later was able to
lure some tribesmen into going west, the vast majority of
the Shawnees remained in Ohio.[16]

Lewis later complained that Tenskwatawa had assisted
Black Hoof in thwarting his removal plans, but Cass ignored
the charges. Aware that the holy man was still committed
to removal, Cass encouraged him to remain at Wapakoneta.
Following Cass's instructions, during the summer and autumn of 1825 Tenskwatawa traveled among the Shawnee
reservations, carefully promoting emigration. In October he
journeyed to Detroit to inform Cass of his progress, returning to Ohio one month later. At first his efforts seemed unsuccessful. In October, Johnston reported to Cass that the

Indians were "more opposed to moving than at any former time," and that Black Hoof intended to visit the president to secure further guarantees that they could always remain in Ohio.[17]

But during the following winter circumstances changed. Slowly but surely Tenskwatawa's labors produced results. On January 11 Johnston informed Cass that many Shawnees now favored removal, and "the emigrating party [was] fast increasing." Black Hoof still refused to leave Ohio, but the Prophet had weaned almost one hundred Shawnees away from the old chief. During the spring Tenskwatawa's following increased and by April the emigrants were so anxious to leave that Johnston wrote to both Cass and Secretary of War James Barbour urging them to "take an early opportunity of having the necessary means provided. None of the Indians can move without the assistance of the government and I think it would have a bad effect if any would damp the ardor of those who are now willing to go. The Prophet is at the head of the emigrating party."[18]

While Tenskwatawa was recruiting Indians for removal, federal officials finalized plans for a new Shawnee reservation in the west. In November 1825, they conducted a treaty with the Shawnees already residing in Missouri; in it, the Indians gave up their claims to lands near Cape Girardeau in exchange for a tract of land in either southwestern Missouri or in a reservation adjoining the Kansas River. After examining both locations, the Missouri Shawnees chose the lands in Kansas, and in 1826 federal officials prepared to consolidate all the Shawnees on the new reservation. The initial indecision over the reservation's location, complicated by problems in organizing the Ohio Shawnees for the trip west, forced government agents to postpone the removal until the fall of 1826. Meanwhile, Tenskwatawa spent the summer enlisting additional members for the emigration.[19]

Once again the Prophet was successful. By September 1826,

over 250 Shawnees plus a handful of Senecas had assembled at the emigration camp at Wapakoneta. Black Hoof still refused to remove, but the emigrants now counted several prominent young Shawnees, including William Perry, Cornstalk, and Big Snake, in addition to Tenskwatawa and Pachetha, Tecumseh's son, who had remained with his uncle since the War of 1812. Although Johnston had no intention of accompanying the Shawnees, he appointed two other agents, Joseph Park and William Broderick, to lead the Shawnees west. He also supplied the Indians with a quantity of salt pork and ten barrels of flour and provided the agents with funds to furnish the Shawnees until they crossed the Mississippi, where he assumed that William Clark would assist them on the remainder of their journey.[20]

The Indians started west on September 30, 1826, but the removal did not go as planned. Instead of traveling due west across the prairies of northern Indiana, Park and Broderick led their charges southwest, through the broken and hilly country drained by the White River. Since the region was heavily forested, the Shawnees' horses often strayed into the underbrush and they were forced to stop and search for them. Heavy rains and an outbreak of dysentery caused further delays, and they did not reach Vincennes until early December, two months after leaving Wapakoneta. At Vincennes the removal agents purchased additional provisions and the Indians crossed over into Illinois, but they still journeyed at a snail's pace. Johnston had failed to provide adequate funds to purchase grain for their horses, and the animals were so weak they could scarcely travel. The removal had proceeded so slowly that the agents, Park and Broderick, who had been hired on a per diem basis, found that the time allotted for their daily fee had expired. Therefore, when the expedition reached the Embarras River, Broderick turned back. Park remained three days longer, but he too deserted when the Indians approached the Little Wabash, near modern Flora, Illinois. Deprived of removal agents, provisions, and funds, the Shawnees trudged on, selling their clothing to purchase food for their families. They reached Kaskaskia, on the Mississippi River, during the last week of December.[21]

Like the other Shawnees, Tenskwatawa was much disheartened. The entire expedition had no food or money. They had expected federal officials to ferry them across the Mississippi, but when they reached Kaskaskia, they found the river choked with ice and the ferry inoperative. Pierre Menard, the local Indian agent, had not expected them and had received no government funds for their support. To his credit, Menard attempted to provide for the emigrants with the limited resources available at his agency, and was able to furnish them with sparse rations of cornmeal, pork, salt, and tobacco. Since many of the Indians had been forced to sell their clothing, Menard purchased blankets, which he distributed to the more needy of the tribesmen. He also ordered the agency blacksmith to repair their rifles so they could hunt to supplement their rations. Although he had no money to buy grain for their horses, he suggested that the Shawnees withdraw to the "Big Bottom," about twenty miles south of Kaskaskia, where the animals might find enough forage to get them through the winter.[22]

Following Menard's suggestions, the Indians spent the winter of 1827 in the Mississippi River bottoms south of Kaskaskia. There in bark huts they huddled around their fires, supplementing their rations by hunting in the surrounding forests. For Tenskwatawa the cold months must have been a time of bitter reflection. For almost a decade following the War of 1812 he had sat beside similar fires in similar bark houses in Canada, then as now eking out a meager subsistence. Hoping to reassert his leadership, he had returned to the United States and had cooperated with federal officials. For a while his medicine had been good. He had been able to persuade his kinsmen to move west and had even been acknowledged as the leader of the removal. But now his medicine again seemed to be failing, and the emigrants had become disillusioned. Shawnees who had helped each other on the trail now divided into factions. Some talked of returning to their old homes in Ohio. Others complained that Tenskwatawa had misled them and that the government would never honor its promises while the Prophet, a former enemy, spoke for the removal party. And so the winter months passed slowly. The Shawnees were hungry, but they survived. Their horses were not so lucky. The trek west had exhausted the animals and many died before spring. Tenskwatawa also shared in this misfortune. He lost three animals, including the handsome white gelding given to him by Cass only two years earlier.[23]

Conditions improved in the spring. Like Menard, William Clark was surprised at the Shawnees' arrival, and in April he dispatched Indian agent Richard Graham to Kaskaskia to ask the Shawnees why they had come to Illinois and what was detaining them there. Graham met with the Indians for two days in a council dominated by Tenskwatawa. In a lengthy speech on April 2, 1827, the Prophet cataloged the government's promises regarding removal and described their recent journey west. He blamed Johnston's poor planning for many of their problems and asked that William Clark supply them until they could complete their trek to Kansas. He also reminded Graham that before the Indians had left Wapakoneta they had been assured that the government would pay them for cabins and other "improvements" they had left behind, and that both Cass and Johnston had promised that they would receive their share of all Shawnee annuities. Tenskwatawa concluded his speech by pleading, "You see us here now before you, in great want. We ask you to take pity on us."[24]

Graham was no stranger to hardship on the frontier, but he was shocked by the Indians' "miserable condition." He reported, "They are in a wretched state and really require the aid of the Government," and he urged Clark to provide funds for increased rations. The Shawnees already had de-

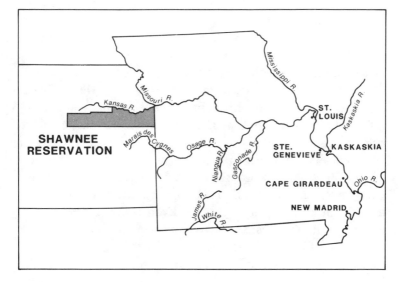

Shawnee Lands in the West

pleted most of the game in the region and Graham feared that they might be forced to kill livestock belonging to settlers. He recommended that the government support the Shawnees until late May or June, when their horses would be recovered and they could travel on to Kansas. He also pointed out that it would be cheaper to keep them at Kaskaskia than to purchase additional horses for their immediate departure or to feed them in Missouri.[25]

Responding to Graham's recommendations, Clark authorized Menard to increase the Shawnees' rations. Meanwhile, he asked federal officials in Washington for funds to support the emigrants on the remainder of their trip west. To his dismay, he found that both the War Department and Congress seemed unaware that the emigration was taking place and had made no plans on the Indians' behalf. Secretary of War James Barbour admitted that "the unfortunate situation of the Shawnees" was "much to be regretted," but since Congress had passed no special appropriation to assist the Indians, no money was available. Even worse, Barbour indicated that he was confused over just which Shawnees were under discussion and that he had no idea of their final destination. Yet he assured Clark that he was pleased that the Indians were going west and authorized him to assist them with such funds as were available at the St. Louis Superintendency.[26]

Unlike Barbour, Clark had a good knowledge of events in the west, but he was afraid that the government's bungling might jeopardize the entire removal. He was particularly concerned that Tenskwatawa and others might become so disillusioned they would refuse to continue on to Kansas and instead would settle with those Shawnees still remaining in Missouri. The latter had relinquished their settlements near Cape Girardeau, but had established new villages on the White River in the south-central region of the state. These Shawnees also had agreed to relocate in Kansas, but an infusion of bitter newcomers opposed to further relocation might prevent them from leaving Missouri. Yet Clark believed that the lands in Kansas were so attractive that if Tenskwatawa and other leaders of the emigrants visited them, they would be eager to settle there. Therefore, during the spring of 1827 he organized an "exploring party" of both Missouri and emigrant Shawnees to examine the region along the Kansas River. He also encouraged delegates from several other eastern tribes, including Kickapoos, Delawares, and Piankashaws, to join the expedition. Since the emigrant Shawnees' horses still could not make such a journey, Clark purchased six mounts so the Prophet and five of his kinsmen could participate in the trip.[27]

The expedition left St. Louis in April, traveled southwest to the James Fork of the White River, where they were joined by the Delawares, and then went northwest along the upper Marais des Cygnes River until they reached the western border of Missouri. Turning north, they rode through prairies interspersed with groves of hardwoods until they reached the juncture of the Kansas and Missouri rivers. They then turned west, ascending the Kansas River Valley about twenty miles, where they made a camp and spent several days exploring the surrounding country. Near modern Bonner Springs they met a creole trapper, who informed them that the Kansas River bottoms were well timbered as far west as Soldier Creek (modern Topeka), but west of that stream wood was scarce. Although Tenskwatawa and the other Shawnees were unaccustomed to such wide prairies, they seemed pleased with the Kansas River Valley and reported that the new reservation was "suitable for the support of [their] families." After selecting sites for villages, the party returned to their homes.[28]

Yet the exploring expedition did not bode well for Tenskwatawa. Although the Prophet had brought the emigrants to Kaskaskia, Clark and other western agents could not forget his role before the War of 1812. During the winter of 1827, while the Shawnees remained camped near Kaskas-

kia, Clark had acquiesced in Tenskwatawa's role as spokesman for the emigrants, but when the exploring party set out
for Kansas, Clark and Graham acknowledged Big Snake and
Cornstalk as the leaders of the emigrant Shawnee delegation. Tenskwatawa also encountered opposition among the
Indians in Missouri. Before the War of 1812 the western
Shawnees had refused to join the holy man's religious movement, and they now scoffed at his attempts to speak for the
tribe. The Delawares were even more adamant. Some of these
tribesmen living on the White River were survivors of Tenskwatawa's witchcraft trials and they viewed his arrival with
considerable alarm. Anderson, the leading chief among the
Missouri Delawares, denounced Tenskwatawa, informing
Clark, "My Brother, this man I no [sic] a long time. He has
been a long time striving to do all the bad things he could."
According to Anderson, the Prophet could not be trusted.
He was secretly formulating plans to lead all the Shawnees
and Delawares south to Texas.[29]

Anderson was only half correct. Tenskwatawa had inquired about Texas not as a refuge from the Americans, but
because several years earlier a party of Shawnees had fled to
the region, where they lived with some Cherokees. The
Prophet had no intention of settling in Texas, but he hoped
that the Texas Shawnees might be induced to unite with the
majority of the tribe on the new reservation. He knew they
were less friendly to the United States than either the Shawnees in Missouri or Ohio, and he hoped that their influence
might neutralize the pro-American sentiments of Black
Hoof's followers. On his return from the exploring expedition, Tenskwatawa visited the Missouri Shawnees and proposed that they meet with their Texas kinsmen and invite
them to Kansas. But the proposal encountered considerable
opposition. The Missouri Shawnees mistrusted his motives
and even many of the emigrant tribesmen at Kaskaskia envisioned the suggestion as nothing more than a scheme by
Tenskwatawa to increase his following on the new reserva-

tion. The proposal split the emigrant Shawnees into two camps, and the rift seemed to follow the old band or village divisions. A large majority of the emigrants traced their ancestry to the Maykujay division, and, led by Cornstalk and Big Snake, they opposed the Prophet's initiative. A minority composed of Kispokotha and Piqua people evidently favored the plan. Unquestionably, Tenskwatawa was eager to increase his following, but he was too politically astute to pursue the proposal in the face of such overwhelming opposition. When the charges of self-aggrandizement were leveled against him, he temporarily abandoned the plan.[30]

While the Prophet was failing in his efforts to recruit more followers, the emigrant Shawnees prepared to continue their journey. Although they originally had intended to leave Illinois during late May or early June, their horses did not recover as quickly as anticipated. During the summer of 1827 several delegations from the emigrants visited Clark in St. Louis. He was anxious for them to move to Kansas, but he calculated that it still remained cheaper to sustain the Shawnees at Kaskaskia than to purchase additional horses for their removal. Moreover, since the Indians would be arriving at their new reservation too late in the season to plant any corn, Clark realized that the government again would be forced to provide rations to the emigrants, regardless of where they spent the upcoming winter. Yet Clark wanted them to resume the journey to Kansas during the summer of 1827, even if they couldn't complete the trip. They could at least establish a winter camp in western Missouri. From there they would be able to reach the reservation in the early spring, in ample time to plant their crops for the following winter.[31]

Finally, in August 1827, the emigrants resumed their journey. They arrived in St. Louis in three parties on August 6 and 7, and spent the next three weeks camped on the outskirts of the city, evidently enjoying Clark's hospitality. On August 23 Cornstalk and Big Snake met with Clark and apologized for their lengthy stay, explaining that they had "repairs to be done," but they assured him, "We are anxious to start and so soon as we can get off, we want to go." Cornstalk admitted that the emigrants had quarreled over the Prophet's proposals, but he asserted that now the Shawnees were "all of one fire" and anxious to proceed to the west. He also asked Clark to provide them with further assistance until they could become self-sufficient in Kansas.[32]

Cornstalk's claims of Shawnee unity could not hide the division that still split the emigrants' camp. Tenskwatawa attended Cornstalk's conference with Clark, but he remained silent. On August 29, however, the Shawnees again met with the agent, and this time Tenskwatawa spoke at length. Although he also gave lip service to the emigrants' unity, he still was eager to promote his scheme of bringing all the Shawnees to Kansas. He informed Clark that Cornstalk had spoken for the Maykujays, but that he would speak for the Piquas and Kispokothas. Lamenting the fact that "the Shawnees were scattered all through the country," Tenskwatawa urged Clark to unite the entire tribe in Kansas: "If they were all on one spot of ground, your words could be known to us easier." Vowing that he was indeed a "principal chief," the Prophet took great pains to assert that he continued to use his influence in behalf of the government. He admitted that he had wanted to contact the Texas Shawnees, but only to bring them "under the protection of their Great Father." If Clark had heard otherwise, such allegations were false, for, according to Tenskwatawa, "I never told a lie. . . . I am a man of truth." The Prophet concluded his harangue with requests for additional assistance, including guns, tents, saddles, shoes, and even garters, "for without garters, the women cannot dance."[33]

In reply, Clark reminded the Indians that Congress had not passed any specific appropriation to provide for their subsistence, but he promised that he would support them as best he could. He did assure them that they would receive their fair share of all annuities and suggested that he advance them $750 from his general funds, which they could pay back when their annuities arrived. The Shawnees spent the night of August 29 discussing the proposal, and on the following morning Tenskwatawa agreed to the terms, but asked that they be given $1,000, rather than the sum Clark had suggested. Clark honored their request and the Prophet asked him to keep the money and to purchase supplies for the Shawnees as they were needed. Otherwise, Tenskwatawa noted, the Indians "might be imposed upon by persons from whom [they purchased]," and would spend the money foolishly.[34]

On September 8, 1827, the Prophet and the other Shawnees left St. Louis, en route for Kansas. They followed the southern bank of the Missouri River as far west as the mouth of the Osage, then turned southwest, seeking a winter camp near the confluence of the Osage and Niangua. There, beyond the American settlements, they spent the winter comfortably, grazing their horses in the river bottoms and supplementing their rations with game. In the spring Richard Graham arrived at their village and on April 25, they resumed the journey toward their new reservation. Tenskwatawa and the other emigrants arrived in Kansas on May 14, 1828.[35]

Chapter Nine

Epilogue

During the summer of 1828 the emigrant Shawnees established a series of small villages along the south bank of the Kansas River, from eight to twenty miles west of the Missouri state line. The government continued to provide them with limited rations and also furnished them agricultural implements and seed so they could plant their corn and produce a crop that would meet their needs for the following winter. In October, missionary Isaac McCoy passed through their villages enroute to St. Louis, and reported that they were harvesting their corn and had erected comfortable bark houses. The Shawnees' difficulties seemed to be over. They had found the promised land in Kansas.[1]

But not Tenskwatawa. William Clark remained reluctant to acknowledge him as a legitimate leader, and after he arrived in Kansas the holy man's influence declined. Federal officials continued to recognize Cornstalk, Big Snake, Perry, and others as the government chiefs, and rations and annuities were funneled through their hands. Of course the Prophet was awarded his share, but only as an individual Shawnee, not as a patron who dispensed such blessings to his followers. He established a separate village, but the population soon shrank as inhabitants left the settlement to pitch their lodges in the towns of more influential leaders. By 1830 his following again numbered only his immediate family, and this time even Pachetha, Tecumseh's son, abandoned him and returned to Missouri.[2]

In August 1830, Isaac McCoy again passed through the Shawnee villages. McCoy was eager to open a mission among the Shawnees and on August 23 he met in council with the Indians, formally proposing that the Baptists erect both a church and a school on the reservation. Many of the Shawnees seemed indifferent to the missionary, but to McCoy's surprise the Prophet spoke at some length in favor of the plan. Tenskwatawa's motivation remains unknown, but since a mission and its emphasis on acculturation contradicted much of his earlier teaching, it is doubtful that he supported the proposal through any sincere belief in its merit. It is more likely that the Prophet was attempting to curry favor from a white man whom he envisioned as both influential and a close friend of William Clark. But even here he failed. McCoy distrusted the Shawnee and reported he had "no doubt [that Tenskwatawa] secretly was opposed to every thing like education or religion."[3]

Meanwhile, the Prophet was surrounded by his former enemies. By 1830 many of the Missouri Shawnees had moved to the new reservation, and in the years that followed, the exodus of Shawnees from Ohio to Kansas quickened. In 1832 about 350 tribesmen from Wapakoneta and neighboring villages arrived in the west and during the next year additional members of the tribe also moved to Kansas. None of the newcomers attached themselves to the holy man and although he tried to assert himself in council, few Shawnees paid him any attention. Embittered, Tenskwatawa withdrew from his kinsmen and established a new "Prophetstown" near a natural spring in what is now the Argentine district of modern Kansas City, Kansas. There he lived with his family, an outcast among his people.[4]

Yet the Prophet was still to have one last moment in the limelight. In 1832 artist George Catlin journeyed up the Missouri River as far as North Dakota, and on his return he stopped at Fort Leavenworth, where he painted several portraits of neighboring Indians. Although Catlin did not paint Cornstalk, or Big Snake, or Perry, among the half dozen Shawnees whom he asked to sit for his portraits was Tenskwatawa. Flattered, the aging holy man readily agreed and during the autumn of 1832 he posed for the artist. Catlin's portrait reveals that Tenskwatawa already had developed a sense of his place in the history of his people. Unlike the earlier portrait by James Otto Lewis, in which the Prophet had sought to present a more acculturated image and had dressed in several garments of European or American manufacture, Tenskwatawa posed for Catlin in more traditional garb, bare chested except for an animal skin thrown over his shoulders. Around his head was wound a cloth turban, common among Shawnees of the period, while through the lobe of his left ear two small arrows and a feather had been thrust, their points lying along his left cheek, just below the hairline. He wore many of the same earbobs, gorgets, and bracelets that he had worn for Lewis, but in Catlin's portrait he is conspicuously displaying his old sacraments, his former badges of office. In his right hand the Prophet held what Catlin called his "medicine fire," a short rod ornamented with feathers and wampum, which may have been one of his prayer sticks. In his left hand were the sacred strings of beans, mystical symbols through which his disciples once "shook hands with the Prophet" as they were converted to his teachings. Aware of his diminished stature, Tenskwatawa obviously was eager to be portrayed as he had been in the past, a holy man whose influence had dominated the tribes.[5]

Catlin's painting also shows something else. The Prophet had aged considerably since 1825. Now almost sixty, Tenskwatawa had grown corpulent, with sagging flesh and dark circles under his eyes. Although Catlin considered the Shawnee to be "shrewd and influential, perhaps one of the most remarkable men, who [had] flourished on these frontiers for some time past," he also commented that "circumstances [had] destroyed him." The once vociferous holy man now seemed "silent and melancholy."[6]

Following Catlin's visit, the Prophet quickly faded into obscurity. He did oppose the missions that opened near the reservation, and other Shawnees occasionally sought his advice on medical matters, but he spent his days close to his lodge and took no part in tribal politics. After 1832, reports by Indian agents and missionaries scarcely mention him. The Prophet's time was past. Younger men more favored by the government now led the Shawnees. Tenskwatawa died in November 1836. He lies buried somewhere under modern Kansas City, Kansas.[7]

In retrospect, the Prophet's life was a microcosm of the Indian experience in the Old Northwest during the period 1775–1840. Like other Native Americans, his world was permanently altered by the circumstances of the American Revolution, and in the postwar years he was forced to adapt to dramatic social and economic changes. Although some tribesmen (Black Hoof, Five Medals, and others) chose to walk the white man's road, the majority, including Tenskwatawa, rejected such acculturation and clung to the ways of their fathers. Of course his role in the religious movement was unique, for he dominated the movement before the Treaty of Fort Wayne, but the religious revivalism he espoused was a natural outgrowth of Indian desperation. Other tribesmen, both before and after the Prophet, have founded similar movements. If Tenskwatawa had not emerged it is probable that another religious leader eventually would have stepped forward to champion the Indians' cause.

Like most of his followers, Tenskwatawa participated in the War of 1812, and in the postwar period he also found himself dependent on white men. Although he was forced to spend a decade in exile, his relationship with the British Indian Department resembled his kinsmen's reliance on the

American annuity system. During these decades successful Indian leaders cooperated with the government, and Tenskwatawa was willing to become a government chief if such collaboration would prove to his advantage. American suspicions prevented his return to prominence, and he was forced to share in the suffering encountered by thousands of other Indians on their ill-planned treks west. Removed beyond the Mississippi, he died in obscurity, ignored by those who now occupied his old homeland.

Although Harrison, Wells, and other Americans condemned Tenskwatawa as a charlatan, at first he believed in his faith. Unquestionably, in the years before Tippecanoe he was convinced that the Master of Life had chosen him to lead the Indians back toward the ways of their fathers. In addition to his visions, his sincerity was the quality that attracted and held his followers in his camp. After Tippecanoe he must have harbored doubts, but by that time he had enjoyed six years of leadership and was determined to retain his prominence. He no longer functioned as a religious leader, but spent the remainder of his life attempting to regain a portion of the political power he had exercised as the charismatic Prophet. American officials who knew him after 1825 portrayed Tenskwatawa as a shallow opportunist, but they encountered a person much changed from the Shawnee holy man who had mesmerized the Indians two decades earlier.

White men always had misunderstood him, even in the years before Tippecanoe. American officials could never comprehend the religious movement that swept through the tribes, and they refused to recognize Tenskwatawa's legitimate role in its inception. To understand the movement, Harrison and others would have been forced to examine the conditions that produced the new faith, and they were unwilling to do so. It was irrelevant that Tenskwatawa's teachings were quite logical within the framework of Shawnee culture; Indian religious beliefs were considered inferior to

Christianity, and white Americans refused to take them seriously. Moreover, any close scrutiny of the movement's broad appeal would have required whites to address the validity of Indian complaints. Since American frontiersmen were responsible for the majority of them, such an examination was not forthcoming. It was much easier, therefore, to condemn Tenskwatawa as a pretender and to picture his movement as a religious digression, entirely secondary to the political and military aspirations of Tecumseh.

In contrast, Tecumseh always has appealed to white Americans. His efforts attracted his white contemporaries and have intrigued historians ever since. Both have admired his foresight and his ability to rise above tribal politics. In 1811 Harrison referred to him as a genius, and reported that "if it were not for the vicinity of the United States, he would, perhaps, be the founder of an empire that would rival Mexico or Peru." Indeed, Americans always have been fascinated with Tecumseh's attempts to unify the tribes. His struggle seemed logical to whites because it was what *they* would have done. His plans reflect a white solution to the Indians' problems. Unfortunately, they were much less appealing to the Indians. Although centralized authority and political unity were characteristic of Euro-American political traditions, they were foreign to the tribesmen. Tecumseh may have dreamed of a pan-Indian union, but most of his followers remained a tribal people. They still saw their world from a tribal perspective.[8]

Tecumseh has continued to appeal to white Americans for other reasons. More than any other Indian in American history, he fits the American conception of the noble savage. His stirring speeches and his efforts in behalf of American prisoners during the War of 1812 (although the latter was contradictory to Indian practices) were praised by his adversaries. Even his death at the Battle of the Thames, the Indian Armageddon, added to his mystique, for his body was never found, but was carried away and buried secretly by his followers. Since his death his reputation has grown, and like other American folk heroes much of the image is apocryphal. Contrary to popular belief, he was not a tall, lean man and his skin was not a lighter color than other Shawnees. Neither did he have a love affair with a frontier maiden, Rebecca Galloway. Yet all of the above have been attributed to him and have been incorporated into his biographies.[9]

Tenskwatawa was much less romantic, but his response to the problems besetting the tribes was much more Indian. His religious revitalization was never understood by white Americans because they had little insight into traditional Indian culture. The Prophet was not a handsome man, and many of his qualities, although very human, were not admirable. His conduct in the postwar years did little to enhance his image, for his influence markedly declined and familiarity bred contempt in the eyes of his white contemporaries. Since his death most historians have continued to portray him in a secondary role. But in the first decade of the nineteenth century his teachings struck a responsive chord among his fellow tribesmen, and it was Tenskwatawa rather than Tecumseh who provided the basis for Indian resistance in the years before the war.

Notes

Chapter One

1. William Henry Harrison to the Secretary of War, July 15, 1801, in Logan Esarey, ed., *Messages and Letters of William Henry Harrison*, 2 vols. (Indianapolis: Indiana Historical Commission, 1922), 1:25–31; "Conference held with the Delaware and Shawnee Deputation, February 5–10, 1802," Shawnee File, Great Lakes-Ohio Valley Indian Archives, Glenn A. Black Laboratory of Archaeology, Bloomington, Indiana; William Burnett to Robert Innes and Co., December 20, 1798, in Wilbur Cunningham, ed., *Letter Book of William Burnett* (n.p.: Fort Miami Heritage Society of Michigan, 1967), 112; Burnett to George Gillespie, May 30, 1800, ibid., 129.

2. Harrison to the Secretary of War, July 15, 1801, Esarey, *Harrison Letters*, 1:25–31; Secretary of War to Harrison, February 23, 1802, in Clarence E. Carter, ed., *The Territorial Papers of the United States*, 27 vols. (Washington, D.C.: Government Printing Office, 1934–), 7:48–50.

3. George Ironside to Prideaux Selby, December 25, 1804, *Collections of the Michigan Pioneer and Historical Society*, 40 vols. (Lansing: Thorp and Godfrey and others, 1874–1929), 23:37; John Heckewelder, *History, Manners, and Customs of the Indian Nations* (Philadelphia: Historical Society of Philadelphia, 1876), 220–23; Speech by Little Turtle, December 1801, in Gerrard Hopkins, *A Mission to the Indians from the Committee of the Baltimore Meeting to Fort Wayne in 1804* (Philadelphia: T. Elwood Zell, 1862), 171. For an excellent discussion of the impact of European diseases on Native Americans, see Alfred Crosby, *The Columbian Exchange* (Westport, Conn.: Greenwood Press, 1971).

4. Harrison to the Secretary of War, June 15, 1801, Esarey, *Harrison Letters*, 1:25–31; Harrison to the Indian Council, August 12, 1802, ibid., 52–54; James Wilkinson to Winthrop Sargent, November 17, 1797, Winthrop Sargent Papers, Massachusetts Historical Society, Boston, roll 4, 473–8 (microfilm); Henry Dearborn to John Johnston, September 14, 1802, Frank E. Jones Collection, Cincinnati Historical Society; Secretary of War to William Wells, May 13, 1804, Letters Sent by the Secretary of War Relating to Indian Affairs, National Archives, M15, roll 2, 4 (microfilm).

5. Hopkins, *A Mission to the Indians*, 160–75; Paul Woehrmann, *At the Headwaters of the Maumee* (Indianapolis: Indiana Historical Society, 1971), 110–41.

6. Harrison to Dearborn, July 10, 1805, Potawatomi File, Great Lakes Indian Archives; Report of Ellicott and Hopkins, October 15, 1804, ibid.; Woehrmann, *At the Headwaters of the Maumee*, 149; Gayle Thornbrough, ed., *Letter Book of the Indian Agency at Fort Wayne, 1809–1815* (Indianapolis: Indiana Historical Society, 1961), 20.

7. Frederick W. Hodge, ed., *Handbook of American Indians North of Mexico*, Bureau of American Ethnology Bulletin no. 30, 2 vols. (New York: Rowman and Littlefield, 1971), 2:530–6; Charles Callender, "Shawnee," in Bruce G. Trigger, ed., *Handbook of North American Indians: Northeast* (Washington, D.C.: Smithsonian Institution, 1978), 630–31; Noel W. Schutz, Jr., "The Study of Shawnee Myth in an Ethnographic and Ethnohistorical Perspective" (Ph.D. dissertation, Indiana University, 1975), 463–4.

8. The functions of the various divisions of the Shawnees changed through the years, and there is much confusion over these roles. See Thomas Wildcat Alford, *Civilization and the Story of the Absentee Shawnees* (Norman: University of Oklahoma Press, 1936), 21; William Albert Galloway, *Old Chillicothe: Shawnee and Pioneer History* (Xenia, Ohio: Buckeye Press, 1934), 180–81; Vernon Kinietz and Erminie Wheeler-Voegelin, eds., *"Shawnese Traditions": C. C. Trowbridge's Account. Occasional Contributions from the Museum of Anthropology of the University of Michigan, No. 9* (Ann Arbor: University of Michigan Press, 1939), xiii–xiv, 8; Callender, "Shawnee," 623–4; James H. Howard, *Shawnee!: The Ceremonialism of a Native American Tribe and Its Cultural Background* (Athens: Ohio University Press, 1981), 24–30; Schutz, "Shawnee Myth," 476–78.

9. "Account of the Affair on the Belle Riviere, July 6–9, 1755," Shawnee File, Great Lakes Indian Archives; Edward P. Hamilton,

ed., *Adventures in the Wilderness: The American Journals of Louis Antoine de Bougainville, 1756–1760* (Norman: University of Oklahoma Press, 1964), 90, 105, 114, 196.

10. Francis Parkman, *The Conspiracy of Pontiac* (New York: Collier Books, 1962), 329, 398, 405–34; Jack Sosin, *The Revolutionary Frontier* (New York: Holt, Rinehart and Winston, 1967), 6–7.

11. Anthony Wallace, *The Death and Rebirth of the Seneca* (New York: Alfred A. Knopf, 1970), 122–23; Sosin, *Revolutionary Frontier*, 84–85.

12. Reuben G. Thwaites and Louise P. Kellogg, eds., *Documentary History of Dunmore's War* (Madison: State Historical Society of Wisconsin, 1905), xii–xiii; "Reminiscences of Judge Henry Jolly," ibid., 9–14; Wallace, *Death and Rebirth of the Seneca*, 123–24.

13. Logan to Michael Cresap, July 21, 1774, Thwaites and Kellogg, *Dunmore's War*, 246–47; Colonel William Fleming's Journal, September–October 1774, ibid., 281–91. Several eyewitness accounts of the battle can be found in ibid., 253–97. Also see Andrew Scott Withers, *Chronicles of Border Warfare*, ed. Reuben G. Thwaites (Cincinnati: Robert Clarke, 1895), 165–74; Sosin, *Revolutionary Frontier*, 86–87.

14. William Christian to William Preston, November 8, 1774, Thwaites and Kellogg, *Dunmore's War*, 301–7; Reginald Horsman, *Matthew Elliott, British Indian Agent* (Detroit: Wayne State University Press, 1964), 5–6; Schutz, "Shawnee Myth," 464; Jack Sosin, "The British Indian Department and Dunmore's War," *Virginia Magazine of History and Biography* 74 (January 1966): 34–50.

15. Speech by Cornstalk, October 10, 1775, Reuben G. Thwaites and Louise P. Kellogg, eds., *The Revolution on the Upper Ohio, 1775–1777* (Madison: Wisconsin Historical Society, 1908), 106; James H. O'Donnell, *Southern Indians in the American Revolution* (Knoxville: University of Tennessee Press, 1973), 40–41; Withers, *Chronicles of Border Warfare*, 209–14; Sosin, *Revolutionary Frontier*, 111, 123.

16. Daniel Broadhead to Timothy Pickering, November 3, 1779, Shawnee File, Great Lakes Indian Archives; Alford, *Civilization*, 201. Also see Don Francisco Cruzat to Estevan Miro, March 19, 1782, in Louis Houck, ed., *The Spanish Regime in Missouri*, 2 vols. (New York: Arno Press, 1971), 1:209; Lawrence Kinniard, ed., *Spain in the Mississippi Valley, 1765–1794, Annual Report of the American Historical Association for the Year, 1945*, 4 vols. (Washington, D.C.: Government Printing Office, 1946), 4:xxx–xxxi; Shawnee

chiefs to the President, March 29, 1811, Records of the Secretary of War, Letters Received Relating to Indian Affairs, M271, roll 1, 550–51, National Archives (microfilm).

17. Captain Killbuck to Daniel Broadhead, June 7, 1780, Louise P. Kellogg, ed., *Frontier Retreat on the Upper Ohio, 1779–1781* (Madison: State Historical Society of Wisconsin, 1917), 190–91; Broadhead to George Washington, August 21, 1780, ibid., 249–50; Consul Wilshire Butterfield, *History of the Girtys* (Cincinnati: Robert Clarke, 1890), 198; Horsman, *Matthew Elliott*, 36–39, 42.

18. Minutes of the Transactions with Indians at Sandusky, August 26–September 7, 1783, *Michigan Historical Collections* 20:175–83. Also see Reginald Horsman, *Expansion and American Indian Policy, 1783–1812* (East Lansing: Michigan State University Press, 1967), 3–15.

19. "Articles of a Treaty concluded at the mouth of the Great Miami," January 31, 1786, *American State Papers: Indian Affairs,* 2 vols. (Washington, D.C.: Gales and Seaton, 1832–34), 1:11–12; Randolph C. Downes, *Council Fires on the Upper Ohio* (Pittsburgh: University of Pittsburgh Press, 1940), 297–98.

20. Downes, *Council Fires on the Upper Ohio,* 298; Josiah Harmar to the Secretary of War, November 5, 1786, William Henry Smith, ed., *The St. Clair Papers,* 2 vols. (Freeport, N.Y.: Books for Libraries Press, 1970), 2:19.

21. Speech of the Indians at Detroit, December 18, 1786, *American State Papers: Indian Affairs,* 1:8.

22. St. Clair to the President, May 2, 1789, Smith, *St. Clair Papers,* 2:111–13.

23. "General Orders," November 4, 1790, *American State Papers: Indian Affairs,* 2:106.

24. St. Clair to the Secretary of War, November 9, 1791, *St. Clair Papers,* 2:262–67.

25. Correspondence regarding this conference, including the "Journal of the Treaty Commissioners," can be found in *American State Papers: Indian Affairs,* 1:340–59.

26. Anthony Wayne to the Secretary of War, July 7, 1794, *American State Papers: Indian Affairs,* 1:487–88; Wayne to the Secretary of War, August 28, 1794, ibid., 491; "A treaty of peace between the United States and the tribes of Indians," December 10, 1795, ibid., 562–63; Horsman, *Matthew Elliott,* 90–102; Francis Paul Prucha, *The Sword of the Republic: The United States Army on the Frontier, 1783–1845* (London, Ontario: Collier-Macmillan, 1969), 35–38.

27. Schutz, "Shawnee Myth," 420–21.

28. Speech by Black Hoof, February 5, 1802, Shawnee File, Great Lakes Indian Archives.

29. Speech by Dearborn to the Shawnees, February 10, 1802, ibid.

30. Jefferson to the Chiefs of the Shawnee Nation, February 9, 1807, Andrew A. Lipscomb, ed., *The Writings of Thomas Jefferson*, 20 vols. (Washington, D.C.: Thomas Jefferson Memorial Association, 1903–4), 16:421–25; William Wells to Harrison, June, 1807, Esarey, *Harrison Letters*, 1:218.

31. Kirk to Dearborn, July 20, 1807, Letters Received by the Secretary of War, Main Series, National Archives, M221, roll 9, 2874–78 (microfilm); Kirk to Dearborn, April 12, 1808, ibid., roll 25, 8114–15.

32. Kirk to Dearborn, April 12, 1808, ibid., roll 25, 8114–15; Citizens of Ohio to the President and Secretary of War, September 25, 1808, ibid., 8147.

33. Shawnee Chiefs to the President and the Secretary of War, December 1, 1808, ibid., roll 25, 8148–50; F. Duchoquet to the Secretary of War, December 4, 1808, ibid., 8145; John Johnston to the Secretary of War, April 15, 1809, Thornbrough, *Letter Book*, 33–36.

34. Speech by the Shawnees to Kirk, April 14, 1809, M221, roll 25, 8188–90; Citizens of Champaign County, Ohio, to the President, April 12, 1809, ibid., 8212; Kirk to Dearborn, February 12, 1809, ibid., 8157; Shawnee Chiefs to the President and Secretary of War, April 10, 1809, Thornbrough, *Letter Book*, 46–48.

35. "John Johnston's Recollections," Jones Collection, Cincinnati Historical Society; Thomas Ashe, *Travels in America Performed in 1806* (London: R. Phillips, 1808), 243; Conference with the Delawares and Shawnees, February 1802, Shawnee File, Great Lakes Indian Archives.

36. Secretary of War to Harrison, February 2, 1802, Carter, *Territorial Papers*, 7:48–50; Jefferson to Harrison, February 27, 1803, Esarey, *Harrison Letters*, 1:69–73.

37. Johnston to William Irvine, August 9, 1804, Jones Collection, Cincinnati Historical Society; Johnston to Dearborn, May 4, 1805, ibid.; Horsman, *Matthew Elliott*, 146.

38. Speech by the Shawnee chiefs, February, 1802, Shawnee File, Great Lakes Indian Archives.

39. Ibid.; Address of St. Clair to the Territorial Legislature, November 5, 1800, Smith, *The St. Clair Papers*, 2:501–10.

40. Speech by the Shawnee chiefs, February 1802, Shawnee File, Great Lakes Indian Archives; St. Clair to James Smith, June 4, 1800, *The St. Clair Papers*, 2:495–96; Jacob Burnet to St. Clair,

August 20, 1800, ibid., 525–26. The fate of the child remains unknown.

41. Moses Dawson, *A Historical Narrative of the Civil and Military Services of Major General William H. Harrison* (Cincinnati: M. Dawson, 1824), 45; Wallace A. Brice, *History of Fort Wayne* (Ft. Wayne: D. W. Jones and Sons, 1868), 166–68; Address of St. Clair to the Territorial Legislature, November 5, 1800, Smith, *The St. Clair Papers*, 2:501–10.

42. Dearborn to Wells, May 18, 1804, Shawnee File, Great Lakes Indian Archives; Ashe, *Travels in America*, 243; "Diary of the Journey of Br. and Sr. Kluge and Br. Lukenbach from Goshen on the Muskingum to White River, March 24 to May 25, 1801," Lawrence Henry Gipson, ed., *The Moravian Indian Mission on the White River* (Indianapolis: Indiana Historical Bureau, 1938), 92–96; "Diary of the Little Indian Congregation on the White River for the Year 1802," ibid., 164–65.

43. Harrison to the Secretary of War, July 15, 1801, Esarey, *Harrison Letters*, 1:25–31; "Diary of the Little Indian Congregation on the White River for the Year 1805," Gipson, *Moravian Indian Mission on the White River*, 327–98.

44. George and Louise Spindler, "American Indian Personality Types and Their Sociocultural Roots" in Deward E. Walker, ed., *The Emergent Native, Americans: A Reader in Cultural Contact* (Boston: Little, Brown and Co., 1972), 502–13; Schutz, "Shawnee Myth," 233.

45. Kinietz and Voegelin, *Shawnee Traditions*, 1–7, 43–46; Schutz, "Shawnee Myth," 228–30.

46. Schutz, "Shawnee Myth," 187–95, 233–35. Also see C. F. Voegelin, John Yegerlehner, and Florence Robinett, "Shawnee Laws: Perceptual Statements for the Language and for the Content," in Harry Hoijer, ed., *American Anthropological Association Memoirs* 56 (December 1954): 32–46.

47. Bernard Barber, "Acculturation and Messianic Movements," *American Sociological Review* 6 (October 1941): 664–65.

48. Ibid.; Anthony F. C. Wallace, "Revitalization Movements," *American Anthropologist*, 58 (May 1956): 266–69.

49. Diary of George Bluejacket, October 29, 1829, Manuscripts Department, Lilly Library, Indiana University; Speech by the Shawnee Chief, 1803, in Benjamin B. Thatcher, *Indian Biography* (New York: J. Harper, 1832), 190–91; Kinietz and Wheeler-Voegelin, *Shawnese Traditions*, 59, 61; Schutz, "Shawnee Myth," 144.

50. Bluejacket's Narrative, in Joab Spencer, "The Shawnee Indians: Their Customs, Traditions, and Folk-Lore," *Transactions of*

the *Kansas State Historical Society* (Topeka: State Printing Office, 1908), 10:384; Johnston to Lyman Draper, September 13, 1847, Tecumseh Papers, Draper Manuscripts, State Historical Society of Wisconsin, 11YY31 (microfilm); Speech by the Shawnee Chief, 1803, Thatcher, *Indian Biography*, 190–91; Schutz, "Shawnee Myth," 211, 479–81.

Chapter Two

1. Benson Lossing, *The Pictorial Field-Book of the War of 1812* (New York: Harper and Brothers, 1869), 188–89; J. P. MacLean, "Shaker Mission to the Shawnee Indians," *Ohio Archaeological and Historical Publications* 11 (June 1903): 223. Historians and anthropologists previously have asserted that Lalawethika's initial vision occurred during the fall of 1805, but evidence in the Shawnee File, Great Lakes Indian Archives, indicates otherwise. See Hendrick Apaumut to Dearborn, May 21, 1805, in ibid.

2. Much confusion exists regarding Lalawethika's and Tecumseh's family and genealogy. Some historians argue that Methoataske was a Shawnee, but overwhelming evidence, including an assertion by the Prophet, indicates that she was a Creek, Tecumpease, the oldest daughter, played a prominent role in both Lalawethika's and Tecumseh's lives; another sister moved west with most of the Kispokotha Shawnees in 1779. The third sister, Nehaaeemo (or her daughter), eventually married the British Indian trader Geroge Ironside. The oldest son, Chiksika, was killed in 1788. Sauwauseekau, the second son, fell at the Battle of Fallen Timbers. C. C. Trowbridge recorded that the Prophet informed Cass that both of his triplet brothers had died shortly after birth, but Trowbridge must have been mistaken. Kumskaukau may have been dead by 1825, but documentary evidence indicates he was living in Tenskwatawa's village in 1807. See MacLean, "Shaker Mission," 221–26, and Richard McNemar, *The Kentucky revival, or a short history of the extraordinary out-pouring of the Spirit of God in the Western States of America* (Albany: E. and E. Hosford, 1808), 111–18. Also see Tecumseh Papers, Draper Manuscripts, 1YY2, 1YY5, 1YY92–93, 1YY121, 2YY1–2, 2YY134–139; Tecumseh File, Fort Malden Historic Park, Amherstburg, Ontario; Kinietz and Wheeler-Voegelin, *Shawnese Traditions*, 30; Benjamin Drake, *Life of Tecumseh* (New York: Arno Press, 1969), 61–65; Glenn Tucker, *Tecumseh: Vision of Glory* (New York: Russell and Russell, 1973),

19–27; George Ironside Papers, Burton Collection, Detroit Public Library.

3. Tecumseh Papers, Draper Manuscripts, 1YY8; Drake, *Life of Tecumseh*, 65; Tucker, *Tecumseh*, 39.

4. Schutz, "Shawnee Myth," 39. Accounts of Tecumseh's childhood stress the close relationship between Tecumseh and both Tecumpease and Chiksika, but make little mention of either adult devoting time to Lalawethika. See Drake, *Life of Tecumseh*, 62; Tucker, *Tecumseh*, 37.

5. Tecumseh Papers, Draper Manuscripts, 2YY134–139; Drake, *Life of Tecumseh*, 61–62, 67–69; Tucker, *Tecumseh*, 37.

6. Tecumseh Papers, Draper Manuscripts, 1YY14–15; Tucker, *Tecumseh*, 89; Drake, *Life of Tecumseh*, 62.

7. Tecumseh File, Fort Malden Historic Park; Drake, *Life of Tecumseh*, 81–83.

8. "Anthony Shane's Statement," 1821, Tecumseh Papers, Draper Manuscripts, 12YY44–67; Harry Emilius Stocker, *A History of the Moravian Mission among the Indians on the White River in Indiana* (Bethlehem, Pa: Times Publishing, 1917), 105.

9. Tecumseh Papers, Draper Manuscripts, 1YY95, 3YY112–115, 4YY62; Thomas Forsyth Papers, ibid., 9T51–54; Drake, *Life of Tecumseh*, 86. For a description of Lalawethika's discussion of Shawnee medical practices, see Kinietz and Wheeler-Voegelin, *Shawnese Traditions*, 35–36. Lalawethika's admission of his alcoholism can be found in Paul Radin, *The Winnebago Tribe* (Lincoln: University of Nebraska Press, 1970), 22–23.

10. Lossing, *Pictorial Field-Book*, 189; Wilson D. Wallis, *Messiahs: Their Role in Civilizations* (Washington: American Council on Public Affairs, 1943), 107; Kinietz and Wheeler-Voegelin, *Shawnese Traditions*, 24.

11. James Mooney, *The Ghost Dance Religion and the Sioux Outbreak of 1890*, Fourteenth Annual Report of the Bureau of American Ethnology 2 pts. (Washington, D.C.: Bureau of American Ethnology, 1896), 2:672–73; Lossing, *Pictorial Field-Book*, 188–89; Kinietz and Wheeler-Voegelin, *Shawnese Traditions*, 41–42; Drake, *Life of Tecumseh*, 87. A slightly different description of Lalawethika's vision can be found in MacLean, "Shaker Mission," 223–24. The impact of Christian theology on Lalawethika's description of hell is obvious.

12. The George Winter Papers, Tippecanoe County Historical Society, Lafayette, Indiana; MacLean, "Shaker Mission," 224. Also see C. F. Voegelin and E. Wheeler-Voegelin, "Shawnee Name Groups," *American Anthropologist* 37 (October 1935): 626.

13. Entries for July 18–28, 1805, Diary of the Little Indian Con-

gregation on the White River for the Year 1805, *Indiana Historical Collections* 23:368–69; J. P. Kluge to Brother Loskiel, September 17, 1805, ibid., 543–45; MacLean, "Shaker Mission," 224.

14. Entry for December 3, 1805, Diary of the Little Indian Congregation on the White River for the Year 1805, *Indiana Historical Collections* 23:392; Thatcher, *Indian Biography*, 204; Mooney, *The Ghost Dance* 2:672; Drake, *Life of Tecumseh*, 87.

15. Thomas Forsyth to William Clark, January 15, 1827, Forsyth Papers, Draper Manuscripts, 9T51–54; Tecumseh Papers, ibid., 2YY25; John Tanner, *Narrative of the Captivity and Adventures of John Tanner during Thirty years Residence among the Indians in the Interior of North America* (New York: G. C. H. Carvill, 1830), 156–57.

16. Forsyth to Clark, January 15, 1827, Forsyth Papers, Draper Manuscripts, 9T51–54; Tanner, *Narrative*, 155–56; Mooney, *The Ghost Dance*, 2:677; Howard, *Shawnee*, 204–7.

17. Tecumseh Papers, Draper Manuscripts, 6YY123; William H. Keating, *Narrative of an Expedition to the Source of St. Peters River*, 2 vols. (London: George S. Whittaker, 1825), 2:230–31; Substance of a Talk by Le Maigouis, May 4, 1807, Letters Received by the Secretary of War, Unregistered Series, National Archives, M222, roll 2, 859–61 (microfilm).

18. Speech by Le Maigouis, May 4, 1807, M222, roll 2, 859–61, National Archives; Mooney, *The Ghost Dance*, 672.

19. Forsyth to Clark, January 15, 1827, Forsyth Papers, Draper Manuscripts, 9T51–54; Speech by Le Maigouis, May 4, 1807, M222, roll 2, 859–61, National Archives.

20. Entry for December 3, 1805, Diary of the Little Indian Congregation on the White River for the Year 1805, *Indiana Historical Collections* 23:392; Speech by Le Maigouis, May 4, 1807, M222, roll 2, 859–61, National Archives. Also see Henry Schoolcraft, *Discourse Delivered before the Historical Society of Michigan* (Detroit: G. L. Whitney, 1830).

21. Forsyth to Clark, January 15, 1827, Forsyth Papers, Draper Manuscripts, 9T51–54; Kinnietz and Wheeler-Voegelin, *Shawnese Traditions*, 3; Speech by Le Maigouis, May 4, 1807, M222, roll 2, 859–61, National Archives; Deposition by Joseph Watson, July 8, 1807, M221, roll 9, 2808, National Archives.

22. Stocker, *History of the Moravian Mission*, 106; Speech by Le Maigouis, May 4, 1807, M222, roll 2, 859–61, National Archives.

23. Forsyth to Clark, January 15, 1827, Forsyth Papers, Draper Manuscripts, 9T51–54; Speech by Le Maigouis, May 4, 1897, M222, roll 2, 859–61, National Archives.

24. Schutz, "Shawnee Myth," 178–79, 235; Forsyth to Clark,

January 15, 1827, Forsyth Papers, Draper Manuscripts, 9T51–54.

25. Tecumseh Papers, Draper Manuscripts, 6YY123; Maclean, "Shaker Mission," 224–25; Tanner, *Narrative*, 157; Speech by Le Maigouis, May 4, 1807, M222, roll 2, 859–61, National Archives.

26. Entry for December 3, 1805, Diary of the Little Indian Congregation on the White River for the Year 1805, *Indiana Historical Collections*, 23:392. Much of Tenskwatawa's teachings resemble the initial doctrines of the Seneca visionary Handsome Lake. Handsome Lake experienced a vision in 1799 that provided him with apocalyptic insight into the problems besetting the Senecas, and he too instructed his followers to return to the old ways. But in 1801 Handsome Lake espoused a new doctrine, urging his disciples to adopt many tenets of American culture. Handsome Lake's influence on Tenskwatawa, if any, is hard to ascertain. There is no evidence to suggest that the Seneca's followers made any attempts to spread the faith among the Shawnees, although some of the latter may have visited him in New York. In the years preceding the War of 1812 Handsome Lake joined with other Iroquois leaders to oppose Tenskwatawa and Tecumseh. Tenskwatawa also may have been influenced by the doctrines of Neolin, the Delaware Prophet, who was active just before Pontiac's Rebellion. Regardless of these peripheral influences, Tenskwatawa's teachings fit into a pattern of Native American revitalization characterized by the activities of all of the above, and by the doctrines of Wovoka, the Paiute prophet of the 1890s. See Wallace, *The Death and Rebirth of the Seneca*, 117–21, 239–302, and Mooney, *The Ghost Dance*, passim.

Chapter Three

1. Entry for January 25, 1806, Diary of the Little Indian Congregation on the White River for the Year 1806, *Indiana Historical Collections*, 23:401–3. For a good survey of Delaware history, see Clifton A. Weslager, *The Delaware Indians: A History* (New Brunswick: Rutgers University Press, 1972).

2. "Autobiography of Abraham Luckenbach," in *Indiana Historical Collections*, 23:618.

3. Entry for March 16, 1806, Diary of the Little Indian Congregation on the White River for the Year 1806, ibid., 414.

4. Ibid., 415; Stocker, *History of the Moravian Mission*, 115.

5. J. P. Kluge to Brother Loskiel, April 1, 1806, *Indiana Historical Collections*, 23:558; Drake, *Life of Tecumseh*, 88.

6. Entry for March 17, 1806, Diary of the Little Indian Congregation on the White River for the Year 1806, *Indiana Historical Collections*, 23:415–16; John Heckewelder, *A Narrative of the Mission of the United Brethren among the Delaware and Mohegan Indians, from Its Commencement, in the Year 1740, to the Close of the Year 1808* (New York: Arno Press, 1971), 410–11.

7. Heckewelder, *Narrative*, 413–15; "Autobiography of Abraham Luckenbach," *Indiana Historical Collections*, 23:620–21; Kluge to Loskiel, April 1, 1806, ibid., 557–61.

8. Stocker, *History of the Moravian Mission*, 115; Thatcher, *Indian Biography*, 198.

9. George Winter Papers, Tippecanoe County Historical Society; Entries for April 1, 9–10, 1806, Diary of the Little Indian Congregation on the White River for the Year 1806, *Indiana Historical Collections*, 23:420; Stocker, *History of the Moravian Mission*, 116.

10. Entry for May 13, 1806, in Joseph Badger, *A Memoir of Joseph Badger* (Hudson, Ohio: Sawyer, Ingersoll and Co., 1851), 145; Basil Meek, "Tarhe—The Crane," *Ohio Archaeological and Historical Society Publications* 20 (January 1911): 67.

11. Harrison to the Delawares, 1806, Esarey, *Harrison Letters*, 1:182–84; "On the Prophet," George Winter Papers, Tippecanoe County Historical Society; Entry for April 18, 1806, Diary of the Little Indian Congregation on the White River for the Year 1806, *Indiana Historical Collections*, 23:421–22.

12. Entry for April 18, 1806, Diary of the Little Indian Congregation on the White River for the Year 1806, *Indiana Historical Collections*, 23:422; "Autobiography of Abraham Lukenbach," ibid., 623.

13. Tucker, *Tecumseh*, 99; Kinietz and Wheeler-Voegelein, *Shawnese Traditions*, 37.

14. "On the Prophet," George Winter Papers, Tippecanoe County Historical Society; Mooney, *The Ghost Dance Religion*, 2:674; Drake, *Life of Tecumseh*, 91; Entry for June 16, 1806, in Badger, *Memoir*, 147.

15. These treaties can be found in Charles J. Kappler, ed., *Indian Affairs, Laws and Treaties*, 2 vols. (Washington, D.C.: Government Printing Office, 1904), 2:70–95. Also see Jacques Lasselle to Jefferson, June 12, 1806, Carter, *Territorial Papers*, 10:59–62; Memorandum of a council held at Saginaw, June 5, 1807, M221, roll 8, 2504, National Archives.

16. Dawson, *Historical Narrative*, 85–87; Harrison to the Kickapoos, July, 1806, Esarey, *Harrison Letters*, 1:193–94; Wells to Harrison, August 20, 1807, ibid., 239–42.

17. William Wells to the Secretary of War, April 25, 1807, Potawatomi File, Great Lakes Indian Archives; Simon Kenton, James McPherson, James Reed, and William Ward to the Governor, 1807, ibid.; Charles Reaume to J. Dunham, June 4, 1807, M221, roll 6, 1805, National Archives; William Wells to Henry Dearborn, August 14, 1807, ibid., roll 15, 4727–28.

18. Wells to the Secretary of War, April 19, 1807, Ottawa File, Great Lakes Indian Archives; Wells to the Secretary of War, April 25, 1807, ibid.; Josiah Dunham to Hull, May 20, 1807, *Michigan Historical Collections*, 40:123–26.

19. Dunham to Hull, May 20, 1807, *Michigan Historical Collections*, 40:123–26; Speech by Le Maigouis, May 4, 1807, M222, roll 2, 859–61, National Archives.

20. Dunham to the Ottawas and Chippewas, May 25, 1807, Ottawa File, Great Lakes Indian Archives; Dunham to Dearborn, June 12, 1807, ibid.; Dunham to Hull, May 20, 1807, *Michigan Historical Collections*, 40:123–26; Hull to Dearborn, June 22, 1807, ibid., 139–42; Charles Askin to John Askin, September 1, 1807, in Milo M. Quaife, ed., *The John Askin Papers*, 2 vols. (Detroit: Detroit Library Commission, 1928–31), 2:568–69.

21. Dunham to Dearborn, June 12, 1807, M221, roll 6, 1808–9, National Archives; Dunham to Dearborn, June 18, 1807, ibid., roll 8, 2508; Speech by Kawachawan, August 24, 1807, ibid., 2550.

22. Schoolcraft, *Discourse*, 103–6; Speech by Le Maigouis, May 4, 1807, M222, roll 2, 859–61, National Archives.

23. William W. Warren, *History of the Ojibway Nation* (Minneapolis: Ross and Haines, 1957), 322–23; Tanner, *Narrative*, 155–58; Edmund J. Danziger, Jr., *The Chippewas of Lake Superior* (Norman: University of Oklahoma Press, 1978), 65–66.

24. Wells to the Secretary of War, August 8, 1807, M221, roll 15, 4732, National Archives; Charles Jouett to Secretary of War, December 7, 1807, M221, roll 9, 2819–20, ibid.; Harrison to Secretary of War, May 19, 1808, Esarey, *Harrison Letters*, 1:290–91; Wells to Dearborn, May 26, 1808, M222, roll 3, 1500, National Archives.

25. Charles Reaume to Dunham, June 4, 1807, M221, roll 6, 1805, National Archives; Jouett to the Secretary of War, December 1, 1807, Carter, *Territorial Papers*, 7:496–97; "Minutes of a Talk given by the Indian Chief near Greenville, September 13, 1807, Mr. Stephen Riddle, Interpreter, delivered by Blue Jacket," Miscellaneous Manuscripts, Ohio Historical Society, Columbus; Louis Phelps Kellogg, *The British Regime in Wisconsin and the Old Northwest* (New York: Da Capo Press, 1971), 274–75.

26. Jouett to the Secretary of War, August 22, 1807, Carter, *Territorial Papers*, 7:472–73; Jouett to the Secretary of War, ibid., 496–97. Also see Radin, *The Winnebago Tribe*, 21–22, and Kellogg, *The British Regime*, 272–73.

27. Frederick Bates to Thomas Hunt, July 27, 1807, Indian Papers, Missouri Historical Society; Wells to Harrison, August 20, 1807, Esarey, *Harrison Letters*, 1:239–43; "Minutes of a talk given by the Indian Chief near Greenville, September 13, 1807, Mr. Stephen Ruddle, Interpreter, delivered by Blue Jacket," Miscellaneous Manuscripts, Ohio Historical Society.

28. Erastus Granger to Dearborn, August 18, 1807, M221, roll 7, 2277, National Archives; Granger to Dearborn, August 25, 1807, in Louis L. Babcock, *The War of 1812 on the Niagara Frontier* (Buffalo: Buffalo Historical Society, 1927), 23–24. Also see Wallace, *Death and Rebirth of the Seneca*, 294.

29. Richard McNemar, *The Kentucky revival, or a short history of the extraordinary out-pouring of the Spirit of God, in the Western States of America* (Albany: E. and E. Hosford, 1808), 111–18; Radin, *The Winnebago Tribe*, 22–24.

30. Harlow Lindley, "The Quaker Contribution to the Old Northwest," (MS), Society of Friends Records, Ohio Historical Society, Columbus; McLean, "Shaker Mission," 221–26; McNemar, *The Kentucky revival*, 119.

31. McLean, "Shaker Mission," 226–29; McNemar, *The Kentucky revival*, 117–19; Wells to Dearborn, July 14, 1807, Carter, *Territorial Papers*, 7:465–66.

32. Depositions by Charles McIlvane, February 16, 1806, Simon Kenton Papers, Draper Manuscripts, 7BB25; Edward Tiffin to the Indians, February 19, 1806, ibid., 7BB28; "Reply to the Governor," March 20, 1806, ibid., 7BB31.

33. Joseph Vance to Benjamin Drake, n.d., Tecumseh Papers, Draper Manuscripts, 2YY108–109; Simon Kenton Papers, ibid., 10BB2; Speech by the Indians, August 11, 1806, Tecumseh Papers, ibid., 3YY60.

34. Drake, *Life of Tecumseh*, 86–92; Anthony Shane's Statement, Tecumseh Papers, Draper Manuscripts, 12YY44–67; J. M. Ruddell to Draper, November 15, 1884, ibid., 8YY43.

35. Wells to the Secretary of War, April 19, 1807, Ottawa File, Great Lakes Indian Archives; Wells to the Secretary of War, April 25, 1807, ibid.

36. Wells to the Secretary of War, April 19, 1807, Ottawa File, Great Lakes Indian Archives; Jefferson to the Chiefs of the Shaw-

nee Nation, February 19, 1807, Lipscomb, *Writings of Jefferson,* 16:421–25; Kirk to Dearborn, July 20, 1807, M221, roll 9, 2874–78, National Archives.

37. Anthony Shane's Statement, 1821, Tecumseh Papers, Draper Manuscripts, 12YY44–67.

38. Ibid.; Wells to the Shawnees at Greenville, April 22, 1807, Shawnee File, Great Lakes Indian Archives.

39. Anthony Shane's Statement, 1821, Tecumseh Papers, Draper Manuscripts, 12YY44–67. William Wells, a white man, had been taken captive by the Miami Indians in Kentucky and raised from childhood by members of the tribe. He was the son-in-law of the noted Miami chief, Little Turtle. See Woehrmann, *Headwaters of the Maumee,* 144–45.

40. Wells to the Secretary of War, June 4, 1807, M221, roll 15, 4662, National Archives; Wells to the Secretary of War, July 14, 1807, ibid., 4710; Wells to the Secretary of War, August 4, 1807, ibid., 4732; Wells to the Secretary of War, August 20, 1807, ibid., roll 8, 2558.

41. Joseph Vance to Benjamin Drake, n.d., Tecumseh Papers, Draper Manuscripts, 2YY108–117; Petition by the citizens of Staunton, July 8, 1807, M221, roll 15, 4728–29, National Archives.

42. Joseph Vance to Benjamin Drake, n.d., Tecumseh Papers, Draper Manuscripts, 2YY108–117; Tecumseh Papers, ibid., 3YY134–136; Simon Kenton Papers, ibid., 9BB1. There is much confusion over the date of the conference at Springfield. Drake places it in the fall of 1807, and Tucker states that it took place in September 1806. Both historians, however, rely on the reminiscences of white observers recorded over a third of a century after the events took place. A close examination of contemporary accounts indicates that the conference was held during late June 1807. See William Kirk to Henry Dearborn, July 7, 1807, M221, roll 9, 2874–78, National Archives; Speech by Roundhead, June 6, 1807, Tecumseh Papers, Draper Manuscripts, 3YY72–73; and Black Hoof and Black Snake to Edward Tiffin, June 28, 1807, Edward Tiffin Papers, Ohio Historical Society, Box 1, folder 4 (microfilm).

43. Hull to Dearborn, September 9, 1807, *Michigan Historical Collections,* 40:197–200; Black Hoof and other Shawnee chiefs to the President, December 8, 1807, Shawnee File, Great Lakes Indian Archives.

44. Joseph Vance to Benjamin Drake, n.d., Tecumseh Papers, Draper Manuscripts, 2YY108–117. Drake, *Life of Tecumseh,* 94. Another delegation of whites led by Simon Kenton attempted to

visit Greenville during late August 1807, but turned back after meeting with white traders. See Kenton et al. to Kirker, September 5, 1807, Simon Kenton Papers, Draper Manuscripts, 7BB45.

45. "Minutes of a talk given by the Indian Chief near Greenville, September 13, 1807, Mr. Stephen Ruddle, Interpreter, delivered by Blue Jacket," Miscellaneous Manuscripts, Ohio Historical Society; Thomas Worthington and Duncan MacArthur to Kirker, September 22, 1807, Simon Kenton Papers, Draper Manuscripts, 7BB48.

46. Worthington and MacArthur to Kirker, September 22, 1807, Simon Kenton Papers, Draper Manuscripts, 7BB48; Drake, *Life of Tecumseh*, 96–97.

47. Harrison to the Secretary of War, September 5, 1807, William Henry Harrison Papers, Burton Collection, Detroit Public Library; Harrison to the Shawnees, August 1807, Esarey, *Harrison Letters*, 1:249–51.

48. The Prophet to Harrison, [September] 1807, Esarey, *Harrison Letters*, 1:251. Although this speech is tentatively dated in August 1807, it obviously was delivered in September. Also see Dawson, *Historical Narrative*, 101–3.

49. The correspondence of Wells and Harrison as well as that of other U.S. officials generally accuses the Prophet of being a British agent. See Wells to Dearborn, August 14, 1807, M221, roll 15, 4727–28, National Archives; Wells to Dearborn, December 5, 1807, ibid., 4856; Wells to Harrison, August 20, 1807, Esarey, *Harrison Letters*, 1:239–43; Harrison to Jefferson, July 11, 1807, Harrison Papers, Burton Collection, Detroit Public Library; Hull to Dearborn, June 22, 1807, M221, roll 8, 2494–95, National Archives.

50. Thomas McKee to William Halton, June 11, 1807, Administrative Records of the Imperial Government, Records of the Governor General and Lieutenant Governors, Upper Canada, Civil Control, Public Archives of Canada, Ottawa, Record Group 10, 2:628; William Claus to John Johnston, November 2, 1807, William Claus Papers, Manuscript Group 19, 9:161, Public Archives of Canada. Hereafter material from these particular record and manuscript groups will be cited by group number. Also see Speech by Kawachawon, August 24, 1807, M221, roll 8, 2550, National Archives.

51. James Henry Craig to Wm. Thornton, December 6, 1807, British Colonial Office Records, Series 42, 136:153–58 (microfilm); Francis Gore to Craig, January 5, 1808, ibid., 167. Hereafter material from the British Colonial Records will be cited by series, volume, and page number (CO 42/136:153–58). Also see Claus to Gore,

February 27, 1808, Claus Papers, MG 19, 9:177–81.

52. R. David Edmunds, *The Potawatomis: Keepers of the Fire* (Norman: University of Oklahoma Press, 1978), 166.

53. Thomas Forsyth to William Clark, January 15, 1827, Forsyth Papers, Draper Manuscripts, 9T53; Tecumseh Papers, ibid., 8YY54.

54. Wells to Dearborn, January 7, 1808, M221, roll 15, 4881, National Archives; Wells to Dearborn, April 20, 1808, Carter, *Territorial Papers*, 7:555–60.

55. Wells to Dearborn, January 23, 1808, M221, roll 15, 4885, National Archives; Wells to Dearborn, March 6, 1808, M221, roll 15, 4935, ibid.; Hendrick Aupaumut to Wells, February 26, 1808, Shawnee File, Great Lakes Indian Archives; Wells to Dearborn, April 20, 1808, Carter, *Territorial Papers*, 7:555–60.

Chapter Four

1. Wells to the Secretary of War, April 22, 1808, Carter, *Territorial Papers*, 7:558–60.

2. Ibid.; Wells to Dearborn, January 23, 1808, M221, roll 15, 4885, National Archives.

3. Worthington and MacArthur to Kirker, September 22, 1807, Simon Kenton Papers, Draper Manuscripts, 7BB48; Wells to the Secretary of War, April 22, 1808, Carter, *Territorial Papers*, 7:558–60; Harrison to the Secretary of War, February 18, 1808, Esarey, *Harrison Letters*, 1:283–84.

4. William Kirk to Dearborn, April 12, 1808, M221, roll 25, 8114–15, National Archives; Statement by John Conner, June 18, 1808, ibid., roll 33, 1016–17.

5. Wells to the Secretary of War, April 22, 1808, Carter, *Territorial Papers*, 7:558–60.

6. Ibid.

7. William Claus to Lieutenant Prideaux Selby, May 3, 1808, A. B. Farney Papers, Fort Malden Historic Park, Amherstburg; Wells to John Gerrard, August 22, 1807, Simon Kenton Papers, Draper Manuscripts, 7BB44.

8. Entry for May 16, 1808, Diary of William Claus, Claus Papers, MG 19, 9:198–99, Public Archives of Canada.

9. Entries for June 10–July 15, 1808, Diary of William Claus, ibid., 206–15; Francis Gore to James Craig, July 27, 1808, Record Group 10, vol. 2 (unnumbered), Public Archives of Canada.

10. James Craig to Lord Castlereagh, July 15, 1808, British Colonial Records, CO 42/136:157–62.

11. David Turpie, *Sketches of My Own Times* (Indianapolis: Bobbs Merrill, 1903), 170–72.

12. Wells to the Secretary of War, June 5, 1808, Shawnee File, Great Lakes Indian Archives; Statement by John Conner, June 18, 1808, M221, roll 23, 1016–17, National Archives.

13. The Prophet to Harrison, June 24, 1808, Esarey, *Harrison Letters*, 1:291–92.

14. Harrison to the Prophet, June 24, 1808, ibid., 292–94.

15. Speech by the Indians, June 24, 1808, ibid., 294–95; Harrison to Dearborn, July 12, 1808, M221, roll 23, 7327, National Archives.

16. Speech by the Prophet, August, 1808, Esarey, *Harrison Letters*, 1:299–300.

17. Dawson, *Historical Narrative*, 107–9; Harrison to Dearborn, September 1, 1808, Esarey, *Harrison Letters*, 1:302; Harrison to Dearborn, February 14, 1809, M221, roll 23, 7538, National Archives.

18. Harrison to Dearborn, May 19, 1808, Esarey, *Harrison Letters*, 1:290–91; Dawson, *Historical Narrative*, 106.

19. Harrison to Dearborn, November 9, 1808, Esarey, *Harrison Letters*, 1:321; Harrison to Dearborn, February 14, 1809, M221, roll 23, 7538, National Archives; Edmunds, *The Potawatomis*, 167–68.

20. Wells to Dearborn, March 31, 1809, Shawnee File, Great Lakes Indian Archives; Wells to Harrison, April 8, 1809, M221, roll 23, 7570, National Archives; Matthew Elliott to Major Hulton, May 19, 1809, Record Group 10, 3:990, Public Archives of Canada.

21. Hull to William Eustis, June 16, 1809, Shawnee File, Great Lakes Indian Archives; Harrison to the Secretary of War, April 26, 1809, M221, roll 23, 7581, National Archives.

22. Hull to Eustis, June 16, 1809, Shawnee File, Great Lakes Indian Archives; Harrison to the Secretary of War, April 26, 1809, M221, roll 23, 7581, National Archives. There is some confusion over the number of Shawnees killed. Harrison reported that only the woman was murdered, but the Ottawas and Chippewas informed Hull that they had killed both the woman the her child.

23. Harrison to the Secretary of War, May 3, 1809, Esarey, *Harrison Letters*, 1:344–45.

24. Hull to Eustis, June 16, 1809, Shawnee File, Great Lakes Indian Archives; Hull to Eustis, August 2, 1809, ibid.

25. Alpha Kingsley to the Secretary of War, April 18, 1809, M221, roll 20, 6175, National Archives; William Clark to the Secretary of

War, April 29, 1809, ibid., 6209–10; Harrison to the Secretary of War, May 3, 1809, Esarey, *Harrison Letters*, 1:344–45; Harrison to John Johnston, July 8, 1809, Jones Collection, Cincinnati Historical Society.

26. Johnston to the Prophet, May 3, 1809, in Thornbrough, *Letter Book*, 49–50; entries for May 25–26, 1809, in ibid., 52; Johnston to William Eustis, July 1, 1809, M221, roll 24, 8062, National Archives.

27. Harrison to the Secretary of War, May 3, 1809, Esarey, *Harrison Letters*, 1:344–45; Harrison to the Secretary of War, May 16, 1809, ibid., 346–47.

28. Harrison to the Secretary of War, July 5, 1809, ibid., 349–55; Harrison to Johnston, July 8, 1809, Jones Collection, Cincinnati Historical Society.

29. Harrison to the Secretary of War, May 16, 1809, Esarey, *Harrison Letters*, 1:346–47; Harrison to the Secretary of War, August 29, 1809, Carter, *Territorial Papers*, 7:670–71; Harrison to Johnston, July 8, 1809, Jones Collection, Cincinnati Historical Society; Secretary of War to Harrison, July 15, 1809, Letters Sent by the Secretary of War Relating to Indian Affairs, National Archives, M6, roll 4, 103 (microfilm).

30. "Journal of the Proceedings at the Indian Treaty at Fort Wayne and Vincennes, September 1 to October 27, 1809," in Esarey, *Harrison Letters*, 1:362–78; "Correct Number of the Indians that attended the treaty of Fort Wayne in September, 1809," December 5, 1809, M221, roll 33, 1579, National Archives; "A treaty between the United States . . . and the tribes of Indians," September 30, 1809, in Kappler, *Indian Affairs: Laws and Treaties*, 2:101–2.

31. Harrison to the Secretary of War, June 14, 1810, in Esarey, *Harrison Letters*, 1:422–30; Johnston to Harrison, October 14, 1810, ibid., 476–80; Harrison to the Secretary of War, December 24, 1810, ibid., 496–500; Johnston to Harrison, June 24, 1810, ibid.

32. Harrison to the Secretary of War, November 3, 1809, ibid., 387–91; Harrison to the Secretary of War, June 14, 1810, ibid. 422–30; *Western Sun* (Vincennes), June 23, 1810, 3, in Shawnee File, Great Lakes Indian Archives; Michael Brouillette to Harrison, June 30, 1810, ibid. Several of Tecumseh's biographers, including Tucker (*Tecumseh*, 131–33), state that both Tecumseh and the Prophet were absent from Indiana during the Treaty of Fort Wayne, soliciting support among the Iroquois. But such an assertion seems apocryphal and is based on a statement by Caleb Atwater, an early Ohio historian, who claimed that he accompanied the Shawnees, serving as their interpreter. In contrast, contemporary accounts make

no mention of either Tecumseh or the Prophet in New York at this time. See Caleb Atwater, *A History of the State of Ohio, Natural and Civil* (Cincinnati: Glezen and Shepard, 1838), 236; and Red Jacket to the Secretary of War, February 10, 1810, M271, roll 1, 529–35, National Archives.

33. Harrison to the Secretary of War, June 26, 1810, Esarey, *Harrison Letters*, 1:433–36; Brouillette to Harrison, June 30, 1810, Shawnee File, Great Lakes Indian Archives.

34. Harrison to the Secretary of War, April 25, 1810, Esarey, *Harrison Letters*, 1:417–19; Harrison to the Secretary of War, May 15, 1810, ibid., 420–22; James Rhea to Jacob Kingsbury, Jacob Kingsbury Papers, Burton Historical Collection, Detroit Public Library.

35. Entry for June 26, 1810, in Thomas Nuttall, "Thomas Nuttall's Travels in the Old Northwest; An Unpublished 1810 Diary," *Chronica Botanica* 14 (Autumn 1951): 57–58; Elliott to Claus, July 9, 1810, British Colonial Records, CO 42/143: 35–36; William Clark to the Secretary of War, July 20, 1810, M221, roll 35, 2577–80, National Archives; Johnston to the Secretary of War, July 25, 1810, M221, roll 38, 4621, ibid.

36. Johnston to Harrison, June 24, 1810, Esarey, *Harrison Letters*, 1:430–32; Johnston to the Secretary of War, July 3, 1810, M221, roll 38, 4614–15, National Archives; Leonard U. Hill, *John Johnston and the Indians in the Land of the Three Miamis* (Piqua, Ohio: Leonard Hill, 1957), 32–33.

37. Samuel Tupper to Eustis, November 13, 1809, M221, roll 32, 800, National Archives; Walk-in-the-Water to Hull, June 25, 1810, Lewis Cass Papers, William Clements Library, Ann Arbor, Michigan.

38. Harrison to the Secretary of War, June 14, 1810, Esarey, *Harrison Letters*, 1:422–30; Hull to Secretary of War, July 12, 1810, Shawnee File, Great Lakes Indian Archives.

39. Wyandots to Hull, n.d., Cass Papers, Clements Library; Wyandots to Hull, June 27, 1810, Shawnee File, Great Lakes Indian Archives; Badger, *Memoir*, 125; Entry for July, 1810, in "Nuttall's Travels," *Chronica Botanica*, 60. Also see William L. Curry, "The Wyandot Chief, Leather Lips," *Ohio Archaeological and Historical Publications*, 12 (January 1903): 30–36; and James B. Finley, *Life among the Indians* (Cincinnati: B. P. Thompson, 1860), 524–28.

40. Harrison to the Secretary of War, June 14, 1810, Esarey, *Harrison Letters*, 1:422–30; Johnston to Harrison, June 24, 1810, ibid., 430–32.

41. Harrison to the Secretary of War, June 14, 1810, ibid., 422–30; Brouillette to Harrison, June 30, 1810, ibid., 436–37; Edmunds, *The Potawatomis*, 181, 183.

42. Harrison to the Secretary of War, July 4, 1810, Esarey, *Harrison Letters*, 1:438–40; John B. Dillon, *A History of Indiana* (Indianapolis: Bingham and Doughty, 1859), 441.

43. Harrison to the Secretary of War, July 11, 1810, Esarey, *Harrison Letters*, 1:444–45; Harrison to the Secretary of War, July 18, 1810, ibid., 446–47; Harrison to the Secretary of War, July 25, 1810; ibid., 449–53.

44. Harrison to the Secretary of War, July 18, 1810, ibid., 446–47; Harrison to the Secretary of War, August 6, 1810, ibid., 456–59; Lossing, *Pictorial Field-Book*, 191; "On the Prophet," George Winter Papers, Tippecanoe County Historical Society.

45. Harrison to the Prophet, July 19, 1810, Esarey, *Harrison Letters*, 1:447–48.

46. *Western Sun* (Vincennes), August 4, 1810, in Shawnee File, Great Lakes Indian Archives; Harrison to the Secretary of War, August 6, 1810, Esarey, *Harrison Letters*, 1:456–59.

47. Harrison to the Secretary of War, August 22, 1810, Esarey, *Harrison Letters*, 1:459–69; Drake, *Life of Tecumseh*, 126–28. Estimates of the number of Indians accompanying Tecumseh to Vincennes vary greatly. Drake, supposedly quoting a contemporary account, lists 400. Yet the editor of the Vincennes *Western Sun*, who took "some pains to inform himself of the substance of what [had] passed at the Councils," reported on August 25 that Tecumseh was "accompanied by about 75 warriors." The latter number seems more accurate. See Drake, *Life of Tecumseh*, 125; and *Western Sun* (Vincennes), August 25, 1810, in Shawnee File, Great Lakes Indian Archives. Tucker claims that Tenskwatawa accompanied Tecumseh, but the Prophet is not mentioned in any contemporary accounts. See Tucker, *Tecumseh*, 159.

48. Harrison to the Secretary of War, August 22, 1810, Esarey, *Harrison Letters*, 1:459–69; Drake, *Life of Tecumseh*, 125–28.

49. Harrison to the Secretary of War, August 22, 1810, Esarey, *Harrison Letters*, 1:459–69; Drake, *Life of Tecumseh*, 129–30.

50. Harrison to the Secretary of War, August 22, 1810, Esarey, *Harrison Letters*, 1:459–69; J. M. Ruddell to Lyman Draper, November 15, 1884, Tecumseh Papers, 8YY43, Draper Manuscripts.

51. Harrison to the Secretary of War, August 6, 1810, Esarey, *Harrison Letters*, 1:456–59.

Chapter Five

1. Harrison to the Secretary of War, October 5, 1810, Esarey, *Harrison Letters*, 1:474–75; Harrison to the Secretary of War, Oc-

tober 17, 1810, ibid., 480–81; Harrison to Jared Mansfield, September 25, 1810, Carter, *Territorial Papers*, 8:48.

2. Speech by Tecumseh, August 20, 1810, Esarey, *Harrison Letters*, 1:463–69; Harrison to the Secretary of War, October 17, 1810, ibid., 480–81; Hull to the Secretary of War, October 4, 1810, Shawnee File, Great Lakes Indian Archives.

3. Speech by Red Jacket, September 24, 1810, Shawnee File, Great Lakes Indian Archives; Chiefs of the Council at Brownstown to the "several Nations we represent," September 26, 1810, ibid.; Chiefs at the Council at Brownstown to the Shawnee, September 26, 1810, ibid.; Hull to the Secretary of War, October 4, 1810, ibid.

4. Johnston to William Eustis, October 20, 1810, ibid.; Johnston to Harrison, October 14, 1810, Esarey, *Harrison Letters*, 1:476–80.

5. Elliott to Claus, October 16, 1810, British Colonial Records, CO 42/143:137–38; Elliott to Claus, November 16, 1810, ibid., 41–42; Francis Gore to Craig, March 2, 1811, ibid., 69–70; Harrison to the Secretary of War, December 24, 1810, Esarey, *Harrison Letters*, 1:496–500.

6. Harrison to the Secretary of War, August 28, 1810, Esarey, *Harrison Letters*, 1:470–71; Nicholas Bolivin to the Secretary of War, August 30, 1810, Carter, *Territorial Papers*, 14:410–11; J. Wetherell to Thomas Palmer, October 13, 1810, in Nuttall, "Nuttall's Travels," 60–61; Hull to Johnston, September 27, 1810, Thornbrough, *Letter Book*, 83–86.

7. Speech by Tecumseh, November 1810, Tecumseh File, Fort Malden Historical Park; Elliott to Claus, November 18, 1810, Farney Papers, ibid.; Elliott to Claus, November 16, 1810, British Colonial Records, CO 42/143:41–42.

8. Gore to Claus, February 2, 1811, British Colonial Records, CO 42/143:71–72; Gore to Claus, February 26, 1811, *Michigan Historical Collections*, 25:282; Craig to the Earl of Liverpool, March 29, 1811, William Wood, ed., *Select British Documents of the War of 1812*, 3 vols. (Toronto: Champlain Society, 1920–26), 1:164–65.

9. Harrison to Eustis, November 7, 1811, Shawnee File, Great Lakes Indian Archives; Harrison to Eustis, January 21, 1811, ibid.; Harrison to Eustis, April 23, 1811, Esarey, *Harrison Letters*, 1:506–10; Harrison to Eustis, June 6, 1811, ibid., 512–17. For a discussion of Wells's reappointment, see Woehrmann, *At the Headwaters of the Maumee*, 164–66.

10. Edmunds, *The Potawatomis*, 173–75; Thomas Forsyth to William Clark, January 1, 1827, Thomas Forsyth Papers, Missouri Historical Society; Harrison to Clark, June 19, 1811, Esarey, *Harrison Letters*, 1:519–21; Harrison to Secretary of War, July 10, 1811, ibid., 532–35.

11. Speech of Monsegoa, May 1, 1811, M221, roll 38, 2892–97, National Archives; John Shaw to Johnston, August 18, 1811, ibid., roll 38, 4625–26; Harrison to the Secretary of War, June 19, 1811, Esarey, *Harrison Letters* 1:518–19. Also see John Bradbury, "Travels in the Interior of America in the Years 1809, 1810, and 1811," in Reuben G. Thwaites, ed., *Early Western Travels, 1748–1846*, 32 vols. (Cleveland: Arthur H. Clark, 1904–7), 5:227; and Carl F. Klinck and James J. Talman, eds., *The Journal of Major John Norton, 1816* (Toronto: Champlain Society, 1970), 286.

12. Harrison to the Secretary of War, April 23, 1811, Esarey, *Harrison Letters*, 1:506–10; Harrison to the Secretary of War, June 6, 1811, ibid., 512–17.

13. Harrison to the Secretary of War, June 6, 1811, ibid., 512–17.

14. Ibid.; Harrison to the Secretary of War, June 19, 1811, ibid., 518–19; Harrison to Clark, June 19, 1811, ibid., 519–21.

15. Harrison to Clark, June 19, 1811, ibid., 519–21; Harrison to the Secretary of War, June 19, 1811, ibid., 518–19; Harrison to Tecumseh, June 24, 1811, ibid., 522–24; Harrison to the Secretary of War, June 25, 1811, ibid., 524–26.

16. Tecumseh to Harrison, July 4, 1811, ibid., 529; Harrison to the Secretary of War, August 6, 1811, ibid., 542–46. Tecumseh had planned to recruit southern tribesmen into his confederacy at least as early as June 1810. See Harrison to the Secretary of War, June 26, 1810, ibid., 433–36.

17. Harrison to the Secretary of War, July 24, 1811, ibid., 537–38; Harrison to the Secretary of War, August 6, 1811, ibid., 542–46; Extract from the *Western Sun* (Vincennes), July 27, 1811, M221, roll 34, 2706, National Archives.

18. Harrison to the Secretary of War, August 6, 1811, Esarey, *Harrison Letters*, 1:542–46; Tecumseh Papers, Draper Manuscripts, 2YY24–36.

19. Harrison to Secretary of War, August 6, 1811, Esarey, *Harrison Letters*, 1:542–46.

20. Ibid.; Harrison to the Secretary of War, August 13, 1811, ibid., 554–55; Secretary of War to Harrison, July 17, 1811, ibid., 535–36; Secretary of War to Harrison, July 20, 1811, ibid., 536–37.

21. Harrison to the Secretary of War, August 7, 1811, ibid., 548–51; Harrison to the Secretary of War, September 17, 1811, ibid., 570–75; "The Battle of Tippecanoe," in Alameda McCollough, ed., *The Battle of Tippecanoe: Conflict of Cultures* (Lafayette: Tippecanoe County Historical Association, 1973), 5.

22. Speech by Little Chief, August 17, 1811, Shawnee File, Great Lakes Indian Archives; Harrison to the Miamis, Eel Rivers, and

Weas, September, 1811, ibid.; Hull to the Ottawas and other northern Indians, September 22, 1811, ibid.; Harrison to Johnston, August 6, 1811, William Henry Harrison Papers, Draper Manuscripts, 1X25.

23. Wesley Whickar, ed., "Shabonee's Account of Tippecanoe," *Indiana Magazine of History* 18 (December 1921): 355; Harrison to the Secretary of War, September 25, 1811, Esarey, *Harrison Letters*, 1:589–92; Harrison to the Secretary of War, September 17, 1811, ibid., 570–75; Report by Edward Hebert, August 1811, M221, roll 36, 3305, National Archives; Forsyth to Clark, November 1, 1811, Thomas Forsyth Papers, Missouri Historical Society.

24. Harrison to the Secretary of War, September 25, 1811, Esarey, *Harrison Letters*, 1:589–92; Harrison to the Secretary of War, October 13, 1811, ibid., 599–603; William Morrison to Joseph Stretch, October 5, 1811, M221, roll 35, 2991, National Archives.

25. Harrison to the Secretary of War, October 13, 1811, Esarey, *Harrison Letters*, 1:599–603; Harrison to Secretary of War, October 28, 1811, Harrison Papers, Draper Manuscripts, 1X38; Robert B. McAfee, *History of the Late War in the Western Country* (Lexington: Worsley and Smith, 1816), 19.

26. Harrison to the Secretary of War, October 13, 1811, Esarey, *Harrison Letters*, 1:599–603; Harrison to the Secretary of War, October 28, 1811, Harrison Papers, Draper Manuscripts, 1X38.

27. John McCoy to his wife, October 26, 1811, John McCoy Letters, Indiana Division, Indiana State Library, Indianapolis; James Miller to Ruth Miller, November 4, 1811, Benson J. Lossing Papers, Burton Historical Collection, Detroit Public Library; Entry for October 20, Adam Walker's Journal, Esarey, *Harrison Letters*, 1:699; Harrison to the Secretary of War, October 13, 1811, ibid., 599–603.

28. Harrison to the Secretary of War, November 2, 1811, Esarey, *Harrison Letters*, 1:606–7; Harrison to the Secretary of War, November 26, 1811, ibid., 648–52; Reed Beard, *The Battle of Tippecanoe* (Lafayette, Ind.: Tippecanoe Publishing, 1889), 54–56.

29. Harrison to the Secretary of War, November 2, 1811, Esarey, *Harrison Letters*, 1:606–7; Harrison to the Secretary of War, November 26, 1811, ibid., 649–52; Whickar, "Shabonee's Account of Tippecanoe," 355–56; Edmunds, *The Potawatomis*, 176.

30. Harrison to the Secretary of War, November 18, 1811, *American State Papers: Indian Affairs*, 1:776–78; Statement by Isaac Naylor, Battle of Tippecanoe—Eyewitness Account File, Tippecanoe Battle Ground Museum, Battleground, Indiana; McAfee, *History of the Late War*, 24–26.

31. Harrison to the Secretary of War, November 18, 1811, *Amer-*

ican State Papers: Indian Affairs, 1:776–78. Also see map in McCollough, *Battle of Tippecanoe*, 7.

32. Harrison to Charles Scott, December 13, 1811, Esarey, *Harrison Letters*, 1:666–72; Harrison to the Secretary of War, December 24, 1811, ibid., 683–85.

33. Report of a meeting between P. B. Whiteman and the Shawnees, December 4, 1811, Tecumseh Papers, Draper Manuscripts, 5YY8; Anthony Shane's Statement, ibid., 12YY8–30; Statement by Joseph Barron, Winter Papers, Tippecanoe County Historical Society; R. I. Snelling to Harrison, November 20, 1811, Esarey, *Harrison Letters*, 1:643–46. Also see Lossing, *Pictorial Field-Book*, 203–4; and Whickar, "Shabonee's Account of Tippecanoe," 358–59.

34. Statement by Isaac Naylor, Eyewitness Account File, Tippecanoe Battleground Museum; Whickar, "Shabonee's Account of Tippecanoe," 358.

35. Jonathan Boyd to Richard Cutts, December 16, 1811, A. G. Mitten Collection, Indiana Historical Society Library; Statement by Isaac Naylor, Eyewitness Account File, Tippecanoe Battleground Museum; Harrison to the Secretary of War, November 18, 1811, *American State Papers: Indian Affairs*, 1:776–78.

36. Harrison to Dr. John Scott, December 1811, Esarey, *Harrison Letters*, 1:689–92; Whickar, "Shabonee's Account of Tippecanoe," 359.

37. Harrison to the Secretary of War, November 18, 1811, *American State Papers: Indian Affairs*, 1:776–78; Florence G. Watts, ed., "Lieutenant Charles Larrabee's Account of the Battle of Tippecanoe, 1811," *Indiana Magazine of History* 57 (September 1961): 243–45.

38. Statement by Joseph Barron, Winter Papers, Tippecanoe Historical Society; Statement by Isaac Naylor, Eyewitness Account File, Tippecanoe Battleground Museum; Snelling to Harrison, November 20, 1811, Esarey, *Harrison Letters*, 1:643–46. Local traditions state that during the battle Tenskwatawa stood on a boulder about one and one-half miles northwest of the American camp, where he prayed and chanted until his warriors' retreat. It is very doubtful that the Prophet would have spent the battle at that location since he would have been vulnerable to an American sortie if his warriors had retreated. For more on the "Prophet's Rock," see McCollough, *Battle of Tippecanoe*, 26.

39. James Miller to Ruth Miller, December 6, 1811, Lossing Papers, Burton Collection, Detroit Public Library; Statement by Isaac Naylor, Eyewitness Account File, Tippecanoe Battleground Mu-

seum; Harrison to the Secretary of War, November 18, 1811, *American State Papers: Indian Affairs*, 1:776–78.

40. Harrison to the Secretary of War, November 8, 1811, Esarey, *Harrison Letters*, 1:614–15; Excerpt from the *Western Sun* (Vincennes), January 4, 1812, in ibid., 680; "A General Return of the Killed and Wounded," November 19, 1811, ibid., 637–43. Also see Alec Gilpin, *The War of 1812 in the Old Northwest* (East Lansing: Michigan State University Press, 1958), 18–19.

41. Horatio Stark to Daniel Bissell, March 8, 1812, M221, roll 42, 7812, National Archives; Johnston to Eustis, May 1, 1812, ibid., roll 46, 1056; James Neeley to Eustis, May 13, 1812, ibid., roll 47, 2238; John Askin to his son, April 27, 1812, John Askin Papers, Burton Collection, Detroit Public Library.

Chapter Six

1. Snelling to Harrison, November 20, 1811, Esarey, *Harrison Letters*, 1:643–46; Harrison to the Secretary of War, December 4, 1811, ibid., 656–58; James Miller to Ruth Miller, December 7, 1811, Lossing Papers, Burton Collection, Detroit Public Library; Hendrick Apaumat to Phillip Thomas, January 9, 1812, M221, roll 348, National Archives.

2. James Miller to Ruth Miller, December 17, 1811, Lossing Papers, Burton Collection, Detroit Public Library; James Miller to Ruth Miller, March 3, 1813, ibid.; Tecumseh Papers, Draper Manuscripts, 1YY38; Proceedings of a Council, June 6, 1812, in Milo M. Quaife, ed., *War on the Detroit: The Chronicles of Thomas Vercheres de Boucherville and the Capitulation by an Ohio Volunteer* (Chicago: Lakeside Press, 1940), 197–207.

3. Report of a meeting between P. B. Whiteman and the Shawnees, December 4, 1811, Tecumseh Papers, Draper Manuscripts, 5YY8; Wells to Johnston, December 3, 1811, M221, roll 49, 3686, National Archives; Johnston to Eustis, December 4, 1811, ibid., roll 46, 994–95; Wells to Eustis, December 20, 1811, ibid., roll 49, 3683.

4. Herbert C. Goltz, "Tecumseh, the Prophet and the Rise of the Northwest Indian Confederation" (Ph.D. dissertation, University of Western Ontario, 1973), 260–67; Drake, *Life of Tecumseh*, 143–45.

5. Goltz, "Tecumseh," 260–67.

6. There is considerable confusion over the date of Tecumseh's

return from the South, but see Little Turtle to Harrison, January 25, 1812, Esarey, *Harrison Letters*, 2:18–19, and Wells to Eustis, February 10, 1812, M221, roll 49, 3709, National Archives. Also see Drake, *Tecumseh*, 156, and Claus to Isaac Brock, June 10, 1812, Record Group 10, 3:1242, Public Archives of Canada.

7. Jacob Lalime to Benjamin Howard, February 4, 1812, Carter, *Territorial Papers*, 14:536–37; Edwards to the Secretary of War, March 3, 1812, ibid., 16:193–94; Thomas Fish and Enos Terry to Return J. Meigs, January 14, 1812, M221, roll 47, 1682–83, National Archives; Jacob Dunn Manuscript, Shawnee File, Great Lakes Indian Archives.

8. Wells to Eustis, February 10, 1812, M221, roll 49, 3709, National Archives; John Shaw to James Rhea, March 1, 1812, ibid., roll 48, 2772; Speech from Tecumseh delivered at Amherstburg, March 13, 1812, Deputy Superintendent General's Office, Correspondence, Record Group 10, 28:16512–13, Public Archives of Canada.

9. Eustis to Harrison, January 17, 1812, Letters Sent by the Secretary of War Relating to Indian Affairs, M15, roll 3, 68, National Archives; James Miller to Ruth Miller, March 3, 1812, Lossing Papers, Burton Collection, Detroit Public Library; Harrison to Eustis, March 4, 1812, Harrison Papers, Draper Manuscripts, 2X17.

10. Harrison to Eustis, March 4, 1812, Harrison Papers, Draper Manuscripts, 2X17; Harrison to Shaw, March 6, 1812, Shawnee File, Great Lakes Indian Archives.

11. Speeches at a council at Fort Wayne, April 18, 1812, Thornbrough, *Letter Book*, 108–10; Benjamin Stickney to Harrison, April 18, 1812, ibid., 102–8; Harrison to Eustis, April 14, 1812, Shawnee File, Great Lakes Indian Archives.

12. Reuben Attwater to William Eustis, January 21, 1812, Shawnee File, Great Lakes Indian Archives.

13. Harrison to Eustis, April 14, 1812, ibid.; Stickney to Hull, *American State Papers: Indian Affairs*, 1:810–11. For the role of the pro-American chiefs in this affair, see R. David Edmunds, "Redefining Red Patriotism: Five Medals of the Potawatomis," *Red River Valley Historical Review* 5 (Spring 1980): 22–23.

14. Speeches of the Indians at the Mississinewa, May 15, 1812, Esarey, *Harrison Papers*, 2:50–53.

15. Ibid.; Stickney to Hull, May 25, 1812, *American State Papers: Indians Affairs*, 1:810–11.

16. Stickney to Hull, May 25, 1812, *American State Papers: Indian Affairs*, 1:810–11; Claus to Brock, June 16, 1812, Farney Papers, Fort Malden Historical Park; Speech by Tecumseh, June 8,

1816, Wood, *British Documents*, 1:312–14. Also see George C. Chalou, "The Red Pawns Go to War: British-American Indian Relations, 1810–1815" (Ph.D. dissertation, University of Indiana, 1971), 58–61.

17. Harrison to the Secretary of War, April 29, 1812, Esarey, *Harrison Papers*, 2:41–44; Harrison to the Secretary of War, May 13, 1812, ibid., 48–49; Snelling to Harrison, April 16, 1812, ibid., 37–38; Edmunds, *The Potawatomis*, 178–81.

18. Forsyth to Clark, May 27, 1812, Thomas Forsyth Papers, Missouri Historical Society; Forsyth to Edwards, June 8, 1812, ibid.; Claus to Brock, June 16, 1812, Farney Papers, Fort Malden Historical Park; Stickney to Eustis, July 19, 1812, Shawnee File, Great Lakes Indian Archives; Samuel Hopkins to Isaac Shelby, November 27, 1812, Esarey, *Harrison Papers*, 2:231–34.

19. Stickney to Hull, June 20, 1812, Thornbrough, *Letter Book*, 140–43; Wells to Harrison, July 22, 1812, Esarey, *Harrison Papers*, 2:76–78; W. H. Merritt, "Journal of Events Principally on the Detroit and Niagara Frontiers," Wood, *British Documents*, 3:549.

20. Gilpin, *The War of 1812*, 23–61.

21. Declaration of Melsello, July 1812, Carter, *Territorial Papers*, 14:578–80; Ninian Edwards to the Secretary of War, July 21, 1812, ibid., 16:244–47; Edwards to Eustis, June 23, 1812, in Ninian W. Edwards, *History of Illinois from 1778 to 1833 and the Life and Times of Ninian Edwards* (New York: Arno Press, 1975), 327–28.

22. Wells to Harrison, July 23, 1812, Esarey, *Harrison Papers*, 2:76–78.

23. Stickney to the Secretary of War, July 19, 1812, Thornbrough, *Letter Book*, 161–65; Speech by the Shawnee Prophet, July 13, 1812, Lewis Cass Papers, William Clements Library.

24. Stickney to the Secretary of War, July 19, 1812, Thornbrough, *Letter Book*, 161–65; Stickney to Harrison, July 21, 1812, ibid., 167–69.

25. Stickney to the Secretary of War, July 19, 1812, ibid., 161–65; Wells to Harrison, July 23, 1812, Esarey, *Harrison Papers*, 2:76–78; Forsyth to Gibson, July 26, 1812, Shawnee File, Great Lakes Indian Archives.

26. Wells to Harrison, July 23, 1812, Esarey, *Harrison Papers*, 2:76–78; Harrison to the Secretary of War, August 12, 1812, Carter, *Territorial Papers*, 8:189–93; Gilpin, *The War of 1812*, 44–128, passim.

27. Stickney to Harrison, June 30, 1812, Thornbrough, *Letter Book*, 149–52; Taylor to Harrison, August 9, 1812, Esarey, *Harrison Papers*, 2:82–83; Harrison to Secretary of War, August 12, 1812,

Carter, *Territorial Papers*, 8:189–93; Forsyth to Howard, September 7, 1812, ibid., 16:261–65.

28. Taylor to Harrison, September 10, 1812, Esarey, *Harrison Papers*, 2:124–28.

29. Ibid.

30. Ibid.; Hiram Beckwith, *The Illinois and Indiana Indians* (Chicago: Fergus Printing, 1884), 134–35; McAfee, *History of the Late War*, 153–55.

31. Edmunds, *The Potawatomis*, 189–91; Harrison to the Secretary of War, October 13, 1812, Esarey, *Harrison Papers*, 2:173–78; Johnston to Harrison, October 23, 1812, ibid., 186–87.

32. Hopkins to Shelby, October 6, 1812, "The Expeditions of Major-General Samuel Hopkins up the Wabash, 1812, and the Letters of Captain Robert Hamilton," *Indiana Magazine of History* 43 (December 1947): 396–99; Hopkins to Shelby, November 27, 1812, ibid., 400–402.

33. Hopkins to Shelby, November 27, 1812, ibid., 400–402; Auguste LaRoche and Louis Chevalier to Howard, April 4, 1813, Carter, *Territorial Papers*, 14:652–55; Edwards to the Secretary of War, April 12, 1813, ibid., 16:312–15; Bert Anson, *The Miami Indians* (Norman: University of Oklahoma Press, 1970), 168–70.

34. Henry Procter to Roger Sheaffe, January 13, 1813, Wood, *British Documents*, 3–5; Alexander Clark Casselman, ed., *John Richardson's War of 1812* (Toronto: Historical Publishing, 1902), 37–134; Harrison to the Secretary of War, February 11, 1813, Esarey, *Harrison Papers*, 2:356–60; George Prevost to the Earl of Bathurst, February 27, 1813, British Colonial Records, CO 42/150:90–92.

35. Elliott to Claus, February 13, 1813, Record Group 10, 28: 16429–30, Public Archives of Canada; Robert Dickson to Noah Freer, March 16, 1813, Record Group 8, C Series, 257: 64–66, ibid.; Dickson to Sheaffe, March 22, 1813, ibid., 67–68; Entry for April 18, 1813, in "Diary of Daniel Cushing," in Harlow Lindley, ed., *Fort Meigs and the War of 1812* (Columbus: Ohio Historical Society, 1975), 114.

36. Harrison to the Secretary of War, April 21, 1813, Esarey, *Harrison Papers*, 2:422–26; Entries for April 24–27, 1813, in "Diary of Peter Chambers," Record Group 8, C Series, 695A:244–45, Public Archives of Canada. Also see Gilpin, *The War of 1812*, 182–83.

37. Harrison to Clay, April 24, 1813, William Henry Harrison Papers, Cincinnati Historical Society; Harrison to the Secretary of War, May 5, 1813, Esarey, *Harrison Papers*, 2:431–33; Procter to Prevost, May 14, 1813, British Colonial Records, CO 42/165:406–8.

38. Entry for May 5, 1813, in "Diary of Peter Chambers," Record Group 8, C Series, 695A:245; Procter to Prevost, May 14, 1813, British Colonial Records, CO 42/165:406–8; Petition of the Militia Captains to Lieutenant Colonel Warburton, May 6, 1813, Fort Meigs File, Fort Malden Historical Park. Detailed eyewitness accounts by survivors of Dudley's Defeat can be found in Tecumseh Papers, Draper Manuscripts, 6YY20–23.

39 Procter to Robert McDouall, May 14, 1813, British Colonial Records, CO 42/165:405; Procter to McDouall, June 16, 1813, ibid., 143; Procter to McDouall, June 29, 1813, Record Group 8, C Series, 679:155, Public Archives of Canada.

40. Procter to Prevost, July 13, 1813, *Michigan Historical Collections*, 15:339–40; J. C. Bartlet to Meigs, Return J. Meigs Papers, roll 3, 548–49 (microfilm), Ohio Historical Society (on deposit from State Library of Ohio); Lossing, *Pictorial Field-Book*, 496–99.

41. Croghan to Harrison, August 5, 1813, Esarey, *Harrison Papers*, 2:514–16; Procter to Prevost, August 9, 1813, British Colonial Records, CO 42/165:420–22; Letter by Black Hawk, August 16, 1813, M222, roll 14, 5529–30, National Archives; Donald Jackson, ed., *Black Hawk: An Autobiography* (Urbana: University of Illinois Press, 1964), 68.

42. Minutes of an Indian Council, August 23, 1813, Record Group 8, C Series, 257:139–42, Public Archives of Canada; Prevost to the Earl of Bath, August 25, 1813, British Colonial Records, CO 42/151:138–44; Harrison to the Secretary of War, September 8, 1813, Esarey, *Harrison Papers*, 2:537–38.

43. Gilpin, *The War of 1812*, 208–12.

44. Procter to DeRottenburg, September 12, 1813, Record Group 8, C Series, 680: 71–74, Public Archives of Canada; Procter to DeRottenburg, October 23, 1813, Wood, *British Documents*, 2:323–27. Also see Victor Lauriston, "The Case for General Procter," in Morris Zaslow, ed., *The Defended Border: Upper Canada and the War of 1812* (Toronto: Macmillan, 1964), 121–27.

45. Speech of Tecumseh, September 18, 1813, Esarey, *Harrison Papers*, 2:541–43.

46. Procter to Prevost, September 21, 1813, British Colonial Records, CO 42/151:217–18; Procter to DeRottenburg, October 23, 1813, Wood, *British Documents*, 2:323–27. Also see Judge Ermatinger, "The Retreat of Proctor and Tecumseh," *Ontario Historical Society, Papers and Records* 17 (1919): 11–21.

47. Harrison to the Secretary of War, September 30, 1813, Esarey, *Harrison Papers* 2:554–56; Procter to DeRottenburg, October 23, 1813, Wood, *British Documents*, 2:323–27. Also see Horsman,

Matthew Elliott, 212–13; and Chalou, "The Red Pawns Go to War," 282–84.

48. Harrison to the Secretary of War, September 27, 1813, Esarey, *Harrison Papers,* 2:550–51; Harrison to the Secretary of War, September 30, 1813, ibid., 554–56. Also see Gilpin, *The War of 1812,* 217–21.

49. Harrison to the Secretary of War, October 9, 1813, M222, roll 8, 3007–13, National Archives; Elliott to Claus, October 24, 1813, William Claus Papers, Manuscript Group 19, F1, 10: 111–13, Public Archives of Canada; Richard Bullock to Major Friend, December 6, 1813, Casselman, *John Richardson's War of 1812,* 230–34. Also see Katherine B. Coutts, "Thamesville and the Battle of the Thames," in Zaslow, *The Defended Border,* 116–17.

50. Procter to DeRottenburg, October 23, 1812, Wood, *British Documents,* 2:323–27; Prevost to Barthurst, October 30, 1813, ibid., 327–29; Tecumseh Papers, Draper Manuscripts, 1YY162.

51. Harrison to the Secretary of War, October 9, 1813, M222, roll 8, 3007–13, National Archives; Procter to DeRottenburg, October 23, 1813, Wood, *British Documents,* 2:323–27; John Hall to Col. Harvey, October 5, 1813, Record Group 8, C Series, 680:205, Public Archives of Canada; G. C. Johnston to Draper, July 28, 1874, Tecumseh Papers, Draper Manuscripts, 11YY2.

Chapter Seven

1. Procter to Harrison, October 8, 1813, Esarey, *Harrison Letters,* 2:557–58; Harrison to the Secretary of War, October 9, 1813, M222, roll 8, 3007–13, National Archives; Procter to DeRottenburg, October 23, 1813, Wood, *British Documents,* 2:323–27; Elliott to Claus, October 24, 1813, Claus Papers, MG 19, F1, 10, 111–13, Public Archives of Canada.

2. Return of the western Indians who have arrived at Dundas, October 26, 1813, RG 8, C Series, 681:10, Public Archives of Canada; DeRottenburg to Major General Vincent, November 1, 1813, ibid., 5–8; Claus to Edward McMahon, November 4, 1813, ibid., 257: 176–77.

3. Sir John Harvey to Phineas Riall, December 29, 1813, Wood, *British Documents,* 2:509–51; Le Breton to Foster, March 8, 1814, ibid., 354–55; James Basden to Alexander Stewart, March 13, 1814, ibid., 359–60.

4. Gordon Drummond to Noah Freer, February 16, 1814, *Michigan Historical Collections,* 15:491–92; Unknown to Captain Fos-

ter, April 27, 1814, Record Group 10, 28:16816–17, Public Archives of Canada; Claus to Captain Loring, May 4, 1814, ibid., 3:1349–50; James Givins to Claus, May 30, 1814, ibid., 28:16909–11; Drake, *Life of Tecumseh*, 62.

5. Drummond to Prevost, April 13, 1814, Record Group 8, C Series, 683:30–34, Public Archives of Canada; Drummond to Prevost, April 19, 1814, *Michigan Historical Collections*, 15:534–35.

6. Claus to Drummond, June 22, 1814, Record Group 10, 28:17037–38, Public Archives of Canada; Extract of a Speech by Colonel William Caldwell, June 14, 1814, Wood, *British Documents*, 3:726–27; Caldwell to Drummond, June 22, 1814, ibid., 727–28. For a good discussion of the long-standing feud between Norton and Claus, see Charles M. Johnston, "William Claus and John Norton: A Struggle for Power in Old Ontario," *Ontario History* 57 (June 1965): 101–8.

7. Givins to Claus, May 11, 1814, Record Group 10, 28:16862–63, Public Archives of Canada; Speech by Naiwash, May 20, 1814, ibid., 16889–90; Claus to Caldwell, June 10, 1814, ibid., 16965.

8. Answer of the Ottaways and Chippewas to their Father's Request about going to Kingston, May 30, 1814, Record Group 10, 28: 16918–19, Public Archives of Canada; William Kern to Major Givens, June 2, 1814, ibid., 16936; Claus to Captain Loring, June 22, 1814, ibid., 17027–28; Claus to Loring, June 8, 1814, ibid., 3:1395.

9. Klinck and Talman, eds., *Journal of John Norton*, 348–52; Major Gregg to Caldwell, July 1, 1814, Record Group 10, 29:17083, Public Archives of Canada; Caldwell to Claus, July 2, 1814, ibid., 17082; D. Cameron to Caldwell, July 4, 1814, ibid., 17085.

10. Klinck and Talman, eds., *Journal of John Norton*, 352; G. F. G. Stanley, "The Significance of the Six Nations' Participation in the War of 1812," *Ontario History* 55 (December 1963): 228.

11. Klinck and Talman, eds., *Journal of John Norton*, 355; Caldwell to Claus, July 23, 1814, Record Group 10, 29:17125–26, Public Archives of Canada; George Ironside to Claus, August 26, 1814, ibid., 17157; Return of the Western Indians, November 1, 1814, ibid., 17328.

12. Duncan MacArthur to Major General George Izard, November 18, 1814, Duncan MacArthur Papers, vol. 19, Library of Congress (microfilm copies at the Ohio State Historical Society); Caldwell to Unknown, November 8, 1814, Record Group 10, 29:17348, Public Archives of Canada; Prevost to Earl Bathurst, November 16, 1814, *Michigan Historical Collections* 25:611–12.

13. Claus to Unknown, October 3, 1814, Record Group 10, 3:1507, Public Archives of Canada; John Byekman to Caldwell, October

12, 1814, ibid., 29: 17268–69; Ironside to Claus, October 22, 1814, ibid., 17306–8; Ironside to Duncan Cameron, October 28, 1814, ibid., 28:17316; Speech by Naiwash, October 6, 1814, Superintendent General's Office Correspondence, ibid., 12:10301.

14. William Elliott to Unknown, December 10, 1814, Record Group 10, 29:17494–17500, Public Archives of Canada.

15. Ibid.; Speech of the Shawnee Prophet, November 20, 1814, ibid., 17381–82; Speech of the Shawnee Prophet, Winter, 1814, ibid., 17518–21; Speech of the Shawnee King, November 21, 1814, ibid., 3:1616–17.

16. Claus to Loring, March 30, 1815, Record Group 10, 4:1726–28, Public Archives of Canada; Speech by Claus, April 24, 1815, ibid., 1716–17; List of Indian payments, April 29, 1815, ibid., 30:17892.

17. Speeches by the Indians, April 26, 27, 1815, Record Group 10, 30:17861–65, Public Archives of Canada.

18. Prevost to Drummond, January 26, 1815, British Colonial Records, CO 42/161:45–46; Drummond to Prevost, February 8, 1815, Record Group 8, C Series, 258:22–24, Public Archives of Canada; Caldwell to Claus, May 1, 1815, Record Group 10, 30:17904.

19. Ironside to Cameron, June 6, 1815, Record Group 10, 30: 18032–34, Public Archives of Canada; Caldwell to Claus, June 15, 1815, ibid., 18051–52; Caldwell to Claus, July 20, 1815, ibid., 31:18206–8.

20. McArthur to Harrison, June 21, 1815, McArthur Papers, vol. 26, Library of Congress; Instructions to Harrison, McArthur, and Graham, June 9, 1815, M221, roll 64, 7786–87, National Archives; Lewis Cass to A. B. Dallas, July 7, 1815, Records of the Superintendencies and Agencies of the Office of Indian Affairs, Michigan, (M1), roll 2, 40–42, ibid. Ironside's exact relationship with Tenskwatawa's family remains uncertain. Tucker asserts that Ironside married Nehaaeemo, an older sister of Tenskwatawa, but information in the Ironside Papers seems to indicate that his wife may have been the Prophet's niece. See Tucker, *Tecumseh*, 23:321; and Ironside Papers, Burton Collection, Detroit Public Library.

21. Shawnee chiefs to John Johnston, April 27, 1815, M221, roll 63, 6471, National Archives; Johnston to the Secretary of War, May 4, 1815, Shawnee File, Great Lakes Indian Archives; Benjamin Stickney to William Crawford, November 12, 1815, ibid.; Speech by the Shawnee Prophet, November 8, 1815, Record Group 10, 31:18625–26, Public Archives of Canada.

22. Speech by the Prophet, August 4, 1815, Record Group 10, 31:18267–71, Public Archives of Canada; Caldwell to Claus, Au-

gust 4, 1815, ibid., 18273–74; Claus to Caldwell, August 15, 1815, ibid., 18307–10; Billy Caldwell to Claus, November 18, 1815, ibid., 18683–84.

23. John Graham to George Graham, August 26, 1815, M222, roll 15, 6232–33, National Archives; Caldwell to Unknown, August 26, 1815, Record Group 10, 31:18342–44, Public Archives of Canada; Proceedings of an Indian Council, August 27, 1815, ibid., 18356–60; Report of an Indian Council, August 28–September 2, 1815, ibid., 18377–79.

24. "Journal of the proceedings of the commissioners appointed to treat with the Northwest Indians at Detroit, August 3–September 8, 1815," *American State Papers: Indian Affairs*, 2:17–25.

25. Ibid.

26. Ibid.; Harrison to William Crawford, September 9, 1815, Harrison Papers, Cincinnati Historical Society; Stickney to Crawford, November 12, 1815, Shawnee File, Great Lakes Indian Archives; James Witherell to Amy Witherell, April 20, 1816, Benjamin F. Witherell Papers, Burton Collection, Detroit Public Library.

27. Speech by William James, September 14, 1815, Record Group 8, C Series, 258:362–69, Public Archives of Canada; Claus to Sir Frederick Robinson, September 18, 1815, ibid., 370–72.

28. Ironside to Claus, October 4, 1815, Record Group 10, 31:18470–73, Public Archives of Canada; Billy Caldwell to Claus, October 6, 1815, ibid., 18493–95; Speech by the Shawnee Prophet, November 8, 1815, ibid., 18625–26; Caldwell to James, October 21, 1815, Record Group 8, C Series, 258:485, Public Archives of Canada.

29. James to Robinson, October 18, 1815, Record Group 10, 31:18549–50, Public Archives of Canada; John Wilson to Duncan Cameron, December 24, 1815, ibid., 18758–59; "Return of the Indians who were Provisioned at Amherstburg," December 25, 1815–June 24, 1816, ibid., 33:19435.

30. Claus to William Halton, November 15, 1815, Record Group 10, 4:1828, Public Archives of Canada; Indian Memoranda by Lt. Col. James, 1816, ibid., 12:10644–61; Speech by the Prophet, February 8, 1816, ibid., 32:18828–29; Caldwell to Claus, December 20, 1815, Record Group 8, C Series, 260: 137–47.

31. Billy Caldwell to Claus, February 15, 1816, Record Group 10, 32:18856–57, Public Archives of Canada; Speech by the Prophet, February 19, 1816, ibid., 18831–32; Claus to Gore, February 22, 1816, ibid., 4:1927–38.

32. Benjamin Witherell to Amy Witherell, April 20, 1816, Witherell Papers, Burton Collection, Detroit Public Library; Cass to the

Secretary of War, April 24, 1816, Carter, *Territorial Papers*, 10:629–31.

33. Benjamin Witherell to Amy Witherell, April 20, 1816, Witherell Papers, Burton Collection, Detroit Public Library.

34. Indian speeches, April 1816, Lewis Cass Papers, William L. Clements Library.

35. Ibid.; Benjamin Witherell to Amy Witherell, April 20, 1816, Witherell Papers, Burton Collection, Detroit Public Library; Cass to the Secretary of War, April 24, 1816, Carter, *Territorial Papers*, 10:629–31; Cass to Johnston, May 22, 1816, Jones Collection, Cincinnati Historical Society.

36. John Whistler to Cass, September 16, 1816, M1, roll 2, 155, National Archives; William Walker to Cass, October 4, 1816, ibid., 161; Stickney to Cass, December 1, 1816, ibid., 195–98.

37. Billy Caldwell to Gabriel Godfroy, July 1, 1816, Record Group 10, 12:10813, Public Archives of Canada; Godfroy to Caldwell, July 5, 1816, ibid., 33:10809–11; Caldwell to Claus, August 12, 1816, ibid., 19296–97; Caldwell to Claus, August 31, 1816, ibid., 12:10818–19.

38. Major Edward Berwick to Major General Wilson, October 25, 1816, Record Group 8, C Series, 260:465–66, Public Archives of Canada; Stickney to Cass, December 1, 1816, M1, roll 2, 195–98, National Archives; Stickney to George Graham, January 4, 1817, Shawnee File, Great Lakes Indian Archives; William Turner to Graham, April 3, 1817, ibid.

39. Whistler to Cass, September 16, 1816, M1, roll 2, 155, National Archives; Stickney to Cass, January 1, 1817, ibid., 202; Berwick to Wilson, October 25, 1816, Record Group 8, C Series, 260:465–66, Public Archives of Canada; Archibald Thompson to Col. Nichols, December 2, 1816, Record Group 10, 33:19509–10, ibid.; Speech by the Indians, March 10, 1817, ibid., 13:11003–6; Minutes of a Council held at Amherstburg, July 4, 1817, ibid., 35:19970–73.

40. Report of a Board of Inquiry, June 22, 1815, Record Group 10, 34:19933–34, Public Archives of Canada; Minutes of a council held at Amherstburg, July 9, 1817, ibid., 35:20070–72; William McKay to Claus, June 30, 1820, ibid., 14:11418–19; H. C. Darling to John Johnston, December 7, 1820, ibid., 11483–84; Claus to H. C. Darling, September 15, 1821, Records of the Military Secretary's Office, ibid., 491:3000–3001; "Statement of the Number of Indians . . . who were not cloathed," George Ironside Papers, Burton Collection, Detroit Public Library.

41. Petition by the Indians, August 31, 1819, Record Group 10,

36:20903–14, Public Archives of Canada; Lalaway and Split Log to Maitland, October 29, 1819, ibid., 489:29582–84; Speech by the Prophet, June 15, 1820, A. B. Farney Papers, Fort Malden National Historic Park.

42. Speech by the Prophet, June 15, 1820, A. B. Farney Papers, Fort Malden National Historic Park; "Extracts from Mr. Ironside's letters to the Deputy Superintendent, 25th May 1820, and 20th June 1820," Record Group 10, 37:21262–63, Public Archives of Canada; Ironside to Claus, June 28, 1820, ibid., 21249–53; William Claus to J. Givens, July 6, 1820, Claus Papers, ibid., 12:63–66.

43. Minutes of a council held at Amherstburg, October 16, 1818, Claus Papers, 11:95–96, Public Archives of Canada; A. McDonnell to Ironside, December 7, 1820, ibid., 12:89–90; "A Statement of Lands purchased by the Crown from Indians in Upper Canada," May 30, 1821, ibid., 97. This document indicates that the Crown purchased 9,735,000 acres of Indian land between 1815 and 1821. Also see Ironside to Claus, November 25, 1820, Record Group 10, 14:11491–93, Public Archives of Canada; Claus to Ironside, June 30, 1823, Ironside Papers, Burton Collection, Detroit Public Library; Speech by the Chippewas, September 24, 1823, ibid.

44. Return of claims of friendly Indians, March 19, 1823, Ironside Papers, Burton Collection, Detroit Public Library; Return of Indians receiving presents at Amherstburg, June 24, 1824, Record Group 10, 42:22527, Public Archives of Canada; Ironside to Claus, July 1, 1824, ibid., 22544.

Chapter Eight

1. Charles Jouett to the Secretary of War, February 1, 1818, Shawnee File, Great Lakes Indian Archives; William Princc to John C. Calhoun, June 23, 1818, ibid.; Minutes of a Council, June 21, 1817, Ironside Papers, Burton Collection, Detroit Public Library; Ironside to Claus, October 24, 1817, ibid.

2. Cass to Calhoun, November 21, 1819, Cass Papers, Burton Collection, Detroit Public Library; Cass to Calhoun, December 25, 1819, Shawnee File, Great Lakes Indian Archives; Johnston to Cass, November 9, 1816, ibid.; Alexander Wolcott to Cass, November 14, 1819, Carter, *Territorial Papers*, 10:855–57; Cass to Secretary of War, November 29, 1816, M1, roll 2, 175–85, National Archives.

3. Ironside to Claus, December 14, 1824, Record Group 10, 42:22707–09, Public Archives of Canada; C. C. Trowbridge to Draper, July 12, 1882, Tecumseh Papers, Draper Manuscripts, 5YY1;

Lewis Cass, "Review of published works on Indians," Cass Papers, William L. Clements Library.

4. Report by James Ellicott and Phillip Thomas, August 1, 1816, Shawnee File, Great Lakes Indian Archives; "Work of Ohio Yearly Meeting for the North American Indians," Society of Friends Records, Ohio Historical Society; Lindley, "Friends and the Shawnee Indians at Wapakoneta," *Ohio State Archaeological and Historical Quarterly* 54 (January 1945): 33–39.

5. Thomas Forsyth to William Clark, September 30, 1818, Forsyth Papers, Missouri Historical Society; Cass to Duncan McArthur, June 13, 1817, M1, roll 3, 83–86, National Archives; Johnston to Cass, July 17, 1819, ibid., roll 6, 165–66.

6. "Articles of a treaty made and concluded, at the foot of the Rapids of the Miami of Lake Erie, between Lewis Cass and Duncan McArthur, . . . and the sachems, chiefs, and warriors of the Wyandot, Seneca, Delaware, Shawanese, Potawatomees, Ottaways, and Chippeway, tribes of Indians," September 29, 1817, in Kappler, *Indian Affairs: Laws and Treaties*, 2:145–55; "Articles of a treaty," September 17, 1818, ibid., 162–63; Josiah Meigs to Calhoun, April 20, 1820, Shawnee File, Great Lakes Indian Archives.

7. Thomas McKenney to J. Cocke, February 24, 1824, Correspondence of the Office of Indian Affairs, Letters Sent, M21, roll 1, 374, National Archives; Johnston to Cass, July 17, 1819, M1, roll 6, 165–66, ibid.; Ironside to Claus, December 14, 1824, Record Group 10, 42:22707–9, Public Archives of Canada. Also see Grant Foreman, *The Last Trek of the Indians* (New York: Russell and Russell, 1972), 48–54.

8. Ironside to Claus, May 22, 1824, Record Group 10, 42:22507, Public Archives of Canada; Ironside to Claus, July 1, 1824, ibid., 22544.

9. C. C. Trowbridge to Draper, December 12, 1882, Tecumseh Papers, Draper Manuscripts, 5YY1; Trowbridge to Draper, May 18, 1868, ibid., 5YY5; Kinietz and Wheeler-Voegelin, *Shawnese Traditions*, viii–xvii, 1–59, passim; McKenney to Cass, January 11, 1825, M21, roll 1, 146, National Archives; Herman J. Viola, *The Indian Legacy of Charles Bird King* (Washington, D.C.: Smithsonian Institution and Doubleday, 1976), 55, 58. Unfortunately, much of the biographical and ethnographic materials collected by Cass during these interviews was lost while Cass served as minister to France. See Trowbridge to Draper, December 12, 1882, Tecumseh Papers, Draper Manuscripts, 5YY1. King's oil painting of Tenskwatawa now belongs to the Thomas Gilcrease Institute of American History and Art, in Tulsa, Oklahoma.

10. Ironside to Claus, December 14, 1824, Record Group 10, 42:22707–9, Public Archives of Canada; Tecumseh Papers, Draper Manuscripts, 3YY19–20; Johnston to Cass, January 25, 1826, M1, roll 18, 14, National Archives; Voucher by the Prophet, 1829, Correspondence of the Office of Indian Affairs, Letters Received, St. Louis Superintendency, M234, roll 749, 698, ibid.

11. Captain Lewis to the Secretary of War, March 9, 1825, M1, roll 28, 175–76, National Archives; Speeches of the Shawnee and Cherokee chiefs, January 7, 1825, M234, roll 747, 177–78, ibid.; Clark to McKenney, January 9, 1825, ibid., 161. The last two entries are erroneously dated 1824; they obviously occurred in January 1825. Also see Foreman, *The Last Trek of the Indians*, 48–50.

12. Clark to McKenney, January 11, 1825, M234, roll 747, 166–69, National Archives; Speech by Lewis, February 28, 1825, M1, roll 28, 172, ibid.; Calhoun to Lewis, March 2, 1825, ibid., 163; McKenney to Cass, March 9, 1825, M21, roll 1, 190, ibid.

13. Johnston to Cass, April 14, 1825, M1, roll 16, 87, National Archives; Johnston to Cass, May 2, 1825, ibid., 111; Johnston to Olmstead, May 30, 1825, *Niles Register*, June 25, 1825, 261; Grant Foreman, *Indians and Pioneers: The Story of the American Southwest before 1830* (Norman: University of Oklahoma Press, 1936), 195.

14. "Minutes of a Council held at Wapaghkonetta, in the State of Ohio, with the Shawnees and Cherokees," May 1825, M1, Roll 28, 148–61, National Archives.

15. Ibid.; "Proceedings in Council with General Clark," November 10, 1825, M234, roll 747, 325–31, ibid.

16. "Minutes of a Council held at Wapaghkonetta, in the State of Ohio, with the Shawnees and Cherokees," May 1825, M1, roll 28, 148–61, National Archives.

17. Peter Menard to Clark, September 30, 1825, M234, roll 747, 356, National Archives; Johnston to Cass, September 28, 1825, M1, roll 17, ibid., 46–47; Johnston to Cass, October 20, 1825, ibid., 83.

18. Johnston to Cass, January 11, 1826, M1, roll 18, 6–7, National Archives; Johnston to Cass, January 25, 1826, ibid., 14; Johnston to Cass, March 30, 1826, ibid., 45.

19. Clark to McKenney, November 7, 1825, M234, roll 747, 321, National Archives; McKenney to Barbour, November 30, 1825, M21, roll 2, ibid., 127–29; "Articles of a convention made between William Clark, Superintendent of Indian Affairs, and the undersigned Chiefs and Head Men of the Shawnee Nation of Indians residing within the State of Missouri," November 7, 1825, Kappler, *Indian*

Affairs: Laws and Treaties, 2:262–64. Also see Voucher by John Johnston, 1826, Johnston Papers, Cincinnati Historical Society; and Louise Barry, ed., *The Beginnings of the West: Annals of the Kansas Gateway to the American West, 1540–1854* (Topeka: Kansas State Historical Society, 1972), 127–28. Angered over Tenskwatawa's cooperation with the Americans, the British Indian Department refused to issue any rations to either the Prophet or his followers after January 1826. See Claus to John Johnston, January 10, 1826, Record Group 8, C Series, vol. 266, Public Archives of Canada.

20. Voucher by John Johnston, Johnston Papers, Cincinnati Historical Society; Johnston to Cass, October 7, 1826, M1, roll 19, 62–63, National Archives; Johnston to the Editor of the *Piqua Gazette,* September 30, 1826, Tecumseh Papers, Draper Manuscripts, 1YY89; Speech by the Shawnee Prophet, April 2, 1827, M234, roll 300, 74–80, National Archives.

21. Johnston to Cass, October 7, 1826, M1, roll 19, 62–63, National Archives; Speech by the Shawnee Prophet, April 2, 1827, M234, roll 300, ibid., 74–80; Pierre Menard to Richard Graham, January 17, 1827, Richard Graham Papers, Missouri Historical Society; *Western Sun* (Vincennes), December 13, 1826, 1.

22. Menard to Graham, January 17, 1827, Graham Papers, Missouri Historical Society; Menard to Clark, February 22, 1827, M234, roll 748, 31–32, National Archives; Clark to Barbour, March 8, 1827, ibid., 29.

23. Speech by the Prophet, April 2, 1827, M234, roll 300, 74–80, National Archives; Voucher by the Prophet, Spring, 1829, ibid., roll 749, 698.

24. Speech by the Prophet, April 2, 1827, M234, roll 300, 74–80, National Archives; Speech from the Shawnee Emigrants, April 3, 1827, ibid., 82–83; Graham to Clark, April 4, 1827, ibid., 70–71.

25. Graham to Clark, April 4, 1827, M234, roll 300, 70–71, National Archives.

26. Clark to Barbour, April 23, 1827, M234, roll 748, 43–44, National Archives; Barbour to Clark, May 17, 1827, M21, roll 4, ibid., 34.

27. Graham to Clark, April 4, 1827, M234, roll 300, 70–71, National Archives; Clark to Barbour, April 23, 1827, ibid., roll 748, 43–44; Tecumseh Papers, Draper Manuscripts, 4YY56.

28. Speeches by the Shawnee chiefs, August 1827, M234, roll 748, 226–39, National Archives; Speech by a Shawnee, November 7, 1827, ibid., 240–41.

29. Clark to Barbour, March 8, 1827, M234, roll 748, 29, Na-

tional Archives; Graham to Clark, April 4, 1827, ibid., roll 300, 70–71; William Anderson to Clark, August 18, 1827, ibid., roll 748, 223; Speech by Cornstalk, August 23, 1827, ibid., 226–31.

30. William Anderson to Clark, August 18, 1827, M234, roll 748, 223, National Archives; Speech by Cornstalk, August 23, 1827, ibid., 226–31; Speech by the Prophet, August 29, 1827, ibid., 231–36.

31. Entries for June and July 1827, in Louise Barry, ed., "William Clark's Diary, May, 1826–February, 1831," *Kansas Historical Quarterly* 16 (February 1948): 27–31; General Abstract of all Disbursements and Expenditures for the year ending August 31, 1827, M234, roll 748, 164–71, National Archives; Clark to McKenney, October 20, 1827, ibid., 179.

32. Entries for August 1827, Barry, "William Clark's Diary," 32–33; Speech by Cornstalk, August 23, 1827, M234, roll 748, 231–36, National Archives.

33. Speech by the Prophet, August 29, 1827, M2334, roll 748, 231–36, National Archives.

34. Entries for August 1827, Barry, "William Clark's Diary," 32–33; Speech by the Prophet, August 30, 1827, M234, roll 748, 237–39, National Archives.

35. Entries for September 1827, Barry, "William Clark's Diary," 33–34; Clark to Barbour, November 23, 1827, M234, roll 748, 207–8, National Archives; Clark to McKenney, February 25, 1828, ibid., 366–70; Clark to McKenney, April 1, 1828, ibid., 388–89; Graham to Clark, June 1, 1828, Richard Graham Papers, Missouri Historical Society.

Chapter Nine

1. Graham to Clark, June 1, 1828, Richard Graham Papers, Missouri Historical Society; John Campbell to Graham, December 27, 1828, ibid.; Isaac McCoy to Clark, October 27, 1828, M234, roll 748, 571–73, National Archives; Entries for September 24–26, 1828, in Lela Barnes, ed., "Journal of Isaac McCoy for the Exploring Expedition of 1828," *Kansas Historical Quarterly* 5 (August 1936): 260–61.

2. William Clark to the Secretary of War, June 22, 1829, vol. 4, William Clark Papers, Kansas State Historical Society, Topeka; Clark to McKenney, July 11, 1829, ibid.; Lela Barnes, ed., "Journal of Isaac McCoy for the Exploring Expedition of 1830," *Kansas Historical Quarterly* 5 (November 1936): 343 n. 12; "An Enumeration of the Shawnees," April 8, 1830, M234, roll 300, 138–39, National

Archives; Speech by the Shawnees to the President, July 20, 1832, ibid., 348–50.

3. Entry for August 23, 1830, in Barnes, "Journal of Isaac McCoy, 1830," 343; Isaac McCoy, *History of the Baptist Indian Missions* (Washington, D.C.: William H. Morrison, 1840), 404–5; George A. Schultz, *An Indian Canaan: Isaac McCoy and the Vision of an Indian State* (Norman: University of Oklahoma Press, 1972), 143.

4. Entry for May 20, 1828, in Barry, "William Clark's Diary," 150; Entry for November 30, 1832, in Barry, *Beginnings of the West,* 223–34; Shawnee chiefs to Richard Cummings, March 21, 1834, M234, roll 300, 626, National Archives; *Kansas City Kansan,* November 21, 1929; ibid., November 24, 1929, Also see Carl G. Klopfenstein, "Westward Ho: Removal of Ohio Shawnees, 1832–1833," *Bulletin of the Historical and Philosophical Society of Ohio* 15 (January 1957): 3–31.

5. George Catlin, *Letters and Notes on the Manners, Customs, and Conditions of North American Indians,* 2 vols. (New York: Dover Publications, 1973), 2:117; William H. Truettner, *The Natural Man Observed: A Study of Catlin's Indian Gallery* (Washington, D.C.: Smithsonian Institution Press, 1979), 229; Harold McCracken, *George Catlin and the Old Frontier* (New York: Dial Press, 1959), 32–33. There is considerable controversy over the date of the Catlin portrait of Tenskwatawa. Through an analysis of the techniques used by Catlin to complete the painting, several authorities argue that Catlin's portrait of the Prophet was completed during the fall of 1830. Although there is no documentation for Catlin being in Kansas at that time, he was in St. Louis, and these authorities argue that he passed unnoticed to the Fort Leavenworth region, where he painted Tenskwatawa and several other subjects. See Truettner, *The Natural Man Observed,* 229; and McCracken, *George Catlin,* 32–33. A close examination of documentary evidence, however, would suggest that the portrait was completed in 1832. Most authorities agree that Catlin painted all six of his Shawnee portraits during one period, but lists of Shawnees in both Kansas and Ohio in April 1830, seem to indicate that two of Catlin's subjects, Lay-law-she-kaw (He Who Goes up the River) and Lay-loo-ah-pe-ai-shee-kaw (The Grass Bush and Blossom), were still residing in Ohio at that time. See Catlin, *Letters and Notes,* 115–17; Barry, *The Beginnings of the West,* 219; and "An Enumeration of the Shawnees remaining in the State of Ohio," April 9, 1830, M234, roll 300, 136, National Archives; "An Enumeration of the Shawnees who have Emigrated west of the Mississippi," April 8, 1830, ibid., 138–39.

6. Catlin, *Letters and Notes*, 118.

7. Barry, *The Beginnings of the West*, 316–17; *Kansas City Kansan*, November 21, 1929; ibid., November 24, 1929; *Kansas City Star*, November 24, 1929.

8. Harrison to the Secretary of War, August 7, 1811, Esarey, *Harrison Letters*, 1:548–51.

9. Carl E. Klinck, ed., *Tecumseh: Fact and Fiction in Early Records* (Englewood Cliffs, N.J.: Prentice-Hall, 1961), 220–31; Robert F. Berkhofer, Jr., *The White Man's Indian* (New York: Alfred A. Knopf, 1978), 86–96. Also see Tucker, *Tecumseh*, passim; Galloway, *Old Chillicothe*, passim; and Alvin M. Josephy, Jr., *The Patriot Chiefs: A Chronicle of American Indian Leadership* (New York: Viking Press, 1961), 131–73.

Bibliography

Manuscript Materials

Amherstburg, Ontario. Fort Malden National Historic Park.
  A. B. Farney Papers.
  Moravian Indian File.
  Potawatomi File.
  Tecumseh File.
  War of 1812, Battle of the Thames File.
  War of 1812, Brownstown File.
  War of 1812, Fort Meigs File.
  War of 1812, Moguago File.
Ann Arbor. University of Michigan. William L. Clements Library.
  Lewis Cass Papers.
  Michigan Papers.
  War of 1812 Papers.
Battleground, Indiana. Tippecanoe Battleground Historical Asso-
  ciation.
  Battle of Tippecanoe—Eyewitness Account File.
Bloomington. Indiana University. Eli Lilly Library.
  Manuscripts Division—Diary of George Bluejacket.
Bloomington. Indiana University. Glenn A. Black Laboratory of
  Archaeology. Great Lakes-Ohio Valley Indian Archives Project.
  Ottawa File.
  Potawatomi File.
  Shawnee File.
Boston. Massachusetts Historical Society.
  Winthrop Sargent Papers.
Chicago. Newberry Library.
  Edward E. Ayer Manuscripts.

Great Lakes Indian Atlas Research Notes.

Cincinnati. Cincinnati Historical Society.
Henry Brown Papers.
John Stites Gano Papers.
William Henry Harrison Papers.
John Johnston Papers.
Frank J. Jones Collection.
John McDonald File.
John Riddle's Account Book.
"A Short Account of a Journey Taken by Volunteers from Gallia County; for the Purpose of Destroying Indians and the Invasion of Canada."

Columbus. Ohio Historical Society.
Thomas Kirker Papers.
August Mahr Papers.
Return J. Meigs Papers.
Miscellaneous Manuscripts—"Minutes of a Talk given by the Indian chiefs near Greenville, September 13, 1807, Mr. Stephen Riddle, Interpreter, delivered by Blue Jacket."
Albert Slager Papers.
Society of Friends Records.
Edward Tiffin Papers.
Upper Sandusky Wyandot Mission of the Methodist Episcopal Church Records.
Mrs. Forest Wilson Papers.
Thomas Worthington Papers.

Detroit. Detroit Public Library. Burton Historical Collections.
John Askin Papers.
Lewis Cass Papers.
Gabriel Godfroy Papers.
William Henry Harrison Papers.
George Ironside Papers.
Jacob Kingsbury Papers.
Benson J. Lossing Papers.
Tecumseh Papers.
Charles Christopher Trowbridge Papers.
Benjamin F. Witherell Papers.

Indianapolis. Indiana Historical Society Library.
William H. English Collection.
William Henry Harrison Miscellaneous Collection.
Indiana Territory Collection.
Letter by Benjamin Stickney to David Jones, January 31, 1816.
A. G. Mitten Collection.

Northwest Territory Collection.
Indianapolis. Indiana State Library.
"Journal of Daniel Dunham."
Jacob Piatt Dunn Collection.
Miscellaneous Collection.
John McCoy Letters.
William Prince Papers.
Lafayette, Indiana. Tippecanoe County Historical Society.
George Winter Papers.
London. Public Records Office. Colonial Office.
Original Correspondence, Secretary of State: Series 42:
Lower Canada. Vols. 135–70.
Upper Canada. Vols. 348–58.
Madison, Wisconsin. State Historical Society of Wisconsin.
Draper Manuscripts.
Thomas Forsyth Papers.
William Henry Harrison Papers.
Simon Kenton Papers.
Tecumseh Papers.
Ottawa. Public Archives of Canada.
Manuscript Group 19. Fur Traders and Indians.
John Askin Papers.
William Claus Papers.
McKee Family Papers.
Record Group 8. British Military and Naval Records.
C Series. Vols. 256–58, 260–69, 676–89, 695–695A.
Record Group 10. Indian Affairs.
Administrative Records of the Imperial Government.
Records of the Governor General.
Upper Canada, Civil Control. Vols. 1–7.
Lower Canada, Civil Control. Vols. 486–87.
General Administration. Vols. 789–92.
Records of the Superintendent's Office.
Correspondence. Vols. 8–21, 26–46.
Letterbooks. Vols. 568, 586.
Military Secretary's Office. Vols. 488–97.
Western Post Records. Vols. 1836–37.
Ministerial Administration Records.
General Headquarters Records.
Governor General's Office, Vols. 268, 782.
Field Office Records.
Western (Sarnia) Superintendency. Correspondence. Vols.
436–41.

Northern Superintendency. Correspondence. Vols. 612–19.
St. Louis. Missouri Historical Society.
John Dougherty Papers.
Thomas Forsyth Papers.
Richard Graham Papers.
Indian Papers.
Topeka. Kansas State Historical Society.
J. A. Chute. "Death of the Shawnee Prophet."
William Clark Papers.
Joab Spencer, "The Shawnee Project."
Washington, D.C. Library of Congress.
Duncan MacArthur Papers.
Washington, D.C. National Archives.
Record Group 75. Records of the Bureau of Indian Affairs.
Letters Received by the Office of Indian Affairs (M234).
 Fort Leavenworth Agency, 1824–38.
 Fort Wayne Agency, 1824–30.
 Indiana Agency, 1824–34.
 Michigan Superintendency, 1824–27.
 Ohio Agency, 1831–38.
 St. Louis Superintendency, 1824–38.
Letters Sent by the Office of Indian Affairs (M21). 1824–36.
Records of the Michigan Superintendency (M1). 1814–28.
Records of the Secretary of War Relating to Indian Affairs.
 Letters Received (M271). 1800–1823.
 Letters Sent (M15). 1800–1824.
Record Group 107. Records of the Office of Secretary of War.
 Letters Received by the Secretary of War, Main Series (M221).
  1801–17, 1825–36.
Letters Received by the Secretary of War, Unregistered Series.
 (M222). 1805–36.
Letters Sent by the Secretary of War Relating to Military Af-
 fairs.
 (M6). 1800–1816.

Primary Sources

ARTICLES

Barnes, Lela, ed. "Journal of Isaac McCoy for the Exploring Expedition of 1828." *Kansas Historical Quarterly* 5 (August 1936):
227–77.

————. "Journal of Isaac McCoy for the Exploring Expedition of 1830." *Kansas Historical Quarterly* 5 (November 1936): 339–77.

Barry, Louise, ed. "William Clark's Diary, May, 1826–February, 1831." *Kansas Historical Quarterly* 16 (February, May, August, November 1948): 1–39, 136–74, 274–306, 384–410.

"The Battle of Tippecanoe as Described by Judge Isaac Naylor, a Participant—A Recently Discovered Account." *Indiana Magazine of History* 2 (December 1906): 163–9.

Crawford, Mary M., ed. "Mrs. Lydia B. Bacon's Journal, 1811–1812." *Indiana Magazine of History* 40–41 (December 1944–March 1945): 367–86, 59–79.

"The Expedition of Major General Samuel Hopkins up the Wabash, 1812: The Letters of Captain Robert Hamilton." *Indiana Magazine of History* 43 (December 1947): 393–402.

Lambert, Robert, ed. "The Conduct of the Militia at Tippecanoe: Elihu Stout's Controversy with Colonel John B. Boyd, January, 1812." *Indiana Magazine of History* 51 (September 1955): 237–50.

McDermott, John Francis, ed. "Isaac McCoy's Second Exploring Trip in 1828." *Kansas Historical Quarterly* 13 (August 1945): 400–462.

Nuttall, Thomas. "Thomas Nuttall's Travels in the Old Northwest; An Unpublished 1810 Diary." *Chronica Botanica* 14 (Autumn 1951): 1–88.

"The Robert Lucas Journal of the War of 1812." *Iowa Journal of History and Politics* 4 (July 1906): 342–437.

Watts, Florence G., ed., "Lieutenant Charles Larabee's Account of the Battle of Tippecanoe, 1811." *Indiana Magazine of History* 57 (September 1961): 225–47.

BOOKS

Alford, Thomas Wildcat. *Civilization and the Story of the Absentee Shawnees*. Norman: University of Oklahoma Press, 1936.

American State Papers: Indian Affairs. 2 vols. Washington, D.C.: Gales and Seaton, 1832–34.

American State Papers: Military Affairs. 7 vols. Washington, D.C.: Gales and Seaton, 1832–61.

Ashe, Thomas. *Travels in America Performed in 1806*. London: R. Phillips, 1808.

Badger, Joseph A. *A Memoir of Joseph Badger*. Hudson, Ohio: Sawyer, Ingersoll and Co., 1851.

Bradbury, John. *Travels in the Interior of America in the Years*

1809, 1810, and 1811. In vol. 5, Reuben G. Thwaites, ed. Early Western Travels. Cleveland: Arthur H. Clark, 1904–1907.

Carter, Clarence E., ed. *The Territorial Papers of the United States.* 27 vols.–Washington, D.C.: Government Printing Office, 1934–.

Casselman, Alexander Clark, ed. *John Richardson's War of 1812.* Toronto: Historical Publishing, 1902.

Catlin, George. *Letters and Notes on the Manners, Customs, and Conditions of North American Indians.* 2 vols. New York: Dover Publications, 1973.

Collections of the Michigan Pioneer and Historical Society. 40 vols. Lansing: Thorp and Godfrey and others, 1874–1929.

Cunningham, Wilbur, ed. *Letter Book of William Burnett.* N.p.: Fort Miami Heritage Society of Michigan, 1967.

Edgar, Matilda. *Ten Years of Upper Canada in Peace and War. 1805–1815: Being the Rideout Letters with Annotations.* Toronto: William Briggs, 1890.

Edwards, Ninian W. *History of Illinois from 1778 to 1833 and the Life and Times of Ninian Edwards.* New York: Arno Press, 1975.

Esarey, Logan, ed. *Messages and Letters of William Henry Harrison.* 2 vols. Indianapolis: Indiana Historical Commission, 1922.

Gipson, Lawrence Henry, ed. *The Moravian Mission on White River: Diaries and Letters, May 5, 1779 to November 12, 1806. Indiana Historical Collections,* vol. 23. Indianapolis: Indiana Historical Bureau, 1938.

Hamilton, Edward P., ed. *Adventures in the Wilderness: The American Journals of Louis Antoine de Bougainville, 1756–1760.* Norman: University of Oklahoma Press, 1964.

Heckewelder, John. *History, Manners, and Customs of the Indian Nations.* Philadelphia: Historical Society of Philadelphia, 1876.

———. *A Narrative of the Mission of the United Brethren among the Delaware and Mohegan Indians, from Its Commencement, in the Year 1740, to the Close of the Year 1808.* New York: Arno Press, 1971.

Hopkins, Gerrard. *A Mission to the Indians from the Committee of the Baltimore Meeting to Fort Wayne in 1804.* Philadelphia: T. Elwood Zell, 1862.

Houck, Louis, ed. *The Spanish Regime in Missouri.* 2 vols. New York: Arno Press, 1971.

Hunter, John D. *Memoirs of a Captivity among the Indians of North America.* London: Longman, Hurst, Rees, Orme, Brown, and Green, 1823.

Jackson, Donald, ed. *Black Hawk: An Autobiography.* Urbana: University of Illinois Press, 1964.

Johnston, Charles M., ed. *The Valley of the Six Nations*. Toronto: Champlain Society, 1964.

Kappler, Charles J., ed. *Indian Affairs, Laws and Treaties*. 2 vols. Washington, D.C.: Government Printing Office, 1904.

Keating, William H. *Narrative of an Expedition to the Source of St. Peters River*. 2 vols. London: George S. Whittaker, 1825.

Kellogg, Louise Phelps, ed. *Frontier Advance on the Upper Ohio, 1778–1779*. Madison: State Historical Society of Wisconsin, 1917.

———. *Frontier Retreat on the Upper Ohio, 1779–1781*. Madison: State Historical Society of Wisconsin, 1917.

Kinietz, Vernon, and Wheeler-Voegelin, Erminie, eds. *"Shawnese Traditions": C. C. Trowbridge's Account. Occasional Contributions from the Museum of Anthropology of the University of Michigan, No. 9*. Ann Arbor: University of Michigan Press, 1939.

Kinniard, Lawrence, ed. *Spain in the Mississippi Valley, 1765–1794, Annual Report of the American Historical Association for the Year, 1945*. 4 vols. Washington, D.C.: Government Printing Office, 1946.

Klinck, Carl F., and Talman, James J., eds. *The Journal of Major John Norton, 1816*. Toronto: Champlain Society, 1970.

Lindley, Harlow, ed. *Fort Meigs and the War of 1812*. Columbus: Ohio Historical Society, 1975.

Lipscomb, Andrew A., ed. *The Writings of Thomas Jefferson*. 20 vols. Washington, D.C.: Thomas Jefferson Memorial Association, 1903–4.

Loudon, Archibald. *A Selection of the Most Interesting Narratives of Outrages Committed by the Indians in their Wars with the White People*. 2 vols. Whitehall, England: Archibald Loudon, 1808.

McCoy, Isaac. *History of the Baptist Indian Missions*. Washington, D.C.: William M. Morrison, 1840.

McKenney, Thomas. *Memoirs, Official and Personal*. 2 vols. New York: Paine and Burgess, 1846.

Quaife, Milo Milton, ed. *The John Askin Papers*. 2 vols. Detroit: Detroit Library Commission, 1928–31.

———. *War on the Detroit: The Chronicles of Thomas Vercheres de Boucherville and the Capitulation by an Ohio Volunteer*. Chicago: Lakeside Press, 1940.

Schoolcraft, Henry Rowe. *Travels Through the Northwestern Regions of the United States*. Albany: E. and F. Hosford, 1821.

Smith, William Henry, ed. *The St. Clair Papers*. 2 vols. Freeport, N.Y.: Books for Libraries Press, 1970.

Spragge, George W., ed. *The John Strachan Letter Book: 1812–1834*.

Toronto: Ontario Historical Society, 1946.

Tanner, John. *Narrative of the Captivity and Adventures of John Tanner during Thirty Years Residence among the Indians in the Interior of North America.* New York: G. C. H. Carvill, 1830.

Thornbrough, Gayle, ed. *Letter Book of the Indian Agency at Fort Wayne, 1809–1815.* Indianapolis: Indiana Historical Society, 1961.

Thwaites, Reuben G., ed. *Early Western Travels, 1748–1846.* 32 vols. Cleveland: Arthur H. Clark, 1904–7.

Thwaites, Reuben G., and Kellogg, Louise Phelps, eds. *Documentary History of Dunmore's War.* Madison: State Historical Society of Wisconsin, 1905.

———. *The Revolution on the Upper Ohio, 1775–1777.* Madison: State Historical Society of Wisconsin, 1908.

Turpie, David. *Sketches of My Own Times.* Indianapolis: Bobbs Merrill, 1903.

Withers, Alexander Scott. *Chronicles of Border Warfare.* Ed. Reuben G. Thwaites. Cincinnati: Robert Clarke, 1895.

Wood, William, ed. *Select British Documents of the War of 1812.* 3 vols. Toronto: Champlain Society, 1920–26.

Secondary Sources

THESES AND DISSERTATIONS

Chalou, George C. "The Red Pawns Go to War: British-American Indian Relations, 1810–1815." Ph.D. dissertation, Indiana University, 1971.

Goltz, Herbert C. "Tecumseh, the Prophet and the Rise of the Northwest Indian Confederation." Ph.D. dissertation, University of Western Ontario, 1973.

Hartman, Paul. "The Vincennes *Western Sun* under the Editorship of Elihu Stout." M.A. thesis, Southern Illinois University, 1967.

Hughes, Paul L. "The Removal of the Shawnee Indians from Ohio." M.A. thesis, Indiana University, 1949.

Schutz, Noel W., Jr. "The Study of Shawnee Myth in an Ethnographic and Ethnohistorical Perspective." Ph.D. dissertation, Indiana University, 1975.

NEWSPAPERS

Kansas City Kansan.
Kansas City Star.

Niles Register.
Western Sun (Vincennes).

ARTICLES

Barber, Bernard. "Acculturation and Messianic Movements." *American Sociological Review* 6 (October 1941): 663–69.

Barce, Elmore. "Tecumseh's Confederacy." *Indiana Magazine of History* 12 (June 1916): 161–74, and 13 (March 1917): 67–91.

Barlow, William. "The Coming of the War of 1812 in Michigan Territory." *Michigan History* 53 (Summer 1969): 91–107.

Berkhofer, Robert F., Jr. "Protestants, Pagans, and Sequences among the North American Indians, 1760–1800." In Deward E. Walker, Jr. *The Emergent Native Americans: A Reader in Cultural Contact.* Boston: Little, Brown and Co., 1972, 370–81.

Bruner, Edward M. "Culture Transmission and Culture Change." In Deward E. Walker, Jr. *The Emergent Native Americans: A Reader in Cultural Contact.* Boston: Little, Brown and Co., 1972, 69–75.

Byrd, Cecil K. "The Northwest Indians and the British Preceding the War of 1812." *Indiana Magazine of History* 38 (March 1924): 31–50.

Callender, Charles. "Shawnee." In Bruce Trigger, ed. *Handbook of North American Indians: Northeast.* Washington, D.C.: Smithsonian Institution, 1978.

Cass, Lewis. "Indians of North America." *North American Review* 22 (January 1826): 57–119.

Coutts, Katherine B. "Thamesville and the Battle of the Thames." In Morris Zaslow, ed. *The Defended Border: Upper Canada and the War of 1812.* Toronto: Macmillan, 1964.

Curry, William L. "The Wyandot Chief, Leather Lips." *Ohio Archaeological and Historical Publications* 12 (January 1903): 30–36.

Edmunds, R. David. "Redefining Red Patriotism: Five Medals of the Potawatomis." *Red River Valley Historical Review* 5 (Spring 1980): 13–24.

Ermatinger, Judge. "The Retreat of Procter and Tecumseh." *Ontario Historical Society, Papers and Records* 17 (1919): 11–21.

Horsman, Reginald. "Western War Aims, 1811–1812." *Indiana Magazine of History,* 53 (March 1957): 1–18.

"The Indian in Ohio." *Ohio Archaeological and Historical Publications* 27 (December 1919): 274–310.

242

Johnston, Charles M. "William Claus and John Norton: A Struggle for Power in Old Ontario." *Ontario History* 57 (June 1965): 101–8.

Klopfenstein, Carl G. "Westward Ho: Removal of Ohio Shawnees, 1832–1833." *Bulletin of the Historical and Philosophical Society of Ohio* 15 (January 1957): 3–31.

Kopytoff, Igor. "Classifications of Religious Movements: Analytical and Synthetic." In June Helm, ed. *Symposium on New Approaches to the Study of Religion, Proceedings of the 1964 Annual Spring Meeting of the American Ethnological Society.* Seattle: University of Washington Press, 1964.

Lauriston, Victor. "The Case for General Procter." In Morris Zaslow, ed. *The Defended Border: Upper Canada and the War of 1812.* Toronto: Macmillan, 1964, 121–27.

Lindley, Harlow. "Friends and the Shawnee Indians at Wapakoneta." *Ohio Archaeological and Historical Quarterly* 54 (January 1945): 33–39.

Linton, Ralph. "Nativistic Movements." *American Anthropologist* 45 (April 1943): 230–40.

MacLean, J. P. "Shaker Mission to the Shawnee Indians." *Ohio Archaeological and Historical Publications* 11 (June 1903): 215–29.

Mahon, John. "British Command Decisions in the Northern Campaigns of the War of 1812." *Canadian Historical Review* 46 (September 1965): 219–37.

Meek, Basil. "Tarhe—The Crane." *Ohio Archaeological and Historical Publications* 20 (January 1911): 64–73.

Moorehead, Warren King. "The Indian Tribes of Ohio." *Ohio Archaeological and Historical Publications* 7 (October 1898): 1–109.

Nash, Philleo. "The Place of Religious Revivalism in the Formation of the Intercultural Community on the Klamath Reservation." In Fred Eagan, ed. *Social Anthropology of North American Tribes.* Chicago: University of Chicago Press, 1937, 377–442.

Parsons, Joseph A., Jr. "Civilizing the Indians of the Old Northwest." *Indiana Magazine of History* 56 (September 1960): 195–216.

Randall, E. O. "Editorialana." *Ohio Archaeological and Historical Publications* 10 (April 1902): 388–90.

———. "Tecumseh, the Shawnee Chief." *Ohio Archaeological and Historical Publications* 15 (December 1906): 418–98.

Schlip, Emil. "Tarhe, the Crane." *Ohio Archaeological and Historical Publications* 14 (June 1905): 132–38.

Skeen, C. Edward. "The Year Without Summer." *Journal of the Early Republic* 1 (Spring 1981): 51–67.

Smith, Dwight. "Wayne's Peace with the Indians of the Old Northwest, 1795." *Ohio Archaeological and Historical Publications* 49 (July 1950): 239–55.

Sosin, Jack. "The British Indian Department and Dunmore's War." *Virginia Magazine of History and Biography* 74 (January 1966): 34–50.

———. "The Use of Indians in the War of the American Revolution: A Reassessment of Responsibility." *Canadian Historical Review* 46 (June 1965): 101–21.

Spencer, Joab. "The Shawnee Indians: Their Customs, Traditions, and Folk-Lore." *Transactions of the Kansas State Historical Society.* Vol. 10. Topeka: State Printing Office, 1908, 382–402.

Spindler, George, and Spindler, Louise. "American Indian Personality Types and Their Sociocultural Roots." In Deward E. Walker, ed. *The Emergent Native Americans: A Reader in Cultural Contact.* Boston: Little, Brown and Co., 1972, 502–13.

Stanley, G. F. G. "The Significance of the Six Nations' Participation in the War of 1812." *Ontario History* 55 (December 1963): 215–32.

Tanner, Helen Hornbeck. "Coocoochee: Mohawk Medicine Woman." *American Indian Culture and Research Journal* 3, no. 3 (1979): 23–41.

Voegelin, Carl F., and Wheeler-Voegelin, Erminie, "The Shawnee Female Deity in Historical Perspective." *American Anthropologist* 46 (August 1944): 370–75.

———. "Shawnee Name Groups." *American Anthropologist* 37 (October 1935): 617–35.

Voegelin, Carl F., Yegerlehner, John, and Robinett, Florence M. "Shawnee Laws: Perceptual Statements for the Language and for the Content." *American Anthropological Association Memoirs* 56 (December 1954): 32–46.

Wallace, Anthony F. C. "New Religions Among the Delaware Indians, 1600–1900." In Deward E. Walker, ed. *The Emergent Americans: A Reader in Cultural Change.* Boston: Little, Brown and Co., 1972, 344–61.

———. "Revitalization Movements." *American Anthropologist* 58 (May 1956): 264–81.

Wallace, Paul W. "The Moravian Records." *Indiana Magazine of History* 48 (June 1952): 141–60.

Watts, Florence G. "Fort Knox: Frontier Outpost on the Wabash,

1787–1816." *Indiana Magazine of History* 42 (March 1966): 51–78.

Wheeler-Voegelin, Erminie. "The Place of Agriculture in the Subsistence of the Shawnee." *Papers of the Michigan Academy of Science, Arts, and Letters.* Vol. 26. Ann Arbor: University of Michigan Press, 1941, 513–20.

Whickar, Wesley, ed. "Shabonee's Account of Tippecanoe." *Indiana Magazine of History* 18 (December 1921): 355–59.

———. "Tecumseh and Pushmataha." *Indiana Magazine of History* 18 (December 1922): 315–31.

———. "Tri-County Historical Itinerary." *Indiana Magazine of History* 12 (March 1916): 37–56.

———. "Zachariah Cicot." *Indiana Magazine of History* 21 (March 1921): 100–108.

Yegerlehner, John. "The First Five Minutes of Shawnee Laws in Multiple Stage Translations." *International Journal of American Linguistics* 20 (October 1954): 281–94.

BOOKS

Anson, Bert. *The Miami Indians.* Norman: University of Oklahoma Press, 1970.

Atwater, Caleb. *A History of the State of Ohio, Natural and Civil.* Cincinnati: Glezen and Shepard, 1838.

Babcock, Louis L. *The War of 1812 on the Niagara Frontier.* Buffalo: Buffalo Historical Society, 1927.

Barry, Louise, ed. *The Beginnings of the West: Annals of the Kansas Gateway to the American West, 1540–1854.* Topeka: Kansas State Historical Society, 1972.

Beard, Reed. *The Battle of Tippecanoe.* Lafayette, Ind.: Tippecanoe Publishing, 1889.

Beckwith, Hiram. *The Illinois and Indiana Indians.* Chicago: Fergus Printing, 1884.

Berkhofer, Robert F., Jr. *The White Man's Indian.* New York: Alfred A. Knopf, 1978.

Brice, Wallace A. *History of Fort Wayne.* Fort Wayne: D. W. Jones and Sons, 1868.

Butterfield, Consul Wilshire. *History of the Girtys.* Cincinnati: Robert Clarke, 1890.

Clark, Jerry E. *The Shawnee.* Lexington: University of Kentucky Press, 1977.

Clift, G. Glenn. *Remember the Raisin!* Frankfort: Kentucky Historical Society, 1961.

Crosby, Alfred. *The Columbian Exchange*. Westport, Conn.: Greenwood Press, 1971.

Danziger, Edmund J. *The Chippewas of Lake Superior*. Norman: University of Oklahoma Press, 1978.

Dawson, Moses. *A Historical Narrative of the Civil and Military Services of Major General William H. Harrison*. Cincinnati: Moses Dawson, 1824.

Dillon, John B. *A History of Indiana*. Indianapolis: Bingham and Doughty, 1859.

Downes, Randolph C. *Council Fires on the Upper Ohio*. Pittsburgh: University of Pittsburgh Press, 1940.

Drake, Benjamin. *Life of Tecumseh*. New York: Arno Press, 1969.

Dunham, Aileen. *Political Unrest in Upper Canada, 1815–1836*. London: Longmans, Green and Co., 1927.

Edmunds, R. David. *The Potawatomis: Keepers of the Fire*. Norman: University of Oklahoma Press, 1978.

Finley, James B. *Life among the Indians*. Cincinnati: B. P. Thompson, 1860.

Flint, Timothy. *The Life and Adventures of Daniel Boone*. New York: Hurst and Co., 1868.

Foreman, Grant. *Indians and Pioneers: The Story of the American Southwest before 1830*. Norman: University of Oklahoma Press, 1936.

———. *The Last Trek of the Indians*. New York: Russell and Russell, 1972.

Galloway, William Albert. *Old Chillicothe: Shawnee and Pioneer History*. Xenia, Ohio: Buckeye Press, 1934.

Gibson, A. M. *The Kickapoos: Lords of the Middle Border*. Norman: University of Oklahoma Press, 1963.

Gilpin, Alec. *The War of 1812 in the Old Northwest*. East Lansing: Michigan State University Press, 1958.

Harvey, Henry. *History of the Shawnee Indians from the Year 1681–1854*. Cincinnati: E. Morgan and Sons, 1855.

Hill, Leonard U. *John Johnston and the Indians in the Land of the Three Miamis*. Piqua, Ohio: Leonard Hill, 1957.

Hodge, Frederick W., ed. *Handbook of American Indians North of Mexico*. Bureau of American Ethnology Bulletin, no. 30. 2 vols. New York: Rowman and Littlefield, 1971.

Horsman, Reginald. *Expansion and American Indian Policy, 1783–1812*. East Lansing: Michigan State University Press, 1967.

———. *Matthew Elliott, British Indian Agent*. Detroit: Wayne State University Press, 1964.

Howard, James H. *Shawnee!: The Ceremonialism of a Native In-

dian Tribe and Its Cultural Background. Athens: Ohio University Press, 1981.

Josephy, Alvin M., Jr. *The Patriot Chiefs: A Chronicle of American Indian Leadership*. New York: Viking Press, 1961.

Kellogg, Louise Phelps. *The British Regime in Wisconsin and the Old Northwest*. New York: Da Capo Press, 1971.

Klinck, Carl, ed. *Tecumseh: Fact and Fiction in Early Records*. Englewood Cliffs, N.J.: Prentice-Hall, 1961.

Lossing, Benson. *The Pictorial Field Book of the War of 1812*. New York: Harper and Brothers, 1869.

McAfee, Robert B. *History of the Late War in the Western Country*. Lexington: Worsley and Smith, 1816.

McCollough, Almeda, ed. *The Battle of Tippecanoe: Conflict of Cultures*. Lafayette: Tippecanoe County Historical Association, 1973.

McCracken, Harold. *George Catlin and the Old Frontier*. New York: Dial Press, 1959.

McInnis, Edgar. *Canada: A Political and Social History*. New York: Rinehart and Co., 1947.

McKenney, Thomas, and Hall, James. *The Indian Tribes of North America with Biographical Sketches and Anecdotes of the Principal Chiefs*. 3 vols. Edinburgh: John Grant, 1933.

McNemar, Richard. *The Kentucky revival, or a short history of the extraordinary out-pouring of the Spirit of God in the Western States of America*. Albany: E. and E. Hosford, 1808.

Mason, Philip P., ed. *After Tippecanoe: Some Aspects of the War of 1812*. East Lansing: Michigan State University Press, 1963.

Mooney, James. *The Ghost Dance Religion and the Sioux Outbreak of 1890*. Fourteenth Annual Report of the Bureau of American Ethnology. 2 pts. Washington, D.C.: Bureau of American Ethnology, 1896.

O'Donnell, James. *Southern Indians in the American Revolution*. Knoxville: University of Tennessee Press, 1973.

Oskison, John. *Tecumseh and His Times*. New York: G. P. Putnam's Sons, 1938.

Parkman, Francis. *The Conspiracy of Pontiac*. New York: Collier Books, 1962.

Prucha, Francis Paul. *The Sword of the Republic: The United States Army on the Frontier, 1783–1845*. London, Ontario: Collier-Macmillan, 1969.

Radin, Paul. *The Winnebago Tribe*. Lincoln: University of Nebraska Press, 1970.

Schoolcraft, Henry R. *Discourse Delivered before the Historical Society of Michigan*. Detroit: G. L. Whitney, 1830.

Schultz, George A. *An Indian Canaan: Isaac McCoy and the Vision of an Indian State*. Norman: University of Oklahoma Press, 1972.

Sosin, Jack. *The Revolutionary Frontier*. New York: Holt, Rinehart and Winston, 1967.

Stocker, Harry Emilius. *A History of the Moravian Mission among the Indians on the White River in Indiana*. Bethlehem, Pa.: Times Publishing, 1917.

Thatcher, Benjamin B. *Indian Biography*. 2 vols. New York: J. Harper, 1832.

Truettner, William H. *The Natural Man Observed: A Study of Catlin's Indian Gallery*. Washington, D.C.: Smithsonian Institution Press, 1979.

Tucker, Glenn. *Tecumseh: Vision of Glory*. New York: Russell and Russell, 1973.

Viola, Herman J. *The Indian Legacy of Charles Bird King*. Washington, D.C.: Smithsonian Institution and Doubleday, 1976.

Walker, Deward E., Jr., ed. *The Emergent Native Americans: A Reader in Cultural Contact*. Boston: Little, Brown and Co., 1972.

Wallace, Anthony. *The Death and Rebirth of the Seneca*. New York: Alfred A. Knopf, 1970.

Wallis, Wilson D. *Messiahs: Their Role in Civilizations*. Washington, D.C.: American Council on Public Affairs, 1943.

Warren, William W. *History of the Ojibway Nation*. Minneapolis: Ross and Haines, 1957.

Weslager, Clifton A. *The Delaware Indians: A History*. New Brunswick: Rutgers University Press, 1972.

Wheeler-Voegelin, Erminie. *Mortuary Customs of the Shawnees and Other Eastern Tribes*. Indianapolis: Indiana Historical Society, 1944.

Woehrman, Paul. *At the Headwaters of the Maumee*. Indianapolis: Indiana Historical Society, 1971.

Zaslow, Morris, ed. *The Defended Border: Upper Canada and the War of 1812*. Toronto: Macmillan, 1964.

Index